LAMINARIA

NEREOCYSTIS

Bowfin Whale

Europe

Asia

Northern Sea Otter

Asian Sea Otter

Papahānaumokuākea Marine National Monument

Hawaii

Takuyo-Daigo Seamount

Coral Triangle Region

Oceanic Whitetip Shark

Chagos Archipelago

Shark Bay

Australia

Sydney Crayweed Forest

Cape Rodney-Okakari Piont Marine Reserve

Great Southern Reef

Lutrawita Giant Kelp Forests

ECKLONIA

Antarctic Krill

NEREOCYSTIS

= Kelp Forests   = Macrocystis   = Laminaria

= Ecklonia   = Nereocystis   = Lessonia

What the Wild Sea Can Be

Also by Helen Scales

Around the Ocean in 80 Fish and Other Sea Life
The Brilliant Abyss
Eye of the Shoal
Octopuses
Eleven Explorations into Life on Earth
Spirals in Time
Poseidon's Steed

Books for younger readers

Shells . . . and what they hide inside
Scientists in the Wild: Antarctica
Return of the Wild
Scientists in the Wild: Galápagos
What a Shell Can Tell
Great Barrier Reef

What the Wild Sea Can Be

The Future of the World's Ocean

HELEN SCALES

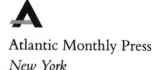

Atlantic Monthly Press
New York

FIRST EDITION

Published simultaneously in Canada
Printed in the United States of America

Book interior designed by Norman E. Tuttle at Alpha Design & Composition.
This book is set in 12-pt. Bembo
by Alpha Design & Composition of Pittsfield, NH.

First Grove Atlantic hardcover edition: July 2024

Library of Congress Cataloging-in-Publication data is available for this title.

ISBN 978-0-8021-6299-1
eISBN 978-0-8021-6300-4

Atlantic Monthly Press
an imprint of Grove Atlantic
154 West 14th Street
New York, NY 10011

Distributed by Publishers Group West

groveatlantic.com

24 25 26 27   10 9 8 7 6 5 4 3 2 1

For Liam Drew and Emma Bryce,
with gratitude for your friendship and for
helping me find words about wild things.

Contents

# Prelude

First, they were bright white dots moving in the distance between sea and sky. Then, as I reached the end of the land at the cliff's edge, the gannets were everywhere. From eyeline to the waterline six hundred feet below, huge birds filled all the available space. They followed invisible contours through the air in every direction and on every horizontal plane. Somehow, silently, they knew to steer to avoid each other, their black-tipped wings never touching. Those not in flight were sitting on every piece of cliff with room to land. They were lined up on ledges, one bird deep, and the flatter patches of scree were studded in nests, always spaced a sharp beak's biting distance apart.

If someone told me this was all the gannets there are, every last one of them, coming to nest on these very cliffs, I might easily have believed it. But other colonies exist on both sides of the Atlantic, some even bigger than this one, and all of them in places where the surrounding ocean contains enough prolific life and food to sustain so many parents and hungry chicks. Gannets dive from great heights to hunt beneath the surface, folding their wings back and piercing the water with their arrowlike heads. Air sacs under their skin, like a subdermal cloak of bubble wrap, protect their bodies from the impact of hundred-foot dives. The ammoniacal tang of guano that wafted from the colony told me about the ocean's immense productivity and all the fish they've been catching.

I came to the gannetry at Hermaness, the northernmost headland on the northernmost inhabited island in Scotland, because I wanted to see an outrageous amount of healthy ocean life. Gannets are the North Atlantic's biggest seabirds, with a six-foot wingspan and bodies more than three feet long. They don't have the vivid blue or red webbed feet of their tropical cousins the boobies, but they have their own understated elegance. Mostly white, the adults have a dusting of peachy-yellow feathers on their neck and head, a long, tapering beak, and striking pale-blue eyes ringed in cobalt—a gleaming swipe of eyeshadow, like Marilyn Monroe in an Andy Warhol print. I had only ever seen an occasional, solitary gannet, usually from afar, and had long wondered what it would be like to see more. When I found out that they gather in enormous colonies in the Shetland Islands, I decided to see for myself tens of thousands of these huge seabirds at once. I wanted to stare and soak up the awe of it all and remind myself that places like this still exist.

That day, July 18, 2022, when gannets lured me to the farthest end of the British Isles, became the day when my outlook on the world changed. It marked the beginning of the United Kingdom's first "red" extreme heat warning. Two days of national emergency had been declared because of a heatwave so severe it put human lives at risk, and people were told their daily routines would have to change. Advice for the worst-hit areas, including my hometown of Cambridge, was to stay indoors, shut and cover windows, and generally slow down. During the hottest day in the United Kingdom on record, runways and roads melted. Train services were suspended. People lay awake throughout the warmest night ever, when temperatures didn't fall below seventy-seven degrees Fahrenheit. And Britain wasn't alone. Extreme heat was engulfing western Europe. Portugal was suffering from a worsening drought, and parts of France and Spain were ablaze with wildfires.

Meanwhile, at Hermaness, a thousand miles north of my home, it was mild and pleasant, but it was strange and unsettling to know that everywhere to the south was far hotter. Missing that heatwave, I think, made it even more disturbing as I tried to imagine what was going on at home. That day, everything felt different. Until that moment, the climate crisis had remained an alarming but still distant threat to me. Suddenly, I realised that the world I had grown up in had gone, that normality had changed and the climate crisis had arrived.

I had booked the trip months earlier and escaped the horrifying heat just by chance. But I also happened to arrive in the middle of another disaster that was hitting northern Scotland far worse than anywhere else.

Standing at the cliff at Hermaness, looking at the scene through binoculars, I watched pairs of gannets sitting together, shaking their long beaks from side to side, and others sitting quietly on their own, waiting for a partner to return from foraging at sea. And there, visible between the nests, were the dead bodies of so many other gannets. More corpses were piled at the base of steep sections of cliff, presumably the ones that fell off their nests.

Avian flu had killed them all. For the first time since the disease appeared in a goose farm in China in 1996, the virus had mutated into a highly contagious and virulent strain and was ripping through populations of wild seabirds. There had been isolated outbreaks of less deadly variants in the wild before, but nothing like this. The epicentre in early summer 2022 was Scotland—in particular, the Shetland Islands.

By the time I visited Hermaness, I had already encountered many dead gannets and other seabirds, several on every beach across the islands, in varying states of decay. Some were little more than feathers ground into the sand. Some were skeletons, archaeopteryx-like, head flung back, and wings outstretched. And some gannets just lay there, intact and perfect, staring blue eyes open, wings folded back as if they had deliberately dived from the sky and landed without a mark on their bodies. Only at the gannet colony were the dead mixed in with living birds. Depending on where I let my gaze rest, this was either a desolate view of ecological breakdown or a stunning scene of natural wonder.

Planet Earth is in the throes of extreme environmental change, a transformation in which the dominant driving force is humanity. In the Anthropocene, the human-dominated epoch in which we're all living, many of the fastest, most dramatic changes are taking place in the ocean.

Within just the past fifty years, as people have been overexploiting species, destroying habitats, and releasing pollutants, the total mass of vertebrate life in the ocean has halved.* In that time, the ocean's chances of being hit by lethal heatwaves, the kind that destroy kelp forests and coral reefs, have doubled. Every decade, the background noise levels in the ocean have also doubled, mirroring the growth in shipping, so that whales and other acoustic animals are having a harder time hearing each other. A plastic fog in the ocean is thickening and now comprises hundreds of trillions of particles. Since records began, the ocean has never been hotter. Sea levels are rising, and polar sea ice is shrinking. Seawater is becoming more acidic. Oxygen is ebbing away.

As humanity wades further into the Anthropocene ocean, changes are happening so quickly it can be hard to keep up with the streams of gloomy news. Scanning the science headlines, you might have come across recent news of a novel disease identified in seabirds caused by inflammation and scarring in their digestive tracts from the build-up of plastics that they swallow. Scientists have named this condition plasticosis. Or you might have caught word of how more marine species are being pushed towards extinction, with dugongs, abalone, and a type of Caribbean coral all recently added to the list of globally endangered species. Or that five out of the top ten

---

*The 2015 Living Blue Planet Report, by the conservation organisation WWF, compiled data on the 5,829 populations of 1,234 mammal, bird, fish, and reptile species that live in the ocean, and found that between 1970 and 2012 their numbers had declined by 49 per cent.

commercially important fish populations in British seas are either overfished or depleted to critically low levels.

At the same time, people are making startling discoveries about what lives in the ocean and how this vast living system works. For instance, scientists recently discovered how northern elephant seals fall asleep while drifting down through the sea, like spiralling leaves, dreaming as they go, and sometimes take naps on the seabed. These enormous marine mammals breathe air, but they know they are in danger at the surface, where predators are more likely to attack, and so they only go to sleep underwater. Not long ago, another team of scientists tracked scalloped hammerhead sharks making regular dives into the twilight zone to search for prey and discovered that while they're thousands of feet down, they hold their breath. These water-breathing fish know to close their gills to avoid cooling their circulating blood in the frigid deep water.

A previously unknown seagrass meadow, full of species like seahorses, scallops, and cuttlefish, was discovered just off the British coast of Cornwall. And in the Bahamas, tiger sharks fitted out with cameras helped discover the world's largest seagrass meadow, extending around thirty-five thousand square miles, the size of the US state of Maine and more than twenty times bigger than the whole of Cornwall.* This finding alone increased the known global area of seagrass habitat by almost half.

I'm often asked by audience members at public talks or by interviewers during radio shows whether I am hopeful for the future of the ocean.† My common response is that it depends on which day you ask me and whether the last piece of news I heard or study I read was depressing or joyful. While I was watching the gannets of

---

*All these discoveries, from snoozing elephant seals to giant seagrass meadows, were made within roughly a half year, in late 2022 and early 2023.

†I am asked this almost as often as that other excellent question, "What is your favourite sea creature?"

Hermaness, it dawned on me that I can hold both perspectives in my mind at once—my optimism and pessimism—and not let one push the other out.

There is no doubt that good and bad things are happening in the ocean, often pressed up tightly together, as the gannets showed me. Many discoveries that offer glorious and hopeful insights into ocean life are also tinged in trouble. In recent times, despite the growing threats of overfishing and warming seas, there are places where manta rays are flourishing; a population of at least a thousand of these magnificent, wide-winged cousins of sharks is swimming around in Komodo National Park in Indonesia; off the coast of Ecuador, a population was recently estimated to be the largest known in the world—by an order of magnitude—with more than twenty-two thousand mantas. And yet in both places, a portion of these animals show scars from collisions with boats and propellors, and many have been tangled in fishing nets or barbed with hooks.

Likewise, strands of hope run through even the most desolate ocean stories. Since I was in Shetland early in the avian flu outbreak, the situation has got far worse, and the virus has spread around the world. Millions of seabirds have died, the virus hitting more bird species in more locations than any previous outbreak. The virus has also jumped into wild mammals, killing foxes, otters, dolphins, and thousands of sea lions. Scientists are beginning to get a handle on how the virus is impacting wild populations, and in the thick of all the carnage, they have found a glimmer of resistance. The world's largest colony of gannets is at Bass Rock in the Firth of Forth off the east coast of Scotland. This gannetry has suffered a huge die-off, but ornithologists have discovered some healthy-looking gannets with avian flu antibodies in their blood. Curiously, many of these survivors have jet-black eyes. It is not yet clear why this happens, or how the flu affects their vision, but for some reason when gannets fight off avian flu and survive, their pale-blue irises turn black.

In the messy midst of the changing ocean, so much has already been damaged and destroyed that discerning what the future may hold requires a careful balance of optimism and pessimism. A worse version of today's ocean is not inevitable, but underestimating the scale of the problems and what needs doing to tackle them would be unwise. It is important to recognise that no place in the ocean is pristine and unspoiled anymore but also to appreciate that all is not lost; none of the ocean's ecosystems and (almost) no species are entirely beyond hope. Many places in the ocean remain tremendously healthy and abundant, and there is still a great deal to fight for. This book, then, sets off with this mind-set on a journey through the Anthropocene ocean to find out what a better future could look like and what it might take to get there.

The starting point is the ocean's distant past, which will root the stories that follow in the context of what happened over many millions of years, long before humans evolved. Keep that outlook in the back of your mind to help measure the changes unfolding in today's ocean and grasp the magnitude of what is happening. For the centrepiece of each of the following chapters, I have picked living species and habitats that are responding in different ways to the Anthropocene. Many are familiar places and beloved animals, and I will dig deeper and uncover how their biology influences their chances of survival and dictates the course of action needed to help them thrive. We will meet species that are at the vanguard of a great modern remixing and conversion of the ocean, moving to new places and adapting to novel conditions, and that stand the greatest chances of surviving by themselves. We will also encounter a suite of species whose glory is already fading fast, the ones that will be the hardest to save and will require the most urgent action. These animals are frantically imperilled by the biggest threats to ocean life and could be the first to succumb in turn to heating seas, overfishing, and pollution. Among them are the polar animals that are disastrously sensitive to rising temperatures and cannot persist without the coldest, frozen seas; the species that grow sedately and to such grand old ages that their exploited populations cannot keep up and replace themselves fast enough; and the apex predators that balance precariously at the top of food chains, where their bodies soak up toxins from the contaminated seas. Together they pose a great challenge but not a hopeless one, of how to reverse their bad fortunes, and they serve as a warning of worse problems that need to be avoided elsewhere in the world.

Ocean wildlife has a tremendous capacity to regenerate and recover from dreadful losses and depletion. Often all that is needed is for the exploitation, destruction, and pollution to stop—a great deal of optimism about the ocean comes from this possibility. Even what seemed to be irredeemable catastrophes have been turned around, including some involving high-priced luxury fish and neglected areas of seabed.

Sometimes the recovery process needs a helping hand to kick-start natural cycles and restore balance. And some habitats face such big problems they will likely require far more deliberate steering and coaxing through the vicissitudes of the Anthropocene ocean. Scientists and conservationists are already working to engineer future-proof species and habitats that can withstand the continuing changes. Their ambitions generally are not to return the ocean to the way it was before humanity began inflicting so many troubles but rather to reach towards a resilient version of the ocean that is still healthy and abundant and, in key ways, different and new—not a rewinding that could ultimately fail but a rewilding that will last.

Together, ocean dwellers and their habitats have a lot to tell us about how the Anthropocene ocean is run through with inequalities. By no means is everything and everyone in the same boat. It is clear that some habitats and wild species—and people too—are already shaping up to be winners and some to be losers in the changing ocean. A critical part of a better future will be to find ways to undo inequalities and build an ocean that is just and fair and that benefits as many people and the greatest portion of nature as possible.

The future of the ocean matters to everyone. No matter where you live and what you do, even if you have never seen the sea in real life, you would not exist—none of us would—without the ocean. When astronomers examine other planets for signs of life, the key feature they search for is liquid water. Here on Earth, the ocean is where life began billions of years ago, and it is what has kept the planet alive ever since. Seawater covers seven-tenths of the planetary surface and plunges to many miles deep, and in its enormity absorbs huge amounts of heat beating down from the sun. Restless ocean currents swirl heat around the globe, preventing the tropics from scorching and supporting the mild mid-latitudes where many people live. The ocean is a rainmaker, providing most of the water that evaporates and falls on land. It generates weather systems and influences the climate we all experience in our daily lives.

The ocean makes the earth habitable not just by the physical presence of water but by the presence of life itself. Half the oxygen we breathe is made by multitudes of minute sun-fixing organisms, the phytoplankton that float through the seas. Phytoplankton also play their part in regulating the climate. They make clouds, which reflect the sun's heat, by releasing particles into the atmosphere that cause water vapour to condense into droplets. Ocean life also mitigates the climate crisis by removing at least a quarter of humanity's carbon emissions from the atmosphere. Phytoplankton absorb carbon dioxide and, when they die, create flurries of organic particles, called marine snow, which settle into the deep. A myriad of other life forms are critical in this drawdown of carbon, from underwater forests and meadows to giant whales and their plankton-fertilising faeces, and the trillions of glittering fish, called myctophids, that migrate each day between the sea surface and the shadowy twilight zone thousands of feet down.

The species and habitats discussed in this book are all vital parts of this life-giving system. They are sentinels of the rapid changes already underway in the Anthropocene ocean, and they forewarn of greater changes to come. In the coming pages, I will focus on what could happen in the next few years and decades, with the end of the century out there on the horizon. I picked this timeframe for a few reasons. On a practical level, 2100 is commonly the date at which scientific models and predictions aim, and so there are many studies that consider what the ocean will be like by then. We will all experience changes unfolding in the next years and decades, as will many of the people we know and care about. And if you think 2100 feels far off, remember that many children born today should still be alive to see the turn of the twenty-second century.

Crucially, the next few years are when decisions made will determine—one way or another—how the next phase of the Anthropocene ocean plays out for a considerable stretch of time to come. Right now, there are choices to be made, but the window of opportunity to meaningfully act is closing. Soon the ocean will reach a point when it heads down a certain path, and it will become harder and harder to change course.

Experts predict that carbon emissions must peak by 2025, at the latest, followed by sharp global reductions, if there is to be any chance of keeping global heating to within 1.5 degrees Celsius* and avoiding the worst-case scenarios for people and the planet. While that target is looking less likely as the present decade wears on and emissions keep climbing, the Intergovernmental Panel on Climate Change (IPCC) has laid out a road map for how those emissions reductions could happen, underscoring the fact that the necessary technologies and solutions already exist. The most promising options

---

*Equivalent to 2.7 degrees Fahrenheit.

are solar and wind energy, as well as preserving intact forests and other carbon-rich habitats, including in the seas.

Exploring the future of the ocean demands a fair amount of mental time travel, both backwards and forwards. The trick to navigating these waters will be to keep a sense of perspective (the ocean has always changed), to not go it alone (share these stories and ideas, talk about them so more people will know what is happening), and to make sure along the way to keep seeing the glory and feeling wonderment in the ocean. I hope this book will offer an antidote to the rising tide of eco-anxiety and fears for the future of the planet. Turn that fear into commitment and initiative. What matters most now is to not look away in anguish but to confront the problems and to know how bad things are and understand why they got this way, while at the same time wanting and hoping for the future ocean to be better.

PART ONE

OCEAN CONVERSION

Chapter 1
Ancient Seas

In a desk drawer, among all sorts of things I'm saving, is a small witness to the changing ocean. The thumb-size piece of slate is etched with narrow silver lines that are smooth along one edge and serrated on the other. I found it at the base of a crumbling cliff that was folded and twisted by an aeon of orogeny. The marks look like the script of some long-lost language pencilled on the rock. In fact, these are fossils of animals that lived 430 million years ago, or thereabouts, and I like them especially for the name they've been given: graptolites—from ancient Greek words *graptos*, meaning "marked with letters," and *lithos*, meaning "stone."

The impressions graptolites left behind hold messages that took palaeontologists a long time to decipher. Many assumed these markings were fossilised plants. Others realised they were animals but had differing views on which kind, variously labelling them as corals, hydroids, or the mossy-looking creatures known as bryozoans. Ultimately the matter was settled, and it was agreed that graptolites belong among an obscure group of ocean dwellers called pterobranchs. Each sawtooth line on my stone was once a colony of tiny animals. They lived together inside a house of interconnected tubes, which they actively built around themselves, like a spider making its web. Their homes were the only parts of graptolites that fossilised, but these are enough to tell us what their colonies looked like and what kind of lives they led. Early on in their evolution, graptolites grew on the seabed, fixed to boulders or rooted in mud. Then in time, some varieties floated away and were among the first animals to become plankton. These abundant drifters colonised open seas all around the world and swiftly evolved into flurries of different-shaped species. Some graptolites were Y-shaped, some poker-straight or two-pronged like a tuning fork, and some grew into spirals that twirled up and down as they sifted floating microbes from the water.

Now, though, the open ocean is empty of graptolites. The last of the planktonic species went extinct around three hundred million years ago. That seemed to be the end of them all, until recently, when a group of tiny animals, the Rhabdopleurida, were deemed to be living graptolites. It wasn't a new finding but a new interpretation of animals that scientists already knew about, microscopic, seafloor-bound colonies, which live all through the ocean, from polar seas to the tropics, from coastlines to a half mile down, and are the colour and translucence of amber. Only five living species have been found, a fragmentary recollection of the once-ubiquitous graptolites, the ghosts of a vanished world.

While contemplating the future of the ocean, it's worth pausing to turn around and look back. The ocean's backstory matters because it provides context for what's happening now. It lets us see what the ocean has been like and how it changed in a prehuman world. Long before us, great tides of ocean dynasties have risen and fallen, and the seas have been both a cradle of evolution and an arena for extinction. Looking back offers a chance to compare humanity against other planetary life-shaping forces. We can search for clues as to what changes lie ahead, note the warnings against misleading assumptions, and seek solace in the fact that, one way or another, life in the ocean goes on.

To think about the past requires an obvious and dizzying shift in perspective, because ocean life stretches behind us for more time than our human brains can instinctively grasp. We must briefly let go of our customary horizons of hours and days, years and decades, centuries and, at a stretch, millennia. Think instead like palaeontologists, who have learned to find ancient moments trapped in stone, then to gather them up and piece together stories that take millions of years to be told. While we try not to get overwhelmed by the scale and intricacy of it all, we can pick out details that tell a wider story of the changing ocean. From there we can begin to sense the rhythm and pace of ocean life.

Trilobites look oddly familiar, as if a pill bug scuttled under a rock and then emerged on the other side much larger, more ornate, and more than a half billion years older. Were I a more skilled and patient fossil hunter, I might find trilobites lodged in rocks not far from my graptolite-embossed slate. There are fossil trilobites on continents across the world. These animals existed in the earliest of three great chapters of complex life on earth—the Palaeozoic, meaning "ancient life," which was followed by the Mesozoic ("middle life") and then the Cenozoic ("new life"). Trilobites in the Palaeozoic weren't the first large animals to evolve, but they were undoubtedly trailblazers. They worried Charles Darwin because they seemed to confound his theory of gradual evolution via natural selection. Trilobites emerged far too quickly, too completely, and too long ago to fit his theory, as perfect creatures pressed into stone.

Trilobites evolved shortly after a three-billion-year prelude in which the only living things were single-celled microbes colonising the ocean, followed in the fullness of time by enigmatic wisps of simple, mostly jelly-based creatures that palaeontologists are still trying to make sense of. Then the Palaeozoic era opened with a dramatic twist in the history of life on earth. This era is divided into six periods; the first was the Cambrian, when evolution suddenly accelerated and ran at full tilt, churning out a mob of animals, including many that looked wildly different to anything alive today, from nozzle-nosed predators to luxuriantly spiky worms. The trigger for this flurry of life, known as the Cambrian explosion, is still a matter of debate. It may have had something to do with the fact that, for a long time leading up to it, the whole planet was frozen. As snowball Earth thawed, likely due to volcanoes spewing planet-heating carbon dioxide, the climate became more favourable for life to flourish. Rocks on land, as yet devoid of living things, began to erode and release nutrients into the ocean that organisms used to grow and build their skeletons, including enormous numbers of trilobites.

Darwin needn't have agonised over trilobites. It was partly a matter of timing. He was quite right when he surmised that ancient seas must surely have been swarming with life, though in his day nobody had yet found any evidence for it. When Darwin was writing and thinking about evolution, most of the world's oldest animal fossils remained unfound underground, including the extraordinary variety of Cambrian life in the Burgess Shale in Canada's Rocky Mountains, which wasn't uncovered until after his death.

A recent study of trilobite fossils has shed light on the timing of the Cambrian explosion and strengthened the idea that evolution can run at different speeds and has sometimes been breathtakingly fast (geologically speaking). A team based at the Natural History Museum in London used a large new collection of Cambrian trilobites to track how their appearance changed over time. The fossils went through an early, short burst of frantic innovation, showing that the Cambrian explosion may have truly gone off with a bang, lasting a brief twenty million years. Once the explosion died down, the rate of evolution among the trilobites levelled off and ticked steadily along.

By the Ordovician, the Palaeozoic period after the Cambrian, the ocean was brimming with trilobites. They ranged from flea-size swimmers to shovel-shaped diggers two and a half feet long, although most species were neatly pocket-size, measuring between one and three inches. Their basic anatomy was a head, thorax, and tail, with a ridged shell divided lengthwise into three sections, hence the name trilobite, and multiple pairs of legs underneath, like a centipede. These simple creatures were moulded and embellished into a phenomenal variety of forms. Many trilobites sprouted impressive spines and barbs, elegant quills, and devil horns. Some were smooth and rounded, like *Bumastus*, which looked just like an armadillo if you popped off its head and hid its tail. And like armadillos and pill bugs, most trilobites could curl up into a ball when they were scared.

From their fossilised remains, it's possible to interpret the ways many trilobites lived their lives. Masses of them scurried across the seabed, leaving footprints as if they had walked over wet cement; these imprints were preserved by rapid burial in sediment and then slowly turned into stone. Fossil trails captured the details of a hunting foray: a line of worm tracks joined by those of a trilobite, and then the trilobite walking off by itself, worm presumably in belly. *Cryptolithus* evolved to be filter-feeding trilobites that stirred up the sediment by scrabbling the seabed with their forelegs, then straining suspended food particles through their perforated, colander-like heads. Others never set a foot down but chased after prey through the water, aided by hydrodynamic shells. Chunks bitten out of their shells show that trilobites were prey for other animals, such as the giant sea scorpions that also roamed the Palaeozoic seas. Planktonic trilobites floated in great midwater swarms, occupying a pelagic niche similar to the one that krill occupy today. In shallow tropical seas, trilobites were beetling around the world's first true coral reefs, which had been built in the Ordovician by horn- and honeycomb-shaped corals. Some trilobites ventured between the tides and foraged on exposed tidal flats, but it seemed they never moved into rivers or lakes or made a permanent move onto land.

Uniquely among animals, trilobites' eyes were made from crystals of the hard mineral calcite, which means they were often exquisitely preserved, and their shapes and arrangements tell us even more about these creatures' lives. From their inception, Cambrian trilobites had complex, multifaceted eyes, similar in general form to the compound eyes of living insects and crustaceans. Some had eyes on long stalks, which scanned for prey while their bodies lay hidden in the mud. *Erbenochile* trilobites had columnar eyes that gave them almost 360-degree vision, each eye with a small, overhanging brow that shaded it in bright light. In deep waters of the twilight zone, where sunlight is dim, *Cyclopyge* trilobites soaked up rare photons with enormous eyes that occupied much of their heads, like the helmet eyes of dragonflies. Deeper still, trilobites evolved to be eyeless and blind, vision serving no purpose in the dark midnight zone.

Some trilobites resembled their nearest living relatives, the horseshoe crabs. *Olenellus* had a rounded, helmetlike head, rearward-pointing body spines, and a long prong for a tail. Not in fact crustaceans, the trilobites and horseshoe crabs are more closely aligned with spiders.

In all, more than twenty-five thousand species of trilobites are known, and more are constantly being found. (For comparison, there are roughly one thousand named dinosaurs.) They were fossilised in the millions, thanks in part to their tough exoskeletons. Trilobites periodically moulted their outer layer, growing new, bigger ones and tossing the casts into the fossil record, duplicating themselves and increasing the chances of being remembered through the passage of time.

The enormous diversity of species and ecology of trilobites show what very early ocean ecosystems were like, with habitats and food webs that are broadly recognisable in the contemporary ocean. More than five hundred million years ago, although the shape of the global ocean was very different, ocean ecology was already working, in many similar ways, as it does today.

Being so prolific and dotted around the planet, trilobites have also helped scientists reconstruct what the entire global ocean used to look like. For much of the Palaeozoic, the Northern Hemisphere was covered in the huge Panthalassic (meaning "all-sea") Ocean, and the continents were located mostly in the Southern Hemisphere. The world was warm, with little ice locking up water, and many of the continents were flooded in shallow seas, each home to a unique assortment of trilobites that didn't cross the deeper ocean in between. Later, when they were long dead and rockbound, fossil trilobites travelled around the planet, pushed by the forces of tectonic drift. Mapping the range of trilobites across modern-day continents is one way palaeontologists have worked out how landmasses moved and the ocean reshaped around them. Through much of the Palaeozoic, a supercontinent, Gondwana, was made up of many of today's continents and subcontinents all clustered together, including Australia, Antarctica, Africa, India, and Madagascar. Today, their shared trilobite fauna is testament to that earlier convergence. For instance, the same tropical species of trilobites have been chipped out of rocks in western Newfoundland, in New York State, and in the Inner Hebrides archipelago in Scotland, showing these lands were all once part of the same ancient continent.

The stories of trilobites have much to tell us about what the ocean used to be like, and together they refute a wider misconception about evolution. Trilobites are proof that life has not simply been advancing from primitive towards ever more advanced forms. They show that since early times, some organisms have been remarkably specialised and sophisticated. And perhaps the most important message from the trilobites is that their early abundance and diversity weren't enough to protect them from the changing ocean. Look all through the seas today, and not a single living trilobite is to be found.

After almost three hundred million years of scurrying and swimming, drifting, digging, and rolling up in balls, trilobites went extinct. They were among the species wiped out by the catastrophic Permian extinction event, which drew the Palaeozoic era to a close. This was the most devastating of the five ancient mass extinctions.* The cause was likely a spell of runaway global warming, triggered by immense volcanic eruptions, which filled the atmosphere with so much carbon dioxide the ocean was cooked, acidified, and sapped of oxygen until most aquatic life suffocated. That was the end of the trilobites, although in fact they had been in decline for much longer.

Trilobite diversity peaked in the late Cambrian and into the early Ordovician, and thereafter this group's splendour had been fading away. For the rest of the Palaeozoic—through the Silurian, Devonian, Carboniferous, and finally Permian periods—trilobites had been relinquishing their dominance in the ocean. Steadily, their diversity diminished until a single family remained, containing a handful of species that were quite plain and small compared to their predecessors.

We have some clarity as to why trilobites were knocked back. For instance, at the end of the Ordovician, the supercontinent Gondwana drifted over the South Pole and became covered in giant ice sheets, pushing the earth deep into an ice age. Sea levels dropped, and when continental seas dried out, crowds of tropical trilobites lost their habitat and went extinct. Those species that happened to be better able to cope with the cold survived. What continues to mystify is why trilobites didn't rebound once the ice age was over and conditions on the earth became more agreeable. New trilobite species were still evolving but not fast enough to replace the older species that were going extinct. No doubt the ocean filling up with new predators had an effect, including the first fish and squid, which were busy chasing after trilobites. Another suggestion is that trilobites weren't

---

*The five mass extinctions of times gone by were in the Ordovician (445 mya [million years ago]), Devonian (375 mya), Permian (252 mya), Triassic (200 mya), and Cretaceous (66 mya).

very good at shedding their exoskeletons. Fossils show that many injured themselves trying to climb out of their old shells, emerging with damaged eyes and misshapen heads.

Nobody has yet found a convincing, single explanation for the trilobites' long-term demise, which suggests it was likely a mix of changes and challenges emerging in their world. Whatever the ultimate causes were, from the end of the Ordovician onwards, trilobites suffered repeated setbacks from which they never fully recovered. Their former success did not predict their future survival.

The second great chapter in prehistoric life, the Mesozoic era, got underway around 250 million years ago in the aftermath of the mass extinction that devastated the earth's biosphere. Trilobites were gone. Huge coral and sponge reefs were gone. So were sea scorpions and spiny sharks called acanthodians. Many other groups of organisms, while not entirely lost, were stripped back to a tiny portion of their former diversity and abundance. In all, fewer than one in ten species survived. For millions of years after the extinction, a disaster fauna, as palaeontologists refer to it, existed on the seabed, made up of species that were just holding on and by no means thriving. The situation was better up in the open water, where shoals of conodonts—eel-like, two-inch-long fish with bulging eyes and no jaws—proliferated. There were also spiral-shelled cephalopods called ammonoids, which looked similar to living chambered nautiluses, as well as an increasing diversity of bony fishes. These animals all became prey for a group of animals whose ancestors had left the ocean more than a hundred million years earlier and in the Mesozoic made a spectacular return to the sea.

Back in the Palaeozoic, a group of fishes had gradually adapted to life beyond the tideline. They already had four legs, which they used while still living at the shallow edges of the sea, and some of them walked out onto land and became the ancestors of all the land-living vertebrates alive today: the amphibians, reptiles, birds, and mammals. Collectively, these vertebrates are known as tetrapods, even the ones that later turned some of their four legs into wings or flippers—and reptiles did both.

By the time the Mesozoic was underway, the reptiles known as dinosaurs* were famously ruling the land, and pterosaurs had taken to the skies. Meanwhile, the ocean was dominated by different groups of reptiles. Having lost their ancestral fishy gills, these animals drew gulps of air into their lungs and then leapt, slithered, and strutted back into the sea and very soon were well acclimatised to their revamped aquatic life. Within a few million years of the end-Permian mass extinction, reptilian apex predators were swimming through all the seas and making a major impression on the rest of ocean life.

These were the real-life embodiment of mythical sea monsters, with all the ferocity and grandeur we might imagine. Cruising around were sixty-five-foot-long ichthyosaurs, some as long as eighty-five feet. They looked like blue whales with elongate, tooth-filled jaws. Other ichthyosaurs were roughly the size and proportions of bottlenose dolphins. *Excalibosaurus* had a rapier-like rostrum, as swordfish do today, and presumably used it in a similar way to slash through shoals of fish. Tylosaurs looked like enormous modern-day orcas, up to twice their size, and may have hunted like them too, subduing prey by ramming into it with their bony snouts and then tearing it apart with razor-sharp teeth.

Plesiosaurs looked like archetypal incarnations of the Loch Ness monster, with a streamlined body, tiny head, and two pairs of long flippers, which they paddled in elegant undulations to fly underwater. Many had phenomenally long necks, some measuring more than twenty feet and taking up two-thirds of their body length. It's tempting to imagine plesiosaurs using their necks to strike out at prey, like a coiled snake, or to grab pterosaurs flying above the

---

* Strictly speaking, these are the non-avian dinosaurs, because birds are living dinosaurs.

waterline. In fact, the plesiosaurs' abundant neck vertebrae were likely quite stiff and didn't flex from side to side. These reptiles may have floated horizontally in the water, dipping their necks below their body to rake fish shoals with a snarl of intermeshed teeth or to root out prey in the seabed.

Swimming through Mesozoic seas were reptiles that looked like monitor lizards, others like giant newts, salamanders, or crocodiles, and huge, long sea snakes with little legs and gently bulging bellies. This was also the era when another group of reptiles, the sea turtles, first evolved, including the biggest ever to exist, the two-ton *Archelon*, which grew to fifteen feet long and would have needed four king-size mattresses to stretch out on.

In all, reptiles retraced their ancestral past and took to the ocean on at least a dozen separate occasions. No one knows for sure what drew them all down to the sea—one idea is that the land was getting crowded with other animals while the ocean offered plenty of space and prey—but clearly reptiles learnt to swim many times over. Their bodies underwent extreme adaptations to enable them to live underwater. Fossils of ichthyosaurs show that their arms gradually became shorter and their hands longer with more fingers—all the better to act as large, swimming flippers. Some ichthyosaurs evolved eyes the size of ten-pin bowling balls, bigger than those of any other animal extinct or alive, which gave them excellent vision as they hunted in the dim waters of the twilight zone. *Thalassodraco* ("sea dragon" in Greek) looked like a dolphin with a huge ribcage, accommodating enormous lungs that let it take great breaths and stay longer underwater.

Occasional food remains preserved in their stomachs and the arrangement and shapes of their teeth tell us Mesozoic marine reptiles had a varied animal-based diet. The most terrifying of all were those that filled an ecological niche that until then had been empty. Hyper-carnivores—predators that eat other predators—hadn't existed until the Mesozoic. It's evident that swimming reptiles were in the habit of eating one another. A fossilised *Diandongosaurus*, a close relative of plesiosaurs, has been found with its hind left flipper missing, likely bitten clean off by a fellow reptilian predator. And a sixteen-foot ichthyosaur swallowed most of a thirteen-foot thalattosaur, another Mesozoic reptile, shortly before it died, as palaeontologists saw when they found a fossil within a fossil.

Not all the swimming reptiles were spine-chilling carnivores. The oldest known plant-eating marine reptile, *Atopodentatus*, had a strange hammerhead skull and may have had an unusual two-step mode of feeding. With its chisel-shaped teeth, it likely scraped at seaweeds on the seabed. It also had a row of needlelike teeth, which formed a mesh and could have sieved fragments stirred into the water column.

And not all these swimming reptiles were giants. Many of the early ichthyosaurs were salmon-sized, including one called *Cartorhynchus*, which had a stubby snout, pebble-shaped teeth for crunching snails and clams, and big flippers with flexible wrists that would have let it move about on land. In life it would have looked rather like a small seal that basked on the shore and dived in the water to feed.

Throughout the 190-million-year span of the Mesozoic, an ebb and flow of marine reptiles occurred, as some went extinct and new forms kept evolving. To begin with, they mostly stayed near the shorelines fringing the coasts of the supercontinent Pangaea, which had formed when other continents collided with Gondwana and spanned both hemispheres. Then, as Pangaea began to break apart, the continents and oceans we know today began taking shape. Volatile seams in the earth's crust opened, and the new Pacific and Atlantic Oceans were born. Marine reptiles swam along the seaways that opened up between continents and soon were living all across the global ocean.

The Mesozoic was more than just an exciting time for its assortment of swimming reptiles. The reign of sea dragons was part of an oceanic revolution that shaped much of life on earth in ways that continue into the present day. The procession of predators triggered an evolutionary arms race as their prey found means of survival and escape, which in turn caused new life forms and lifestyles to flourish.

A major battleground was the seabed, where reptiles as well as bony fishes, sharks, ammonoids, and crabs were all busy searching for shelled creatures and crushing them in their powerful jaws or claws. The prey responded in many different ways. Clam-like bivalves began a long game of hide-and-seek that still goes on today, as they escaped downwards, burrowing into the seafloor and sprouting long breathing tubes.* Sea lilies, umbrella-shaped relatives of starfish, escaped the feeding frenzy by drifting off into open waters. Snails evolved thicker, spinier shells; some also took flight from the dangerous seabed, evolving tiny wings and flitting off into the plankton as sea butterflies. Other snails fled the oceans altogether. The Mesozoic reptiles that went back to the sea and evolved into terrifying sea monsters were part of the forces that drove snails into fresh water and ultimately onto land.

Predators evolved countermeasures to keep up with their prey. They developed excellent vision and camouflage, improving their chances of spotting prey from farther away and sneaking up undetected. And predators evolved new ways of breaking through tough-shelled defences. If you ever find a seashell with a neat, round hole, it contained a creature that was killed and eaten via a mode of attack that first evolved in the Mesozoic, when predatory snails gained the ability to drill through the shells of other molluscs and suck out their soft insides.

Ocean food webs had become a scramble of animals eating and getting eaten. In 1977, mollusc expert Geerat Vermeij proposed this

---

*Look at the enormous, fleshy siphon of a living geoduck clam to see where that development led.

ferocious struggle should be called the Mesozoic marine revolution. Since then, signs of the revolution's effects have been noted in many other animals, but only in 2021 did this transition come into view across the entire fossil record. Earlier fossil studies found obvious signs of the five prehistoric mass extinctions—it's not too difficult to spot the annihilation of more than 90 per cent of all life. But the influence of mounting predation in the Mesozoic was more gradual and didn't clearly show up. With advances in computing power and new ways of analysing enormous fossil data sets, researchers can now extract patterns that were previously hidden from human eyes and minds. Scientists at Umeå University in Sweden built what amounts to an interactive digital map of the entirety of ancient ocean life through space and time. It shows that the Mesozoic marine revolution was indeed a life-shaping force equally as powerful as mass extinctions. Dramatic global catastrophes have caused ocean-wide changes in biodiversity, and so too did the prolonged shift that took place under the influence of marine reptiles and all the other predators roaming through Mesozoic seas.

Today the only reptiles that live a fully oceanic life are sea turtles and sea snakes. All the other fish-like, whale-like, and lizard-like Mesozoic lineages went extinct. The last of the ichthyosaurs were gone by around one hundred million years ago, likely because they weren't evolving quickly enough to adapt to an intense period of climate change. Meanwhile, the plesiosaurs made it to the end of the Mesozoic, then died along with three-quarters of life on earth, extinguished by another mass extinction. That moment, sixty-six million years ago, is the most infamous planetary disaster, one that captures people's imaginations more than any other and shapes the popular view of extinction. An asteroid hit the earth, the skies darkened, and the dinosaurs' days were numbered. A story often told is that once dinosaurs were out of the way, mammals had their chance to arise from their shadows. It's a dusty old theory, challenged by many lines of evidence in the fossil record. And yet, the idea persists that mass extinctions pave the way for new life to rebound—that devastation is a prerequisite for renewal.

Machine learning tools are helping scientists construct another powerful new view of biodiversity through time. By programming computers with artificial intelligence algorithms, biologist Jennifer Cuthill from Essex University (UK) and colleagues have held millions of fossils in their virtual hands and tracked subtle shifts in life from the Cambrian to the present day. Their method detected the same five mass extinctions that everyone else has found, plus seven other major extinction events. They also pinpointed seventeen times in the past when life flourished and evolution surged into action, which they called mass radiations. Critically, they found that mass extinctions and mass radiations don't tend to pair up in the fossil record. There are only two examples of a notable extinction followed right away by a great radiation. On fifteen other occasions, radiations happened nowhere near an extinction event. Rather, they were often associated with evolutionary innovations, such as the development of eyes or the movement of different forms of life onto land. There is little evidence that mass extinctions are a force of creative destruction.

The pace and rhythm of evolution in deep time is not simply driven by dramatic extinctions; life is far more responsive and complex. A catastrophe isn't needed to steer evolution down new avenues and sculpt biodiversity in novel ways. A tangle of other elements is constantly in play, as more gradual and less immediately lethal environmental changes take place. And these intricate responses are evident in the ways ocean life changed through the third great chapter of life, the Cenozoic,* beginning sixty-six million years ago and leading up to now.

---

*The Cenozoic era is divided into seven or eight epochs: the Palaeocene, Eocene, Oligocene, Miocene, Pliocene, Pleistocene, and Holocene, plus arguably the Anthropocene.

When the aftermath of the dinosaur-killing extinction had subsided, roughly ten million years into the Cenozoic, the earth was in the grip of fearsome global warming. There was no ice at the poles. Forests flourished in Antarctica. Flying lemurs leapt through the trees on Ellesmere Island in far northern Canada. The situation suddenly escalated fifty-six million years ago, when the deep sea released a colossal burp of the potent greenhouse gas methane, perhaps because gradual heating had caused seabed sediments to destabilise. Global temperatures spiked by ten degrees Celsius in the ocean surface and five degrees Celsius in the deep sea. The ocean became more acidic, a mass extinction swept through deep-sea ecosystems, species moved towards the poles, and the earth became a tropical hothouse.

Many scientists consider this to be the closest analogue to anthropogenic climate change, and while certainly the most recent such event, it wasn't as extreme as what's happening now. In comparison, changes in ocean chemistry and the rate of carbon release are an order of magnitude higher today because of humankind. Back then, temperatures continued to rise until forty-nine million years ago, when the climate dramatically changed course. Carbon dioxide levels in the atmosphere began to fall, thanks in part to the chemical weathering of continental rocks,* which accelerated when India collided with Asia, building the Himalayan mountain range. Temperatures steadily dropped, and the earth, recovering from its fever, began to descend into an ice house, setting the scene for the climate we live in now.

---

* Carbon dioxide is sucked out of the atmosphere when natural mild acid in rainwater reacts with some rock types, breaking them into compounds such as bicarbonate that wash into the ocean and are used by marine organisms such as phytoplankton to make shells and are eventually deposited as layers of limestone on the seafloor.

The world was also beginning to look much like it does now. The continents had drifted into their approximate current locations, except for some subtle but important tectonic shifts that were still to come. Around thirty-four million years ago, the southern tip of South America pulled away and left Antarctica on its own. This allowed an oceanic current to begin swirling endless clockwise loops around the continent, effectively isolating it from warmer waters in the rest of the ocean. It also happened that the Antarctic continent had come to sit right over the South Pole, putting it in the perfect place to get very cold very fast, and it was soon covered in a giant sheet of ice.

Not until much more recently, around 2.7 million years ago, did the seas at the North Pole begin to turn to ice. The story of how this happened is more complex and disputed than Antarctica's deep freeze. But likewise, continental movements were involved. The gap was gradually closing between North and South America. Where the Central American Seaway had provided a direct connection between the Pacific and Atlantic, now the land bridge of Panama lay in the way, preventing the two oceans from directly mixing. This had profound effects on global ocean circulation and climate, including intensifying the Gulf Stream, which flows from the Caribbean Sea into the northeast Atlantic. The closure was also linked with the strengthening of the global conveyor belt, the ocean circulation that flows around the whole planet today. By pushing moisture-laden air northwards, the Gulf Stream likely played a part in boosting snowfall over Greenland and North America, increasing the size of glaciers that were forming in the Northern Hemisphere as the earth entered a prolonged and volatile ice age.

In the Cenozoic, the ocean settled into its present-day configuration and welcomed the arrival of many life forms that still prevail. A recurring theme during this era was the return of tetrapods to the ocean. Yet again, four-footed land animals gave in to the irresistible lure of the sea, many times over. The main protagonists this time weren't reptiles, as in the Mesozoic. Instead, it was the turn of mammals to go back to their aquatic roots. Seven different types of mammals dipped their hooves, paws, and feet in the water and evolved ways to survive at sea, in time becoming integral parts of ocean ecosystems.

Around fifty million years ago, an assortment of prehistoric mammals walked the shores of the Tethys Ocean, an ancient water body that used to connect the Atlantic and Indian Oceans across northern Africa. Among them were animals that trotted on long, thin legs and had something of the wolf in them. These were archaeocetes, the beginning of a long animal dynasty that led up to modern cetaceans—the whales and dolphins. They were animals with even-toed hooves, a group that today includes giraffes, camels, antelopes, llamas, sheep, pigs, and cows. Modern cetaceans' closest living relatives are hippopotamuses.

Proto-whales went through a series of evolutionary stages, as shown by elegant fossils, at first amphibious then increasingly oceanic. They followed parallel lines of evolution leading them to resemble many of the giant marine reptiles that swam before them. Their legs turned into flippers, and their tails sprouted powerful, wide flukes, although they didn't swing sideways, like the tails of swimming reptiles, but up and down, a throwback to the gait of their terrestrial forebears; contrast a reptilian gecko, which sashays along flexing its spine from side to side, with a cheetah, which bends its back up and down as it runs. It took roughly ten million years for whales to become fully pelagic, with nostrils on the tops of their heads (i.e., blowholes) and inner ear bones adapted to hearing well underwater. But the cetacean lineage really took off a while later.

A key point in the evolution of whales was when Antarctica broke away from South America, and the global climate shifted into an ice house. This was when the two main cetacean lineages—the baleen whales (mysticetes) and the toothed whales (odontocetes)—diverged from each other. With Antarctica on its own, a current now whirled around the continent, which not only sent temperatures falling but also triggered deep mixing of the Southern Ocean, stirring nutrients into upper layers of the sea. Consequently, oceanic ecosystems around the world became enormously productive. Plankton proliferated, and the new group of filter-feeding whales with hairy baleen plates in their mouths had plenty to eat. Around that time, toothed whales began to interrogate the ocean with beams of sound, hunting for prey with their new echolocating powers. From these early odontocetes, a lineage of smaller cetaceans separated and began filling seas and rivers with dolphins, porpoises, narwhals, and orcas.*

At the time when the proto-whales were starting to wade and swim, a different group of mammals were splashing along the shores of the Tethys Ocean. Sea cows began as pig-size relatives of elephants with stumpy legs that walked on land and wallowed in the shallows. Also known as sirenians, they spread across the planet and evolved into assorted species of dugongs and manatees, which mostly lived along warm and tropical coasts and spent their days chewing on seagrasses. Some moved into the North Pacific rim and fed on the giant kelp forests that started growing there around thirty million years ago as the ocean was cooling. They shared their kelp forest home with yet another gang of aquatic mammals—desmostylians, stocky, hippo-size animals with two pairs of short, goofy tusks sticking out of their mouths. Like many other herbivorous marine mammals, they had thick, heavy bones that acted as ballast to help them sink while they foraged underwater, especially important when their rotund bellies filled up with digestive gases produced by their plant-based diet. Desmostylians existed for only a narrow window

---

*The Delphinida includes the oceanic dolphins (Delphinidae), the Amazonian dolphins (Iniidae), the South Asian river dolphins (Platanistidae), and the narwhals and belugas (Monodontidae).

of time, between thirty-three and ten million years ago. All the North Pacific sea cows also went extinct, including, most recently, the biggest ever to evolve. Steller's sea cow grew up to thirty feet long, several times the size of living sea cows. This giant was named after the German explorer Georg Wilhelm Steller, who encountered it in the 1740s while shipwrecked on the Commander Islands, off Kamchatka, Russia. By then the species was already on its way out, driven into decline by the changing climate during the last ice age. When sea levels dropped during glaciations, much of its kelp habitat became fragmented. Human hunters played a part in the Steller's sea cows' annihilation, killing the last of them for their oil and for their meat, which apparently tasted like corned beef.

Outliving the kelp-dwelling sea cows and desmostylians are mammals that much more recently took to the ocean. Sea otters evolved in the North Pacific from weasel-like ancestors only in the past two to three million years, and at up to a hundred pounds, they're the heaviest mustelids but the smallest marine mammals.

Farther south, seagrass meadows along the South American coast were grazed by giant swimming sloths. Five species of *Thalassocnus* were related to the giant ground sloths that lumbered around the pampas grasslands. These aquatic sloths grew up to eleven feet long from snout to tail, longer than a bison, and they bounded along the seabed, steering with their tails like beavers. Giant sloths swam about for fewer than five million years, a brief moment in the ocean's history. When the Central American Seaway closed, the changing ocean currents and falling temperatures killed off swaths of seagrasses along the South American coasts. With little to eat and no blubber to keep them warm, the furry, swimming sloths came to an end.

The same climatic shift caused a major stir among the cetaceans too, with the arrival of conditions that favoured outrageously big whales. When the Northern Hemisphere froze over, sea levels dropped, and patches of rich seasonal food developed in the ocean.

Smaller baleen whales were confined to the coasts, where the seawater was draining away, and many of them went extinct around three million years ago. Meanwhile, much bigger whales were thriving. They set off on long journeys, cruising between high-latitude feeding and low-latitude, tropical breeding grounds. Today, enormous whales migrate every year to feed in the Arctic or Antarctic, the fifty-foot humpbacks and grey whales, the eighty-foot fin whales, and the largest animals known to have existed, the hundred-foot blue whales.

The Cenozoic also saw several other mammal groups take to the ocean. Pinnipeds originated in the Arctic at least twenty-four million years ago from a similar group of ancestors to the sea otters. Indeed, early on they looked a lot like three-foot-long otters, but their fossilised teeth give away that they were in fact seals. Three groups of pinnipeds have since diverged and moved onto shores around the world: the seals, sea lions, and walruses.* In the Arctic, walruses and seals haul out on the sea ice to rest and raise their young, all the while watching out for polar bears, the mammals that most recently took to the sea. Polar bears diverged from brown bears and began prowling the Arctic ice within the past half million years.

For seals in Antarctica, there are no polar bears to fear, and they share the Southern Ocean with another gaggle of vertebrates that also dived into the Cenozoic ocean and became Antarctic specialists. Direct ancestors of modern-day penguins evolved twenty million years ago on temperate coasts and islands of Aotearoa (New Zealand)† and Australia. From there they moved south and took advantage of Antarctica's circumpolar current to disperse around the continent, gradually adapting along the way to the freezing climate and diverging into new species. First to evolve were the biggest living species, which stand waist-high to a human: the emperor and

---

*The phocids, otariids, and odobenids.

†Aotearoa is the name the Māori people use for New Zealand, their native islands. I have included aboriginal and dual place names and spellings throughout the book.

king penguins. Then came gentoos, chinstraps, and Adélies.* All of
them eat krill, the finger-size swimming crustaceans that evolved at
a similar time and became the staple diet of most Southern Ocean
animals. Later, around eleven million years ago, the Antarctic current
strengthened and propelled penguins northwards to warmer climes,
including back to Aotearoa and even as far as the equatorial Galápagos Islands, but they've not made it as far as the Arctic. Penguins
remain resolutely Southern Hemisphere species.

The many new arrivals in the Cenozoic ocean joined a mix of marine
life that had survived from earlier epochs and was busy shifting into
a modern guise. During the Cenozoic, modern day coral reefs took
shape. Previously, reefs had been built by various kinds of corals as
well as sponges and shells. Then, after millions of years of coming
and going through multiple mass extinctions, the scleractinian corals finally gained a firm footing in the ocean, and their diversity
steadily increased. Individual corals are tiny, flower-like polyps that
construct around themselves exoskeletons of limestone, hence their
other name, the stony corals. In great colonies, they form the main
foundation for tropical reefs today.

The Cenozoic also saw a huge proliferation of fish species, in particular the group known as the spiny-rayed fishes because they have
sharp bony spines in their fins.† Flatfish, tuna, swordfish, rockfish,
mackerel, and cod are just some of the many abundant spiny-rays in
the ocean today. Coral reefs are brimming with spiny-rayed fishes,
among them the butterflyfish and angelfish, parrotfish, pufferfish,

---

*Adélie penguins (*Pygoscelis adeliae*) were named after Adèle Dumont d'Urville, who
was married to a nineteenth-century Antarctic explorer from France, Adélie being an
alternative way to spell Adèle.

†Also called acanthomorphs, these fishes have sharp bony spines on their dorsal and
anal fins, which they can use as protection from predators; they can also protrude their
jaws to snap up food.

and groupers. Seahorses evolved in the Cenozoic when seagrass meadows spread between Australia and Indonesia. Their unusual upright posture, horses' heads, and curling, gripping tails were all adaptations seahorses evolved that camouflage them and help them navigate through the grass blades.

While bony fishes with spiny rays were doing very well in the Cenozoic, another group of fishes, with bendy, cartilaginous skeletons, were not so lucky. Sharks had been swimming through the ocean for hundreds of millions of years but almost went extinct nineteen million years ago. This near-extinction was discovered only in 2021, from a study of their toothlike scales, called denticles, which dropped down onto the deep seabed and became trapped in sediments. Close to three-quarters of shark species disappeared, and it's not obvious why. Fossils suggest that sharks have never been as abundant as they once were, but within a few million years they began to regain their diversity and to get a lot larger. The megatooth shark lineage was made up of species that gradually got bigger through the Cenozoic, with the unrivalled giants evolving around sixteen million years ago. Megalodons* had seven-inch-long teeth and ten-foot-wide jaws and from head to tail were between fifty and sixty feet long, roughly two full-size school buses parked bumper to bumper. The species went extinct 3.6 million years ago, shortly after the arrival of a newcomer, the great white shark. It's possible great whites pushed their competitors towards extinction by hunting the same prey as young megalodons.

At odds with the popular idea that sharks are prehistoric creatures that haven't changed much in millions of years, new species have evolved relatively recently in the Cenozoic. The youngest belong to a group known as the walking sharks, which live in shallow seas of Papua New Guinea, Indonesia, and northern Australia. These

---

* *Otodus megalodon* was previously thought to belong to the Lamnidae, the same family as great white sharks, but is now placed within a separate sister group, the Otodontidae, or megatooth sharks.

three-foot-long sharks spend their days resting on the seabed, then set off at night to hunt, using their pectoral and pelvic fins as rudimentary legs, strutting along in a gecko-like gait. With their leisurely strolling and reluctance to swim, these sharks never move too far under their own steam. The most westerly species arrived in its current location in Indonesia not by swimming but by riding on its home island. That's how sedentary these sharks are—they use the geological forces of tectonic drift to get around. This means walking-shark populations are easily cut off from one another, between one island and the next, increasing the chances of splitting into separate species. All nine known species of walking sharks evolved in the past nine million years, and the youngest species split apart only two million years ago.

The view we now have back through deep time tells us that life on earth and in the ocean has always been turbulent and ever changing. Life has been sculpted by life itself and steered by powerful external forces that shift currents and continents and alter the climate. Now, in the present moment we've reached in the Cenozoic era, a single global force has come into effect. The Anthropocene, the age of humans, is underway.

Homo sapiens has been modifying the earth for millennia, by hunting other animals, felling forests, burning vegetation, and domesticating animals and crops. But only in recent times have humans been altering the planet on such vast scales and in so many ways. The word *Anthropocene* is intended to embrace the accumulating and accelerating ways human activities have become dominant agents of global change, from chemical pollution to climate change, from the mass rearing of livestock to the rampant destruction of biodiversity.

When exactly the Anthropocene began is a rather esoteric matter, one that a team of geologists, the Anthropocene Working Group, has been considering since 2009. In 2023, they proposed that a lake in Canada serve as the marker for the start of the Anthropocene, with the idea it will be identifiable thousands of years in the future. Crawford Lake, near Toronto, is six acres in area and almost eighty feet deep, and contains layers of undisturbed sediment that gently sink down into it, including key molecules that indicate when human activities shifted gear to a world-altering scale. A thin layer laid down in 1952 contains plutonium particles from the hydrogen bomb tests that drifted around the world. There are also spherical particles of carbon released by the widespread burning of fossil fuels, and nitrates released by the flood of chemical fertilisers. For Crawford Lake to be officially adopted will require three more committees of geologists to vote in favour, but already the idea of the Anthropocene has taken hold.★

A critical part of anthropogenic change is the endangerment of thousands of species that is driving the earth's sixth mass extinction. Humans have already caused countless species to disappear, ranging from documented extirpations, like that of Steller's sea cow, to the hidden extinctions as species slip away when entire ecosystems are demolished. One way to get a sense of the scale of what's happening now is to compare current extinction rates against the background rate at which species have steadily been lost from the fossil record in aeons gone by when there wasn't a mass extinction raging. Whichever way you slice the data, the rate of extinction is now far higher, perhaps a hundred times, than during those peaceful intermissions of the past. A contemporary mass extinction is in full swing.

Messages from deep time warn that there will be no creative destruction, no wiping clean of the slate to make way for a flourishing new era of biodiversity. New radiations of species will happen in time, but they're unlikely to be the direct result of Anthropocene extinctions. There will be no swift recovery of lost species,

---

★An alternative suggestion is the *Capitalocene*, a term that emphasises the global change associated with the history of capitalism and colonialism and recognises the uneven distribution of costs and benefits in this age of humans.

and certainly not on timescales relevant to human lives. Following even the milder mass extinctions of the past, biodiversity has taken hundreds of thousands of years to recover. If our collective impact comes close to the worst extinctions, life on earth will be diminished for millions of years to come. Decisions made now in the Anthropocene will set changes in motion that will alter the path of life far beyond the likely lifespan of humanity itself.

There's no telling who the survivors in the long term will be and what kind of new living worlds they will build together in the ocean. If the past is anything to go by, probably predators and prey will continue to exist, as will animals swimming around with hydrodynamic bodies and quite possibly flippers and tails. There's no telling which group of animals might take on those roles, any more than we could have guessed that an ocean filled with trilobites scurrying and paddling around would be replaced by a realm ruled by giant swimming reptiles, then much later by a similar-looking crowd of mammals.

Perhaps another group of vertebrates will fill niches vacated by the sixth mass extinction; maybe birds will become the next underwater giants, or perhaps an age of oceanic amphibians will dawn and frogs, toads, and salamanders will follow their ancestors back to the seas. Or it could be the turn of invertebrates to become the ocean's dominant predators once again. Octopuses or squid could rise up and diversify into blood-chilling apex predators or gentle filter feeders. Reefs too could keep growing along the edges of continents and islands, built by new kinds of builders; maybe a different group of corals, shells, or seaweeds will take on that role, or maybe sea stars or sea urchins will press their hard skeletons together in great colonies and shoulder the ramparts of new reefs. Until the ocean enters a post-Anthropocene era, we can only guess what will come next.

What we can do is meaningfully consider the changes that will likely happen within our own lifetimes and that people in future generations will witness. We can contemplate who the likely winners and losers will be, human and nonhuman, and look for effective ways to overcome the challenges facing the ocean. And we can recognise the fundamental difference between what's happening in the Anthropocene and everything else that came before. Past changes have had multiple, often unidentifiable triggers. This time a single species is to blame, one that's aware, at least to some extent, of the trouble being caused. Humans are in the unique position of having a chance to make conscious decisions about the future of the earth's biodiversity and with it our own future.

Chapter 2
Remixing Seas

Ten years ago or so, I met a lionfish that I couldn't bring myself to kill. Hunkered under a coral overhang on a reef in the Bahamas, it was one foot long, striped like a zebra in white and red, its fans of long fins folded back against its body. I'd heard about how lionfish had been set free from aquarium tanks and were spreading across the Caribbean and western Atlantic. And yet, coming face to face with a species I had last seen half a world away, I felt more unsettled and conflicted than I'd expected. In that moment, the so-called lionfish invasion shifted in my mind from a textbook example of how people are meddling with the ocean into this one beautiful yet misplaced animal. This fish wasn't to blame for the troubles going on; it was not an individual animal to victimise but simply one caught up in our human ways. Here was unavoidable proof of the changing seas, gazing right back at me.

Some years had passed since I had scuba dived in the Caribbean. Last time I had been there, I wouldn't have seen a lionfish no matter how hard I might have searched. Most of my research had taken me to the Indian and Pacific Oceans, the native range of lionfish. I've always liked seeing them underwater, and only once have I encountered their darker side. In Madagascar, on a small sand island off the west coast, I met a fisherman who a few days earlier had caught a lionfish and been stung by one of its venom-tipped fins. He held out a horribly swollen, discoloured hand. We helped him into our boat and gave him a ride to the mainland to get medical attention.

Now, here I was on a Bahamian reef, staring at a fearless lionfish that wasn't about to swim away from me. I had never tried my hand at spearfishing before, but I'd been informed that shooting lionfish is easy. Generally, they are slow, fluttering fish that aren't easily scared off, relying on their bright colours to warn intruders away from their venomous spines. I was working as part of a research team studying the effects of lionfish on Caribbean coral reefs. We weren't there to catch as many lionfish as possible; we were gathering samples to unpick the contents of their stomachs. As I clutched the spear, held taut with a giant rubber band, I found myself quite unable to let go and send it flying through the water to put an end to that fish.

The order of the ocean's fauna and flora used to be shaped just by climate, ecology, and geography. Now it's being directly shaped by people too. Not so long ago, there were places that were home to only certain combinations of species, with well-traversed routes and highways where they roamed. Now, a turbulent remixing is underway, making it a daunting prospect to work out what the future ocean will look like.

One way this happens is when people deliberately move species, usually with some economic goal in mind. Land-based bids to do this have often gone badly wrong and spiralled out of control, like when giant African land snails were introduced to oceanic islands in the South Pacific. The idea was for people to farm and consume these massive molluscs, which can reach twelve inches long, but instead the snails escaped and began demolishing wild vegetation. So, people released another foreign snail species, the carnivorous Florida rosy wolfsnail, which they hoped would eat the giant snails. But that plan didn't work out either. Instead, the wolfsnails turned their attention to the islands' endemic tree snails, which live nowhere else on earth and soon were being hunted to extinction. The story was playing out like the children's rhyme about the old lady who swallowed a fly, then a spider to catch the fly, and we know how that went in the end. Conservationists arrived in French Polynesia just in time to gather up the remaining tree snails and whisk them away to safety in zoos around the world. Still, this and other catastrophic cases from land ecosystems haven't been enough to put people off from deliberately moving species around the planet, including in the seas.

Red king crabs are formidable, spiny crustaceans with legs that can stretch almost six feet across and ochre-coloured shells that brighten to scarlet when they're cooked. Their native range stretches across the North Pacific, from the coasts of Korea and Japan across the Bering Sea to Alaska and Vancouver Island. For the past few decades, they've also been living much farther away. In the 1960s, Russians gathered up red king crabs from the Sea of Okhotsk, off Kamchatka, and moved them more than three thousand miles to the Barents Sea, in the far northwest of Russia. They translocated a total of 1.5 million larvae, ten thousand young crabs, and close to three thousand adults. The aim was to establish a commercial crab fishery in waters that are more easily accessible to Russian fishing fleets—and it worked. But of course the crabs didn't stay where they were put, and soon they were breeding and spreading.

Thirty years later, fishers in Norway, to the west of Russia, began pulling huge red crabs from their nets and traps. At first, Norwegians feared the invading crabs would ruin their livelihoods and tear apart their fishing gear, until many of them realised they were looking at a lucrative new source of income. This was before *Deadliest Catch* became a hit television series about the Alaskan fishery of the red king crab in its native range in the Bering Sea, but people still knew about the high prices these crustaceans could command, especially when kept alive and shipped to high-end restaurants around the world. So that's what Norwegian fishers started doing.

Wrestling king crabs from icy seas is not an easy way to make a living, but it pays. The new red king crab fisheries have transformed many people's lives in Norway, and the export fishery is now worth tens of millions of euros every year. But the crabs are also a major cause for concern. These are large, omnivorous generalists that make a mark on their surroundings. Adult king crabs grab prey in their powerful pincers and tear it to shreds. When the crabs arrived in the Barents Sea, many other species dramatically declined. In some places, the newcomers completely wiped out mussels and starfish. King crabs also eat a lot of worms, which are important for digging and stirring up sediments. When there are fewer worms, less oxygen is mixed into the seabed, altering the ecosystem and making it harder for other animals to survive.

There are also concerns for other fisheries. King crabs may compete for food with commercially fished species like Atlantic cod, plaice, and haddock, and they eat the eggs of capelin, a key fish species in the Barents Sea food web. What's more, leeches that are hosts to a type of parasite that infects cod like to fix themselves onto the king crabs' spiny shells.

The red king crabs have already reached the Norwegian city of Tromsø, and they could continue along the Scandinavian peninsula and offshore to the Lofoten Islands and there threaten major seasonal cod fisheries. And so, in an attempt to halt this westerly march of the king crabs, Norwegian fisheries officers have drawn a line. The twenty-sixth meridian east runs through Magerøya Island near Knivskjellodden, the northernmost part of mainland Norway, 150 miles from the Russian border. On each side of that line, different stories about king crabs are playing out.

To the east, the fishery is run with the aim of operating for years to come. Quotas are set for the total weight of king crabs a fisher can take each year, and fishers are permitted to keep only those with shells bigger than five inches across. Crabs any smaller go back in the sea to carry on growing and reproducing. Fishers commonly fill their quotas within a few weeks, then some spend the rest of the year running tours, bringing tourists to the fjords to see and taste the king crabs.

West of that line of longitude, fishers can keep all the king crabs they catch. Here, no crabs go back in the sea. This westerly free-for-all is technically known as an eradication fishery, the aim of which is to remove as many crabs as possible as quickly as possible.

It would be far-fetched to assume the eradication fishery will entirely halt the king crabs in their tracks. Their larvae will keep drifting, and adults will keep walking, and not all of them will end up in nets and traps. Fishers farther west are anticipating their arrival. In January 2022, fishers in the north of England pulled up their crab pots and found inside spiny red giants. The news that invading Russian crabs had made it all the way across the North Sea sparked shock and excitement in the UK fishing industry; some fishers worried about local ecosystems and their regular catches of brown crabs, while others began dreaming of export markets. However, experts from London's Natural History Museum later confirmed these were not in fact red king crabs but a similar species, the Norway king crab, a North Sea native, although rarely caught in British fisheries. Still, there's a good chance the red kings will make their way over.

On occasion, ocean species simply show up out of the blue and with no obvious human help. Solitary animals arrive in places where they're not normally expected, such as a huge male walrus that recently left the Arctic and toured the coasts of Europe, gaining an entourage of fans who spotted him in Ireland, England, France, and Spain, then back up north in Iceland. They nicknamed him Wally.* However, when a single unusual animal is followed by another and

---

* If Wally had shown up in North America, he probably would have been named Waldo.

another until they can no longer be considered occasional visitors, then humans are usually involved.

Ships are a major source of long-distance travellers, their hulls encrusted with hangers-on and their ballast water tanks twitching with hitchhiking larvae and microbes, which get picked up in one place and dumped elsewhere. Not all the transported species survive the journey or thrive when they arrive, but many that do end up causing trouble. This was how, in the 1980s, sea walnuts, a species of comb jelly, moved from North American waters to the Black Sea. So many were stowed away in ballast tanks and released thousands of miles from their native waters that their numbers soon exploded. Superabundant sea walnuts ate so much plankton that many fish went hungry, triggering the collapse of local fisheries.

Adding to the drip-feed of species that people are accidentally moving great distances, a wave of climate migrants is making its own way across the ocean. With temperatures rising, much ocean life is on the move.

Along both the east and west coasts of North America, large shark species are swimming to places where they were not normally seen in the past. Historically, the waters off the northeast coast were too cold for tiger sharks, cold-blooded apex predators that need to stay in warm waters. Back in the summers of the 1980s, they would ride the Gulf Stream from the Caribbean and spend time off the coast of Florida. Now the ocean is warmer, and tiger sharks are venturing hundreds of miles farther north. Large congregations now form off the coast of North Carolina, and tigers swim as far north as Cape Cod, Massachusetts. This northerly shift is making tiger sharks more vulnerable to fishing, because they're now swimming outside of marine protected areas and coming within range of longline fisheries.

In the west, on the central California coast, great white sharks have started showing up. In 2014, sightings in Monterey Bay rose dramatically. Drone cameras photographed a half dozen at a time cruising together. Strangely, these were all relatively small sharks, around eight feet long, making them juveniles between three and four years old, which don't normally swim this far north. Even though this shark species is warm-blooded, young great whites are usually confined to warmer waters because they are less chunky than adults and easily get chilled. The arrival of young sharks in Monterey Bay coincided with a huge marine heatwave that struck the Pacific coast.

Around the world, a cavalcade of ocean migrants are escaping to higher latitudes, from lobsters to flounders, pipefish, and starfish. In the Pacific, the Humboldt squid is expanding its range on either side of the equator, to both the north and south. Collectively, ocean species are moving towards the poles, travelling at a global average pace of forty-five miles per decade. This is a coarse figure, obscuring details gathered from masses of tracking studies that follow individual animals and species moving this way and that, but it speaks to the immensity of the changes already taking place.

On land, the pace of climate migration is an order of magnitude slower than in the sea. The ocean offers far fewer obvious boundaries and obstacles for migrating species to overcome. And the seas are full of organisms that during some portion of their lives—from egg to larva to mobile, swimming adult—make use of their free-flowing liquid realm to find mates and new territories to settle and grow. In the sea, it's common for species to end up living a long way from where they were born, giving them an inbuilt capacity for shifting to cooler climes as the ocean around them heats.

Ocean dwellers in a warming world also need to move more urgently than land dwellers because they tend to live within narrow thermal safety margins. They're not used to getting either much hotter or colder, as they evolved to live at temperatures that fluctuate very little on a daily or seasonal basis. Air temperatures can swing by tens of degrees between day and night, while the thermal inertia of water keeps conditions in the sea much more stable. Consequently, ocean species are highly sensitive to warming. Even small changes in their surrounding temperature can be lethal.

To make matters worse, there's nowhere easy to hide from heat in the ocean. Terrestrial animals can stay more or less where they are and adapt their behaviour to hot conditions—for example, by lurking somewhere cool during the day and coming out only at night. More elaborate adaptations include those of fogstand beetles in Africa's Namib Desert, which survive on sands that reach 140 degrees Fahrenheit by climbing to the tops of dunes in the cool hours of the morning and raising their bodies so that fog blowing off the sea condenses on their bumpy exoskeletons. In the sea, there's no point in sweating or panting, digging burrows or retreating to the shade when the water warms. The only real option is to move somewhere cooler, by either travelling towards the poles, tracking cold currents, or retreating to greater depths.

It's simple enough to foresee that ocean species will generally tend to strike out for chillier waters, but a range of factors influences who moves, when, how far, and how fast. Ocean mixing is happening in a disorderly fashion. There's no mass relocation with entire assemblages moving together in one go. Some species move quickly, and some stay behind; some spread to new territories while also maintaining old haunts; some move on and abandon their former ranges; some slide down deeper, and others hold their depth.

In the Mediterranean, hound sharks and spiny dogfish, unihorn* and musky octopuses, and jewel and flying squid are among the species that in recent years have been increasing their maximum depth. In contrast, bony fishes and crustaceans are staying nearer the surface. It could be that the sharks and octopuses are more sensitive to rising temperatures and have greater need to sink, or they are better equipped to cope in deeper waters, where sunlight dwindles, less food is available, and the pressure ramps up. But just because those

---

*Yes, unihorn, not unicorn.

animals are the first and fastest to move downwards, doesn't mean they will survive in the longer term. Once they reach the bottom of the sea, they'll have nowhere deeper to go.

For many sea-dwelling animals, climate change not only brings the direct stress of rising temperatures but also forces them to shift their range in order to keep breathing. Since the middle of the twentieth century, average oxygen levels throughout the ocean have fallen by around 2 per cent; by the end of the twenty-first century, it's expected the ocean will have deoxygenated by between 3 and 4 per cent. This is happening, in part, because of the simple fact that warmer water can hold less dissolved oxygen. Other factors also make oxygen loss far worse in certain areas. In coastal waters, fertilisers and sewage washing off land in rainfall runoff and rivers stimulate great blooms of phytoplankton, often painting the sea livid green or red. When these dense patches of microscopic algae die and decompose, the water is stripped of oxygen. Pollution from land also explains why enclosed seas, such as the Black Sea and the Baltic Sea, are notoriously oxygen poor, and now they're joined by regions of open ocean much farther from shore. Low-oxygen zones are expanding and intensifying in the eastern Pacific, off the west coast of Africa, and in the Arabian Sea and Bay of Bengal. This is happening because climate change is altering wind patterns and currents, reducing the amount of oxygen circulating through the ocean.

Hit hardest by deoxygenation are the fast-swimming animals with racing metabolic rates. Tuna, marlin, and sailfish are already losing part of their vertical habitat because of declining oxygen levels in deeper waters. They are forced to stay closer to the surface, where oxygen levels in the water are higher. Bluefin and yellowfin tuna are expected to shift their ranges polewards in the coming years to seek out enough oxygen.

Among the multitudes of ocean migrants are likely winners and losers. Species that require conditions to be just right will find it harder to survive—the clownfish that can't survive without its anemone home; the sea slugs that eat just one type of sponge or seaweed, and nothing else will do. If their food and homes don't move with them, these animals will be in trouble.

Other species are better suited to travel and more ready to adapt and fit into new neighbourhoods. Many of them share key characteristics. They tend to be generalists and aren't choosy about their food and habitats, and they either spend prolonged periods drifting as larvae or swim great distances as adults.

Climate change is doing some oceanic travellers a favour. Wandering and Laysan albatrosses set off on great soaring journeys above the waves, riding the winds and gathering food for their chicks. Now the heating ocean is intensifying winds, and albatrosses are flying farther and faster, and coming back quicker to feed their chicks, and as a result more of them are surviving.

On the list of likely survivors are lionfish, which are inadvertently being tested for their place in future seas. In the process, they're stirring a great deal of unease while also confirming that it's not an easy matter to predict the environmental impacts of migrant species.

A dozen species of lionfish are native to the Indian and Pacific Oceans. Two that are especially difficult to tell apart just by looking at them are the devil firefish and the red lionfish.* The farthest they naturally roam is Oeno, a tiny, uninhabited Pacific island roughly four thousand miles due west of the South American coast. Now, though, these two lionfish species also live together in a troublesome jumble in the Atlantic Ocean.

In the twentieth century, aquarium keepers enchanted by these striking fish brought them into captivity, adopted them as pets, and

---

* *Pterois miles* and *Pterois volitans*.

put them on public display. No one is absolutely sure where or when it happened, but both devil firefish and red lionfish were set free in the warm waters of the western Atlantic, and they found conditions much to their liking. A single lionfish was spotted in Florida waters in 1985. In the ensuing decades, following multiple releases in different places, lionfish have spread along the US East Coast from Florida to North Carolina, all through the islands of the Caribbean, into the Gulf of Mexico, and as far south as Brazil.

The successful spread of two lionfish species through this new range comes down to various quirks of their biology. Females reach breeding age when they're one year old and from then on can spawn every few days, laying as many as two million eggs a year. Larvae drift for up to a month, riding currents, getting blown about by hurricanes, and travelling for hundreds of miles. And for fish that are not built for speed like tuna and marlin are, adult lionfish swim surprisingly long distances, at least six miles a day. Also in their favour is the fact that lionfish are not fussy about where they live. Normally considered coral-reef species, they're also quite at home on seagrass meadows, in mangrove forests, and in estuaries. They've been seen a thousand feet down in Bermuda and Honduras, even beneath the murky plume of the Amazon River as it flows into the Atlantic.

When unfamiliar lionfish move into new places, the animals around them respond in different ways. Sharks, groupers, and other predators tend to ignore them and rarely try to eat them. Smaller fish aren't scared of them. Damselfish carefully tend their seaweed farms and usually chase off intruders, even human scuba divers, but they don't accost lionfish. Young reef fish that normally swim away when they see and smell predators are not bothered by lionfish. In fact, some have adopted the unfortunate habit of swimming towards them, perhaps mistaking their elaborate fins for somewhere to hide.

For these ambush predators, life in their new home is easy because their prey tends not to swim away from them. Stories have emerged of lionfish in the Caribbean finding it so effortless to hunt they were suffering from fatty liver disease, a condition usually seen in overfed pet fish. In many places, as lionfish arrived, conservationists and fishers watched in horror as the predators tucked into a naive Atlantic smorgasbord.

Similar worries of ecological turmoil were unleashed when lionfish moved into another new region. This one was caused not by releases from aquariums but by the opening of a new swimming route for wild fish. When the Suez Canal was built in 1869, it was a human enterprise on par with tectonic forces. The Mediterranean and Red Seas were connected for the first time since the eastern portion of the ancient Tethys Ocean closed around fourteen million years earlier. Historically, marine species were blocked from navigating the canal by the hypersaline Bitter Lakes midway along it. But since the canal has been successively enlarged to make way for more shipping and move more commodities around the planet, the lakes have been diluted, and hundreds of marine species have made the journey with the prevailing current from the Red Sea to the Mediterranean. Known as Lessepsian migration,* the procession of species includes lionfish from the Red Sea. The first arrivals were briefly spotted in Israel in 1991, but lionfish weren't seen again until 2012, when a new wave of them began rapidly spreading through the Mediterranean. Within a decade, lionfish had reached the coasts of Lebanon, Cyprus, Libya, Syria, Tunisia, Turkey, Greece, and Italy.

Lionfish are restricted by wintertime temperatures and generally survive only if the sea is warmer than fifty degrees Fahrenheit. The warming Mediterranean has let them survive year-round, and as temperatures continue to rise, their range will expand. By century's end, it's likely lionfish will occupy most of the Mediterranean basin and slip through the Strait of Gibraltar and out into the eastern Atlantic.

---

*Named after Ferdinand de Lesseps, the French diplomat in charge of building the Suez Canal.

On the opposite side of the Atlantic, the warm waters of the Gulf Stream currently offer winter refuge for lionfish along the shelf break off the southeastern US coast. Tropical larvae ride the Gulf Stream, and occasionally young lionfish make a summertime appearance as far north as Long Island, New York. If winters become warm enough as temperatures rise, lionfish will gradually make a year–round move farther inshore and northwards on the American coastline.

Early on, when the two lionfish invasions were getting underway in the Caribbean and the Mediterranean, the prognosis for the environment looked bleak. A worst-case scenario predicted that native fish would be replaced wholesale by lionfish, leaving habitats depleted and stripped of biodiversity, ruining fisheries and tourism, transforming ecosystems into something completely different and unappealing. However, as time has passed and more lionfish studies are being carried out, a more nuanced and complex picture is emerging.

The direst impacts of the lionfish influx have been happening in the northern parts of their new Atlantic range. Prey species have been hit hard in the Bahamas, where lionfish exist at densities five times higher than in their native ranges, the equivalent of around two hundred roaming a football field.

Off New Providence Island in the Bahamas, as lionfish numbers increased, native species of prey fish were reduced by 65 per cent. In Exuma Sound, scientists set up experimental patches of corals and saw that where lionfish were present, far fewer young fish of other species came in and settled. Presumably, lionfish were eating almost all the other little fish as soon as they arrived on the coral patches.

Where lionfish numbers are high, it's possible other species could be wiped out. Lionfish are especially fond of eating fairy basslets, finger-length fish with a front half neon pink and back half golden yellow. The predators keep on hunting these colourful snacks even when there are very few left, raising the chance that the basslet could become locally extinct. There are also major concerns for the social wrasse, a highly endangered species that lives only around a few mangrove islands in Belize. There it makes up more than half the diet of the newly arrived lionfish.

In contrast, farther south in the Caribbean, fish populations seem to cope much better with lionfish, although no one is sure exactly why. In Panama, lionfish are still outnumbered on coral reefs by native predatory fish, and local prey face no greater threat of being eaten than they did before. In Venezuela, native fish living inside a marine reserve were still doing just fine three years after lionfish moved in. When ecosystems are in good health, they seem to better resist the impacts of lionfish.

Gladly, the arrival of lionfish hasn't always triggered instant environmental disaster, as some people originally feared they would. The situation is complicated and difficult to predict. Even though lionfish are so obviously good at surviving and thriving in new places—with ravenous, unfussy appetites and formidable defences against other predators—no simple scenario exists for how they will influence other species that get drawn into their orbit.

When species move to new places, people often keenly respond. In 2022, a female walrus, this one nicknamed Freya, swam into the harbour of the Norwegian capital, Oslo, and attracted huge crowds of curious onlookers. Government authorities sparked outrage when they killed the thirteen-hundred-pound walrus after she was deemed to be a danger to the public. A statue of Freya has been raised in her honour. In contrast, soon after lionfish began settling into the waters of Florida and the Caribbean, people labelled them evil invaders, and the overwhelming reaction was to do whatever it took to get rid of them.

Thankfully, nobody has suggested releasing another species to try to swallow the proverbial fly, but various other ways of killing lionfish have been tried out. Divers tried persuading sharks and groupers that lionfish was good to eat by offering them a speared lionfish. All that did was give predators the dangerous idea of sniffing around after scuba divers to get a free feed. There are reports of groupers learning to lead divers towards a lionfish and hang around for their dinner to be served on a spike.

Bounties have been put on lionfish to encourage people to catch them. In Belize, the price per lionfish was twenty-five Belizean dollars, and in the US state of Mississippi, people were paid five dollars for every lionfish pulled out of the Gulf of Mexico. The problem is that very quickly the money ran out—there are simply too many lionfish.

More successful are lionfish derbies. During dawn-to-dusk bonanzas, competitive fishers and spearfishers go searching for lionfish. Prizes are handed out for the biggest and smallest and the greatest number brought in. The Emerald Coast Open, held in Destin, Florida, is the largest annual tournament, where competing divers have killed as many as fourteen thousand lionfish in two days. Routine lionfish removals are also carried out, especially in areas popular with tourists. In Honduras, wardens at the Roatan Marine Park hand out spears to visitors and teach them how to hunt lionfish.

There's also money to be made killing and selling lionfish. They happen to be delicious and are safe to handle and eat once their venomous spines have been cut off. The meat sells for a decent price, similar to that of other high-end reef fish such as snappers. People make frilly jewellery from lionfish fins and leather from their skin.

In Florida, people are being encouraged to trap live lionfish. Many of those captives follow in their ancestors' wake and find themselves in aquarium displays, only now the spectators gazing at them have thoughts of evil invaders on their minds and no plans to set them free.

While triumphant spearfishers hold up their trophy catches, and seafood diners do their bit by eating unwanted invasive species, it's important not to forget that these are fish that human actions have turned into problems. Not only did humans originally introduce them to places they aren't welcome, but the impacts of lionfish are made worse by other human disruptions to the environment. Climate change will encourage lionfish to invade new waters. And if other predators like groupers and sharks weren't already so widely overfished, they could be more effective in controlling lionfish outbreaks, not necessarily by eating them but by scaring them. While a lionfish is hiding, it's not hunting and growing fatter and more fecund.

It is too late to do away entirely with lionfish in their new ranges. For one thing, they soon get wise to human hunters and learn to avoid spear-wielding divers, and so they have become harder to catch. Efforts to control lionfish will carry on, and this can help reduce impacts in the most vulnerable locations. The methods may change, especially if somebody invents an effective lionfish trap or successfully sends out platoons of underwater robots to zap them with electric shocks, as has been proposed. But there's no escaping the fact that lionfish are now a permanent part of these Atlantic, Caribbean, and Mediterranean ecosystems, as are many other species that are on the move. Some, like lionfish, have become a nuisance. The silver-cheeked toadfish is among the Lessepsian migrants that ventured through the Suez Canal and are stirring trouble in the Mediterranean, already as far west as the Strait of Gibraltar. A species of pufferfish, it grows between one and three feet long and has a silver blotch in front of its eyes, and its sharp teeth easily damage fishing nets and bite through fishing lines. It's no good to eat because it's laced with deadly tetrodotoxin. Other migrants are far more benign, and they've found a place in their new ecosystems and fisheries without too much bother. When asked in 2020 about what lives in their waters, fishers from the Mediterranean island of Cyprus identified the toadfish as a new and troublesome arrival, but they considered various other species as natives, even though they originally came from the Red Sea. Rabbitfish, lizardfish, barracuda, and squirrelfish are all mostly harmless, edible fish and have been living around Cyprus since the 1960s, time enough for local fishers, aged on average in their late forties, to get quite used to them.

This is the sort of story about the changing ocean that will doubtless become more common in the years ahead. It can take less than a generation for fishing communities to become accustomed to new assemblies of species, welcoming in those that are profitable, shunning those that are tasteless, toxic, or otherwise disagreeable. Terms like *native* and *non-native* will prove not to be fixed and universal but will slip from species to species and from place to place. Ideas of what belongs where in the ocean will continue to be shaped by human wants and needs. And as species move, some will inevitably disappear altogether. Their ghosts will linger for a while, and then memories will fade too, until perhaps no one will recall they were ever there at all.

As the ocean continues to warm, and species move farther and faster, there are going to be far-reaching changes in the way fisheries operate. Which species are available to eat, and where in the ocean they come from, will alter markedly. At higher latitudes, new species that offer new commercial opportunities are already appearing. Fishers in the North Sea now catch squid and anchovies, which not long ago seemed exotic for the region. Along the US East Coast, trawl fisheries have started targeting species such as fluke (also known as summer flounder), which is shifting polewards as the ocean warms. In the decades ahead, territories in the far north stand to gain tremendously from the reorganising ocean. By 2050, catches around the Arctic could increase by as much as 30 per cent relative to the early 2000s.

Farther south, most notably in the tropics, fishing is going to become much more challenging. In a widening band on either side of the equator, the seas are already becoming too hot for many species to survive. Since the 1970s, the diversity of ocean species living at the equator has been falling. Animals are escaping to cooler waters in the north and south, and none are moving in to take their places. The global pattern of marine biodiversity used to peak at the equator; now there's a pronounced dip. This is especially true for the swimming pelagic animals, the type that fishers generally target.

Predictions extending to 2050 show that in many countries in West Africa, Southeast Asia, and the Pacific islands, fish catches could be less than half what they were at the start of the century. In these countries, coastal communities rely on wild fish for their nutrition and livelihoods. Not only will there be fewer species to fish, but those that do survive in tropical waters will be smaller, owing to the combined effects of rising temperatures and falling oxygen, making it even harder for fishers to make a living and feed their families.

The changing availability of seafood in the warming ocean will add to growing global inequalities and widen the gap in income and food security between rich and poor. If industrialised nations continue with business as usual and fail to curb carbon emissions, it will lead to the worst possible outcome for tropical countries, which had little to do with creating the climate crisis. However, devastating declines of fisheries at lower latitudes are avoidable. If carbon emissions are sharply reduced and global temperature rise is kept below two degrees Celsius by the end of the century, fishery losses will not be nearly as widespread or extreme.

In contemplating the future of the Anthropocene ocean, it is hard to get a clear idea of how species in new combinations will interact with each other and how the novel ecosystems they create will work. Researchers have built all manner of computer models to project future distributions of ocean life, and most often they focus on one species at a time, leaving out the complex dynamics of food webs. And yet, the ways species respond to each other will influence how reshuffling the ocean will pan out. Migrating prey animals could escape from traditional predators and expand their ranges quickly, or they might run into new enemies and slow down. One study predicts that these kinds of food-web interactions will hamper species' abilities to shift their ranges and will thereby impede the polewards march through the ocean.

Some species will have a major impact on the ocean when climate change forces them to move. Outsize megafauna, the big-bodied animals, often play outsize roles in their ecosystems. Whales affect the ocean around them in many ways: seabirds feed on shoals of fish that whales drive towards the surface as they hunt; whale faeces fertilise plankton, which nourish food webs and draw carbon down into the deep ocean; and when whales die and sink into the deep, they nurture long-lived ecosystems dotted across the seabed like stepping stones, which are occupied by many animals that live nowhere else, such as *Osedax*, the bone-eating worms. All these connections could change—links could break and new ones form as whales respond to warming seas and alter the timing and routes of their migrations, which is already happening in many cetaceans, especially in the far north.

The Arctic Ocean is one of the fastest-heating regions of the planet, thanks to a feedback loop tied to the sea ice. As temperatures rise, the bright white frozen surface of the sea melts and reveals the dark ocean underneath; more heat from the sun is absorbed into seawater and less is reflected from the ice, accelerating heating and melting in dangerous synchrony. In response to the rapid warming, Arctic ecosystems are in flux. Species are moving; ecological interactions are changing.

Bowheads are the only baleen whales endemic to the Arctic. In the past, one population used to spend the winters in the northwest Bering Sea, between Alaska and Russia, then migrate north through the Bering Strait and hundreds of miles into the Chukchi Sea and the Canadian Beaufort Sea in the east. Acoustic studies have been tracking the whales' migrations and finding that some bowheads are no longer going back to the Bering Sea and have started staying in the summer feeding grounds year-round, likely because these waters are not freezing like they used to. Bowheads need open seas to swim through and strain plankton from the water with their enormous mouths. When the sea freezes over in winter, the whales are driven south. As sea ice continues to shrink, more bowheads will stay in the Beaufort Sea, where they'll encounter more container ships, which are also increasingly taking advantage of the low-ice conditions and taking a shorter route across the Arctic between Asia and Europe. The shifting whale populations will alter the ecosystems they feed in and affect the lives of people in Native Alaskan and Canadian communities who rely on bowhead whales for their traditional subsistence hunting.

Orcas are also penetrating farther north into Arctic seas than they used to. They aren't adapted to living in frozen waters, where sea ice can get in the way of their tall dorsal fins when they surface to breathe (Arctic whales, including bowheads and narwhals, have no dorsal fins). As the ice retreats, the orcas' available habitat is expanding, and as they move, these apex predators are impacting the lives of their prey. Around Baffin Island in Canada, newly arrived orcas have started hunting narwhals, the small, long-tusked whales that also live in Arctic seas, in and around the ice. Orcas are now hunting and killing more than fifteen hundred narwhals each year, not enough to threaten the narwhals' future but certainly a big change in their lives. Even those narwhals that aren't getting eaten are altering their behaviour. When orcas are fifty miles away, narwhals abandon the open seas and huddle closer to the shoreline, presumably where there's less risk of attack. Bowhead whales in the region are also responding to orcas by retreating into the dense pack ice, which keeps them safer but takes them away from the open waters where they feed. There's no way the whales can hear the orcas from so far away, or see them, but somehow they're responding to an alarm that goes off through the ecosystem. Perhaps narwhals and bowheads are learning to spot signs of panic among each other and know when it's time to hide.

The climate-driven conversion of the ocean is manifesting in many places as a gradual shift, with species moving bit by bit as the seas warm. Off the North American coasts, for instance, commercial fish catches are changing in line with the rise in local sea temperatures. This can lead to a false sense of security that climate change in the ocean will unfold steadily and in ways that can be forecast and, in time, adapted to. Yet, ocean ecosystems also suffer from sudden shocks, shifting into a completely different state.

One such regime shift has happened in the seas off southeast Greenland, a remote region of the Arctic, four hundred miles west of Iceland and thirteen hundred miles north of Newfoundland. Until twenty years ago, this was one of the most inaccessible parts of the planet because much of it was locked in sea ice. Huge ice packs would drift from frozen seas around the North Pole, a few hundred miles away, and accumulate along the Greenland coast. This was old ice—multiyear ice, as scientists call it—which would have formed when the surface seawater froze several seasons previously and hadn't melted but had grown thicker over time. Throughout centuries of European whaling in the Arctic, ships rarely made it through the pack ice to this part of Greenland. Indigenous people living in a few small, scattered settlements did not make regular contact with the outside world until the end of the nineteenth century.

A diverse mix of cold-adapted, ice-dependent animals thrived in these frozen seas. There were great shoals of polar cod, with natural antifreeze coursing through their blood and covering their skin to prevent them from turning into blocks of ice. Narwhals chased after cod and other fish, perhaps using their elegantly twisted tusks to sense and skewer prey, although the precise role of their singular, long tooth remains a mystery. Hooded seals, ringed seals, and walruses lived on and among the ice packs, using the frozen platforms to rest on and rear their young.

This whole ecosystem changed when the ice disappeared. Seas in this region have warmed by more than two degrees Celsius, ocean currents have shifted, and the procession of pack ice from the North Pole has petered out. Since 2003, summers off southeast Greenland have become almost completely ice-free. In response, cod and narwhals are quickly moving north and could disappear entirely from the Greenland coast in the next few years. Populations of seals and walruses are also declining, as shown by the falling catches taken by indigenous hunters.

At the same time, boreal animals from farther south have been moving in, including an influx of predatory cetaceans. Humpbacks, pilot and minke whales, orcas, and dolphins used to be a rare sight, and now they're commonly seen. They hunt for capelin and mackerel, yet more fish species that are migrating north. Fin whales, the second biggest animals on earth, are also now swimming through these seas, feasting on krill. In all, the new predators are eating around two million tons of food a year, most of it compressed into a few months, triggering changes that are cascading all through the food web.

Eastern Greenland remains incredibly remote, and very few people live there or visit, besides scientists and tourists on cruise ships. Nevertheless, the transformation of the region matters far beyond the borders of these melting seas. It warns of just how swiftly—and sometimes irreversibly—ocean ecosystems can switch into an alternate state. The changes involve not just a species here and there arriving or disappearing but entire ecosystems operating in completely new ways. This could happen elsewhere in the ocean, away from the melting polar seas, if currents drastically alter, or if key habitats like coral reefs find the ocean unbearably warm and acidic and they finally disappear.

Greenland is also a forerunner for the rest of the Arctic Ocean, which is expected to become entirely ice-free in the summertime. Across the North Pole, there are no landmasses, just a vast area of frozen sea, which expands in the winter and shrinks each summer. Since 1978, when scientists began monitoring the polar seas from satellites, the extent of sea ice in the Arctic has shrunk by 13 per cent every decade. This incessant melting is one of the clearest signs of the climate crisis in progress. Experts now think we've passed the point where the Arctic's summer sea ice can be saved—it's just a question of when the entire region will be open ocean for the first time in thousands of years, from Canada and Alaska to Russia. This could be in the 2030s, or as late as the 2050s, depending on how quickly and deeply carbon emissions are reduced.

Already, consequences of the warming Arctic Ocean are being felt by people all around the world. There's increasing evidence that rising temperatures in the Arctic are weakening the jet streams (strong winds that flow high above the earth's surface) and leading to extreme weather events, from flooding to droughts and heatwaves.

The changing Arctic seas are also showing that life will continue and ecosystems will still function in the newly mixing Anthropocene ocean. But some species, such as the narwhal and cold-loving polar cod, although they can migrate and adjust their ranges, will be able to move only so far, and the time will come when they run out of cooler ocean and have nowhere else to go.

PART TWO

VANISHING GLORIES

Chapter 3
Ice Walkers

Antarctica is the coldest, windiest, and brightest continent on earth. It's colder than its northern counterpart, chiefly because, while the Arctic is surrounded by land, Antarctica is bathed in the freezing Southern Ocean, which keeps it cut off from the warmth of the rest of the planet. Here, life is dominated by two seasons. The long summer begins in October, when the midnight sun hangs low on the horizon, and temperatures in some places rise above freezing. Then around March, the sun sets, and winter comes. The switch from light to dark happens because the earth's tilt brings the polar regions into the shade and farther from the sun, the north and south taking turns. Wintertime temperatures in Antarctica plunge to −76 degrees Fahrenheit. The lowest temperature ever recorded on the earth's surface, −128.6 degrees Fahrenheit, was made in the heart of winter in July 1983 at a research base roughly halfway between Antarctica's coast and the South Pole. Cold, dense air pours off Antarctica's high plateau towards the coasts, driving katabatic winds of more than one hundred miles an hour that whip up blizzards and can roar constantly for days on end. Most living organisms simply could not exist in Antarctica's winter, especially out of the sea and on the exposed ice. But this is where one species comes each year to spend a key part of its life cycle, a feat made possible by its supreme survival skills.

An emperor penguin in peak condition is encased in a life-sustaining suit of feathers. Outermost is a rigid layer, windproof and waterproof, made from long, stiff-vaned plumes called contour feathers; black on the back and head, with characteristic yellow smudges around the cheeks and chin, and white at the front, as if the penguins picked up the colour of snow while tobogganing along on their bellies.

Many scientific reports recount the fact that emperor penguins have the highest density of contour feathers per square inch of skin of any birds. In fact, until recently, nobody had properly checked; instead, it was assumed this must be the case for these birds to be able to survive the extreme conditions of Antarctica. However, the white-throated dipper, a small, plump passerine with a largely European distribution, which dips into near-freezing streams in search of food, beats the emperor penguin in contour-feather density six times over. But the emperors win on the density of downy feathers that lie beneath their outer cocoon.

Fixed near the base of the penguin's contour feathers are fluffy plumes, called after-feathers, and fixed directly to the skin are separate feathery puffs called plumules. In all, an adult emperor penguin has at least 150,000 after-feathers and plumules, which together trap an insulating blanket of air that helps maintain the bird's core body temperature at around one hundred degrees Fahrenheit, no matter the external conditions.

All this fluff also helps penguins to swim and, briefly, to fly. Emperor penguins prowl the Southern Ocean for squid, fish, and krill, swimming at a steady pace of four to five miles per hour and diving for over half an hour, the longest dives of any penguin species, and to depths of at least fifteen hundred feet, deeper than any other animals that rely on fur or feathers for warmth. When it's time to get out, especially if they're being chased by a predatory leopard seal, the penguins' stubby legs are no use for quickly scrambling onto the ice. Instead, emperors shoot towards the sea surface, doubling their speed, then leap clear of the water. Key to their acceleration is the stream of bubbles they leave behind in the sea, like smoke trails. When a penguin dives down, air trapped between its feathers gets compressed as the water pressure pushes in; it then locks its contour feathers in place, trapping the compressed air until the critical moment when it needs a boost. As it races upwards, the air quickly expands as the pressure drops, and the penguin finely adjusts its plumage to let go of bubbles, which fizz out through its fine, downy feathers. The tiny bubbles cloak the body and reduce its drag in the water, helping the penguin swim fast enough to burst into the air, a trick scientists call air lubrication. An especially thick covering of contour feathers across an emperor penguin's chest helps to cushion it as it lands on the ice.

Emperor penguins also have even tinier feathers right next to the contour feathers, known as filoplumes. In birds that fly, these act as sensory devices, which fire when nearby flight feathers are knocked out of alignment, alerting the bird that it needs to preen its plumage back into shape to keep itself efficiently in flight. Penguin experts generally assumed these swimming birds had no need for filoplumes, until 2015, when some keen-eyed researchers spotted the tiny wisps within an emperor penguin's plumage. It's likely the filoplumes signal to the emperors when their contour feathers need preening to ensure their bodies stay hydrodynamic and well insulated.

Ultimately, their exceptional plumage makes emperor penguins' lives possible, and it's what ties them intimately to the frozen edges of Antarctica. There, the surface of the sea forms an icy skin, doubling the continent's size each winter and growing thick enough to support the world's biggest penguins, which can weigh as much as ninety pounds. Feathers keep male and female emperors warm as they march over white expanses of sea ice in March and April to congregate in their colonies. Out on the land-fast sea ice, the stable parts that are frozen to the edges of the continent, the adult penguins perform courtship rituals, bowing and swinging their heads from side to side. Females select a male, usually a different one each year, and the pair gracefully moves in synchrony, mirroring each other's gestures, which reinforces their bonds. Each female produces a single egg, one of fifteen or so she'll lay in her twenty-year lifetime. She quickly transfers it to her partner, and he balances it on his feet to keep it off the ice, pressing it against a bare patch of skin on the underside of his belly and swaddling it in his softest downy feathers. The females return to sea to feed and leave the males to stand for two months through Antarctica's long, dark, perishing night. During storms, the males huddle together to preserve body heat, and their feathers are so good at keeping them warm that now and then they break apart and steam, as if they'd just stepped out of a sauna. While the fasting males wait out the winter with nothing to eat on the empty ice, they run down their fat reserves, and their feathers pack more densely around their shrinking bodies, making their insulation even more effective.

Eventually, the sun rises, the chicks hatch, and the female emperors come back and find their partners. Then parents take turns to fetch food from the ocean, busily to-ing and fro-ing across the ice for several months to nourish their fluff-covered chicks, which grow to be as tall as they are.

Sometime in December or January, the fledgling chicks will shed their fuzz and get their first ocean-ready contour feathers. Later, the adult penguins will catastrophically moult. They drop all their old feathers and grow a whole new set. The rigours of Antarctic life are such that a cloak of feathers can be worn for only a single year before it needs replacing. It's another reason ice matters so very much to emperor penguins. They need a stable platform to perch on for the several weeks it takes for their new feathers to sprout. Only when they have regrown a full coat can they safely go back in the water.

But what happens if the sea ice breaks up too early, before the penguins' feathers are ready? And what will happen when the ice is gone for good?

Emperor penguins are some of the toughest birds on the planet, but with their hardiness comes a paradoxical vulnerability. The ice walkers utterly depend on their frozen sea, a habitat that will soon become harder and harder to find.

For a long time, humans and emperor penguins kept well out of each other's way. Emperors live only around Antarctica, a continent that Europeans only dreamt of for centuries, imagining it as a necessary balance to the known continents in the north. Despite earlier dangerous and expensive efforts to find it, Antarctica was officially sighted by explorers from the Northern Hemisphere only in 1820. Russians were the first of them to see the edges of the ice sheet that covers the continent, a frozen white layer that's between one and three miles thick and contains more than half of all the fresh water in the world. The ice sheet forms from layer upon layer of compacted snow and constantly flows towards the sea, forming glaciers and floating ice shelves like towering white cliffs, which periodically calve off drifting icebergs.

Officers on that Russian naval expedition of 1819–21 navigated their ships through the sea ice, where they were the first people in documented history to lay eyes on emperor penguins. But without a naturalist on board, the explorers assumed these to be the same species as the king penguins already known from South Georgia, a subantarctic island nearly two thousand miles north.

Twenty years later, a British expedition went to Antarctica and brought back several dead, preserved emperor penguins, delivering them to the Natural History Museum in London, where they were officially named as the closest, and slightly taller, relatives of king penguins. The duo was assigned the genus *Aptenodytes*, from Ancient Greek words meaning "diver without wings."

And so, Western scientists became aware of the emperor penguins' existence, but that was really all that was known of them.

The extreme conditions these birds evolved to survive keep most other large-bodied life forms away, humans included. Decades passed before more details of their lives were discovered by people who were prepared to venture into their icy world.

"It is extraordinary how often angels and fools do the same thing in this life, and I have never been able to settle which we were on this journey."

So wrote the British explorer and fledgling zoologist Apsley Cherry-Garrard, known as Cherry, who trekked across the unforgiving Antarctic ice in the winter of 1911. Together with two companions, Edward "Bill" Wilson and Henry "Birdie" Bowers, Cherry was attempting to make a scientific breakthrough. The men hoped to become the first people to find a colony of emperor penguins during the breeding season and to bring back several fertilised and growing emperor penguin eggs. The hope that kept them going as they dragged their sleds towards Cape Crozier was the possibility of uncovering a missing link between birds and dinosaurs.

At around that time, some scientists were keen to test out the theory of recapitulation, which proposed that developing embryos replay the evolutionary stages of their ancestors. Emperor penguins were thought to be the most primitive of living birds (in fact, they are not), and so, the theory went, their embryos could act as virtual time machines, transporting scientists back to when birds first evolved from their reptilian forebears. The only way to get hold of an emperor penguin embryo was to pluck a warm egg from the feet of a brooding male, deep within the cold and dark of the Antarctic winter.

It took the men five weeks to walk around 125 miles from base camp to the emperor colony and back. Cherry, Birdie, and Bill clambered over huge pressure ridges of ice, braved temperatures of minus seventy Fahrenheit, and kept falling down crevasses in the dark. A terrible storm was stirring when they finally arrived at the site of the brooding emperor penguins. The explorers scrambled to grab five eggs and retreated as quickly as they could to the igloo they had built, intending to use it as a base while they made more visits to the penguins. For days, they stayed inside the igloo waiting out the blizzard, huddled around the stove, burning fat from several adult penguins they had also snatched. "The earth was torn in pieces: the indescribable fury and roar of it all cannot be imagined," wrote Cherry of the storm. Eventually they made it back to base camp with three emperor penguin eggs intact, each around four inches long, the size of a Fabergé egg, with its embryonic contents frozen and preserved.

The following year, during the same Antarctic expedition, Bill and Birdie both died, alongside Robert Falcon Scott, during an even worse journey as they endeavoured to become the first men to walk to the geographic South Pole;* they were beaten to it five weeks earlier by Roald Amundsen and four other Norwegians. Cherry had not taken part in the push for the pole and later found his companions' tent with their frozen bodies inside. He returned to London as the sole egg bearer, but at the Natural History Museum he did not get the welcome he anticipated. While the three men were toiling across the Antarctic ice, scientific thinking had moved on, and the theory of recapitulation was slipping out of fashion. The museum's curators showed little interest in the emperor penguin eggs, although in the end they were sent to Cambridge University, where scientist Dorothy Thursby-Pelham drew intricate pencil sketches of a tiny, unborn penguin; it looks as if it's still floating inside its egg, muffled from the cold by its father's feathers. The hard-won eggs didn't lead to great new insights into the origins of birds, but the first emperor penguin eggs brought into the human world do still bear witness to the extraordinary lengths three men went to in the name of science. One of the eggs has recently been put on display at London's Natural History Museum among other

---

*The magnetic south pole wanders about as the earth's molten iron core swirls.

treasures, including the skull of a royal lion, some of Charles Darwin's pigeons, and a moon rock.

Today, it's not such a life-threatening business to watch and study emperor penguins in the wild throughout their entire life cycle. Scientists now have equipment, clothing, and communications that are much better at keeping them alive, and they can retreat to well-insulated base stations that look like giant metal caterpillars standing on the ice.

Many details of emperor penguins' lives have been revealed by scientists who have never actually visited Antarctica and instead are watching the birds from above. Satellites passing overhead take photographs of such high resolution that they reveal guano stains on the ice showing where adult emperors meet, mate, rear their chicks, and defecate. If light conditions are favourable, it's even possible to make out the shadows cast by clusters of these four-foot-tall penguins. Of course, the imagery doesn't have much to show when the sun goes down, while the males overwinter with their eggs on the dark ice. But before and after, on days when there are no clouds in the way, scientists get a clear view of where emperor penguin colonies are—and where they are not.

A map of Antarctica with its present-day covering of the world's largest ice sheet looks something like a human brain. Emperor penguin colonies are dotted around the entire circumference at remarkably regular intervals. By the latest count from satellite images, there are sixty-six breeding colonies spaced roughly 250 miles apart, with a few larger gaps where the biggest ice shelves get in the way.

Since the 1950s, scientists have known of an emperor colony located on the northeast side of the Weddell Sea, at the back of the neck, roughly where the brain's cerebellum would be. Close to one in ten of all the world's emperor penguins had been gathering here, near to where the Brunt Ice Shelf flows off Antarctica's ice sheet at a spot known as Halley Bay. Sheltered spots at the base of the ice shelf had been a good place for them to rear their young, where the sea would freeze and usually stay firm and intact until January, giving enough time for the chicks to fledge. Throughout the sixty-plus years that scientists knew about the Halley Bay colony, the sea ice remained stable and reliable throughout the breeding seasons, and the emperors were doing well. It was one of the largest colonies in Antarctica, with numbers varying each year between around four-teen thousand and twenty-three thousand pairs of adult penguins. Then, in 2016, disaster struck.

In October that year, the weather was unusually stormy. Strong winds whipped along the edges of the ice shelf and broke apart the sea ice. It happened during the emperor penguins' crèche period, when parents begin to leave their young chicks in groups together on the ice while they go to gather food. That year the ice collapsed beneath the chicks' feet, long before they had a chance to grow their waterproof feather coats. All the chicks drowned.

The following year, the sea ice froze over again, and the adult penguins returned. But the ice wasn't strong enough to last, and once again all the chicks perished. In 2018, satellite images showed that only a few hundred adults gathered at the breeding site at Halley Bay, while thousands lingered at the edges of the sea ice, perhaps wondering what to do. Penguins stood among refrozen fragments of brash ice and the slushy soup of grease ice, an early stage in the formation of solid sea ice, which would never have supported their chicks had they produced any. By November, all the sea ice on the northern side of the Brunt Ice Shelf was once again completely gone. After three years of total failure to breed, emperor penguins stopped coming, and the Halley Bay colony was abandoned.

For the adult penguins it was a tragic setback, but more photo-graphs taken from space hint that at least some of them survived.

At around the same time that the Halley Bay colony collapsed, a nearby colony got much bigger. Between 2015 and 2018, the number of emperors at the Dawson-Lambton colony, thirty-five miles to the south, increased from twelve hundred to almost fifteen thousand. It's likely that many of them were adults relocating from Halley Bay after the sea ice disappeared. At first, a lot of them stood scattered in loose groups and were probably not breeding. But by 2018, guano stains showed they were huddled more closely together in two main groups and most likely had settled once again into their breeding rhythm. Some of the missing adults could still be out there somewhere, skipping their breeding and waiting for conditions to improve at Halley Bay (emperor penguins can typically live for around twenty years). Some may have moved away, and maybe one day a new emperor colony will show up on a satellite image.

It's not possible at this stage to blame the climate crisis directly for what happened at Halley Bay, but the year it happened, 2016, was a turning point for Antarctica in the Anthropocene. For quite some time, sea ice surrounding the southern continent seemed to be defying human-driven climate change. While in the Arctic, the sea has steadily become less icy over the past few decades since satellite monitoring began, Antarctic sea ice had been highly variable and in some places had been increasing. Scientists studying this phenomenon identified changing wind patterns as a major cause. Then, in 2016, there was a sudden decline in sea ice all around Antarctica, the beginning of a relentless downward trend. New record lows in sea ice extent were set in the summer of 2021–22. The following year, even more ice was gone by summer's end, so much that it left polar scientists deeply shocked and desperate to understand the complex mix of rising temperatures and shifting winds, ocean currents and salinity that could explain the rapid changes.

Meanwhile, late in 2022, the impact of shrinking sea ice on Antarctica's wildlife became more obvious and tragic than ever. The

region suffering worst from loss of ice was to the west of the Antarctic Peninsula, in the Bellingshausen Sea. Five emperor penguin
breeding sites had been discovered there from satellite images, all of
them smaller than the former Halley Bay colony, and only one of
them visited by scientists. Satellite imagery from 2022 showed the
usual springtime arrival of adult penguins, but then, one by one, the
penguin gatherings disappeared. At the Verdi Inlet colony, the sea
ice usually stayed fast until the New Year, but in 2022 it had broken
apart by November fourth. At other sites, the breakup happened later
in November and into December, coinciding with the end of the
emperor penguins' crèche and fledgling periods. Rothschild Island
was the only colony where the sea ice lasted almost to the end of
the year, giving some of the chicks a chance to safely swim off with
their new feathers fully grown.

Across the Bellingshausen Sea at least seven thousand chicks fell
into the sea too soon for them to survive. The overall death toll was
lower than at Halley Bay, but the catastrophic breeding failure in
2022 was on a scale never seen before, with the four out of the five
colonies abandoned. And unlike at Halley Bay, there are no other
colonies nearby for any surviving adult emperor penguins to easily
relocate to.

The collapse of colonies in the Bellingshausen Sea was precisely
the kind of disaster predicted in the most detailed study to date of
what could happen to emperor penguins as the climate heats and
sea ice vanishes. Analysis conducted in 2019 by Stéphanie Jenouvrier
from Woods Hole Oceanographic Institution in Massachusetts and
her colleagues showed that if humanity blunders on regardless and
allows greenhouse gas emissions to continue unabated, Antarctica's
frozen fringe of sea ice will shrink by around half, and many more
emperor colonies would see their sea ice vanish entirely during the
critical times when females should be laying and males should be car-
ing for eggs balanced on their feet. In this ice-starved, stressed state,
emperor penguin numbers would crash in 80 per cent of colonies,

and the entire species would be shrinking year by year. It would effectively spell the end of the emperor penguin.

Jenouvrier's analysis offers little hope that the situation would improve if emperors in the future do as the Halley Bay penguins did and swim off to join other colonies that aren't faring so badly. Nobody knows for sure how well emperor penguins disperse. Jenouvrier tested out various possibilities, including penguins that disperse either short or long distances and either seek out areas of good habitat where other birds are already breeding well or simply swim about searching at random. The models suggest that regardless of how well penguins disperse and find their way to other colonies, it won't be enough to counteract the declines in the population caused by shrinking sea ice.

We also can't assume emperor penguins will start using other types of ice that will last longer in warming seas. Their legs are not long or strong enough to let them easily climb onto the tall, longer-lasting ice shelves; they can't easily scale the steep edges of icebergs, nor have they any hope of leaping their big bodies that far, even with the added push of bubbles. Occasionally emperors come across a ramp of snow to clamber up onto a high ice shelf, as happened in 2017 in Atka Bay to the east of the Weddell Sea. However, with no easy access to the sea to gather food, the penguins were left stranded and had no other choice but to jump fifteen to thirty feet into the water. For those that hadn't fully molted this was a lethal leap. Moving onto land may not be a good option either, because the penguins would likely be too far from oceanic foraging grounds to feed themselves and their growing chicks. It seems likely that emperor penguins simply don't have it within their biology to save themselves as a species while the Anthropocene changes their world. Their main hope comes from the possibility that human-made carbon emissions won't continue to relentlessly rise.

As sea ice retreats, the precarious future of emperor penguins is tied closely with that of millions of people around the world. Melting sea ice doesn't directly contribute to rising sea levels, just as melting ice cubes don't cause a gin and tonic to spill over the side of the glass. Seawater itself freezes each year, and when it melts, no additional water is added to the ocean. However, sea ice plays a part in protecting coastlines where other forms of ice are attached to the land, helping to buffer ice shelves from waves and storms. When there's less sea ice around, these towering ice platforms flex and bend, and it becomes more likely for icebergs to calve off and the ice sheets to break apart.

Melting glaciers and ice shelves are already causing global sea levels to rise. In Antarctica's Amundsen Sea, Thwaites Glacier (nicknamed the Doomsday Glacier) is melting and retreating because of the warming sea around it. Part of this slab of ice, roughly the size of Great Britain, is braced by a floating ice sheet that is pushed up against an underwater seamount and acts as a giant plug. Recent studies sending autonomous robots under the ice shelf have found deep cracks and crevasses in its underside that are melting fast as warm water flows into them.

If the Thwaites Glacier collapses, scientists predict it could cause more than two feet of sea level rise. And if it drags other glaciers and ice sheets with it, the rise could be as much as ten feet. This catastrophic rise, compared to six inches in the twentieth century, would unfold over the centuries to come and impact the lives of coastal communities all around the world.

Scientists are working hard to predict how Thwaites and other ice forms in Antarctica will behave as the planet continues to heat. A major question is whether the whole ice sheet covering West Antarctica could collapse. Evidence suggesting this happened in the not-so-distant past, and hence could happen again, has come from an unusual source. Turquet's octopuses have lived in waters all the way around Antarctica for the past four million years. A 2023 study of their genetics showed that their seabed-dwelling populations on opposite sides of the continent intermixed with each other roughly 125,000 years ago. This was the most recent time the earth was in a warm phase between ice ages, when global temperatures were between 0.5 and 1.5 degrees Celsius warmer than today. The only likely route to allow those octopuses to mingle would have been a seaway right across Antarctica, between the Weddell Sea and the Ross Sea, which could have happened only if the ice sheet had completely collapsed.

This doesn't mean Antarctica's ice sheet definitely is doomed, but it warns that, the way climate change is going, it could happen. The more swiftly and deeply carbon emissions are reduced, the greater the chance Thwaites Glacier and other critical parts of Antarctica's vast icy landscape will stay intact.

It took a little over a century for emperor penguins to transform in human minds. What was once a kind of near-fabled, otherworldly animal that few people knew about, and explorers risked their lives to find, has become a species imperilled by the changing world. The penguins' future depends on the decisions and actions of people thousands of miles away, leading lives entirely removed from theirs. If climate change is allowed to continue unchecked, and the emperor penguin walks along a pathway towards extinction, as predicted by Jenouvrier's study, it will become a sorrowful symbol of the destructive forces humanity is unleashing on the planet. The potential loss of this beloved animal is a rallying cry to take the climate crisis seriously, and urgently curb emissions—otherwise the emperor penguin could easily go the way of the dodo, and how will people think of them then?

These two oversize, flightless birds have a fair amount in common. Dodos were the biggest members of the pigeon and dove family, the Columbidae, that people ever saw; emperor penguins are the biggest living members of the penguin family, the Spheniscidae. But in other ways the two species will be very differently remembered. Far more is known about the lives of emperor penguins than we will ever know about dodos. No keen-eyed scientists trailed after dodos through the forests of Mauritius noting down the details of their lives, and the species was allowed to disappear without any reliable descriptions or well-preserved specimens. Drawings of dodos from the time when the species was last seen alive, sometime towards the end of the seventeenth century, were often based on overfed captive birds or dead birds badly preserved by taxidermy. What living dodos actually looked like is not clear.

In contrast, emperor penguins are one of the most famous and easily recognisable birds. They are the adored stars of documentaries and animated movies; we can fall asleep in emperor penguin pyjamas while cuddling emperor penguin soft toys that bear more than a passing resemblance to the real thing. My favourite chocolate bar as a kid had an emperor penguin (and a joke) on the wrapper. Real emperor penguins could come to an end, but they would surely live on as avatars in the human world; only their meaning would have to change. People could no longer watch documentary footage and imagine all those birds are somewhere out there, devoted parents surviving in extreme conditions. Instead, the emperors would become memories from a past that is no more accessible than the time of the trilobites, ichthyosaurs, or giant aquatic sloths.

Like dodos, emperor penguins would not be a lone extinction. Through stories and poetry, such as Lewis Carroll's *Alice's Adventures in Wonderland*, dodos have become legendarily extinct, but they shared the tropical forests of Mauritius with many other endemic species that also vanished at a similar time and for similar reasons— those other animals, however, have largely been forgotten about. There were Mauritius blue pigeons, with red face, green beak, and feathers of indigo and shining metallic blue; at the water's edge were Mauritius shelducks with black-and-white wings; stalking through the forests were flightless rails that looked like red-tinted versions of Aotearoa (New Zealand) kiwis; there were broad-billed parrots, Mascarene grey parakeets, Mascarene coots, Mauritius night herons, Mauritian giant skinks, small flying foxes, and two species of giant tortoise. All of them went extinct when people cut down the island's forests, let pigs and cats run wild, and found the native animals gleefully easy to hunt, as none had instincts to fear humans. A few species lasted a while longer, like the Mauritius scops owl, but in the mid-nineteenth century it lost its final fragments of forest to sugarcane plantations.

Just as dodos joined a parade of animals that disappeared along with the Mauritian forests, so emperor penguins are among a rich mix of species that could be lost to the warming waters of the Southern Ocean. A lot of Antarctic animals face an uncertain future because they share with emperor penguins a diet that depends on the icy seas: they all eat a lot of krill.

A single adult Antarctic krill is finger-size, beady-eyed, and mostly transparent except for spots of pigment that give penguin guano its rosy tint. Aptly named *Euphausia superba*, krill sparkle in the dark as bioluminescent patches along their body pulse with blue-green light, perhaps to communicate with mates or help organise themselves in shoals.

Female and male krill meet up in the deep sea, hundreds of yards underwater, where they perform an elaborate mating ritual. A male chases after a female and touches her body with his long antennae. The couple embrace in a clinch of flickering legs, then the male wraps himself around his partner's body in a sideways loop, and for a few seconds they spin together in circles. While all that is going on, the male transfers sperm to the female.

Sometime later, she releases into the sea thousands of fertilised eggs, which drift off and hatch into larvae. At first, the young krill look like fat spiders with only six legs; then, for several months, they keep reinventing themselves, casting off a dozen versions of their exoskeletons and reshaping their bodies, gradually taking on their shrimplike adult form.

By the time the Antarctic winter arrives, the adolescent krill have made their way to the surface to seek shelter and food on the underside of floating sea ice. In channels and cracks, they hide from predators while raking over the ice with the bristly ends of their legs to feed on a layer of microscopic algae.* During the rest of the year, krill eat planktonic algae floating in the water column, using their forelegs as a filtering device. But their overwintering grounds contain little plankton, and they get most of their food from ice algae. Here, the more sea ice there is and the longer it lasts, the more krill there are. And when Antarctic krill are doing well, they can be fantastically abundant.

Drop a bucket over the side of a ship in the Southern Ocean, and if you're in the middle of a squirming pink shoal, you could easily catch a hundred krill in a single scoop. Typically, a shoal is the length of a football field, extends thirty feet deep, and contains more than one hundred million krill. They inhabit the entire circular loop of the Southern Ocean, all the way around the Antarctic continent. Collectively, the biomass of these little crustaceans adds up to an estimated half gigaton, making them the most abundant species on the planet that you don't need a microscope to see.

In their colossal abundance, krill lie at the heart of Southern Ocean ecosystems. They harness energy from plankton and ice algae and create a vast pool of biological energy on which most other large animals in Antarctica depend.

Krill are food for elephant seals and fur seals, squid, and silverfish. Krill are plucked from above by a great many seabirds, including Wilson's storm petrels, southern fulmars, and snow and Antarctic

---

* The main types of algae that krill eat are diatoms, including those of the genus *Nitzschia*.

petrels, which in turn get their food stolen in midair by scavenging skuas. Many penguin species, not just emperors, hunt for krill as they dive through the Southern Ocean.

Whales are another major group of krill consumers. Southern right whales and humpbacks, sei and fin whales all come to Antarctica to eat krill and replenish their energy stores. Minke whales skim along just under the sea ice, lunging dozens of times on each dive, swallowing down great mouthfuls of krill. A single blue whale, the species with the biggest mouth of all, can gulp 3.6 million krill every day.

Curiously misnamed, crabeater seals don't in fact consume crabs but have the whale-like habit of straining krill from the sea. To do so, they evolved the most specialised teeth of any carnivore, with multiple curved cusps that interlock to act as a sieve. A crabeater seal swims through a shoal of krill, mouth open, then snaps its jaws shut and pushes out the seawater through its teeth, holding back the krill and then swallowing them.

No other ecosystem on earth relies so much on a single species. Even apex predators, such as orcas and leopard seals, are no more than one step away from krill when they chase after fish, squid, and penguins.

How all this will change as the climate crisis bears down is not an easy matter to get a handle on, especially as krill populations naturally fluctuate year by year. Even so, plenty of studies cast grim predictions for the future of krill because of their reliance on sea ice and their need for cold, productive waters. Female krill need to eat a lot during the summer to build up their body reserves and store enough energy to successfully spawn the following year. The way ecosystems are changing, female krill could soon struggle to get the food they need to see them through the year. It's likely that individual krill will grow to less than half the size they are now. The total population of krill could shrink by a third by the end of the century. Add in the impacts of the ocean absorbing more carbon dioxide and becoming increasingly acidic, and *Euphausia superba* could collapse altogether in three hundred years or so.

Currently, enough krill swarm around Antarctica that there are no pressing concerns for their extinction. But as certain parts of Antarctica are showing, what matters is where exactly krill are at their most plentiful.

The term *global warming* can give the misleading impression that the whole planet is heating gradually by the same amount everywhere. Changes already taking place in the global climate are by no means uniform. The Antarctic Peninsula is one of the fastest-warming places on the planet. This thousand-mile finger of icy land and islands—which points towards Tierra del Fuego, South America's southern tip—is the spinal column on the brain map of Antarctica. Since the 1950s, the air temperature here has risen by three degrees Celsius, and the surface seas by one degree. During a heatwave in February 2020, a new record for the Antarctic continent was set at the peninsula's northern tip, where the air temperature reached 64.94 degrees Fahrenheit (normally, summer temperatures don't rise more than a few degrees above freezing). It's no great surprise that the sea ice here is rapidly melting, and krill populations are retreating pole-wards, tracking their icy habitat to the south. At the same time, two krill-eating penguin species that used to live all along the peninsula are now in drastic decline.

Adélie penguins are small and sleek, their whole heads black, as if dipped in paint, leaving a white-ringed eye. They're easy to tell apart from their close relatives the chinstrap penguins, whose black cap appears to be held in place by a dark band secured neatly under the chin. Colonies of both species, which used to be noisy with thousands of nesting birds, are growing increasingly sparse and quiet. On several subantarctic islands north of the peninsula, chinstrap numbers are less than half what they were in the 1970s. Adélie colonies are similarly collapsing. The number coming to nest near the American Palmer research base has dropped by around 80 per cent.

Chinstrap and Adélie penguins are not at imminent risk of going extinct. Across the whole of Antarctica, there are between six and seven million birds of each species living in hundreds of colonies. In the more stable parts of Antarctica, including the Ross Sea, numbers of Adélies are still healthy; chinstrap colonies in parts of the South Orkney Islands are increasing in size. Even so, their dire status along the peninsula is worrying enough, in and of itself, and it's an ominous sign of what could lie ahead.

Penguin experts don't yet understand precisely what is going wrong with the peninsula's chinstraps and Adélies. It must have something to do with the shifting ice and krill populations, particularly during the nesting season, when penguins rely on a nearby supply of krill to feed their chicks. If there aren't enough krill in the neighbourhood, then foraging adults are forced to set off on longer journeys to search for food, and they risk leaving their chicks to go hungry for too long.

Further complicating matters is the fact that whales, seabirds, seals, squid, and penguins aren't the only ones hunting for krill. Now humans are too. The immense biomass of krill around Antarctica has proven too tempting for industrialists to resist. Factory ships, notably from Norway and China, head south to scoop up Antarctica's krill. Specially designed trawl nets are lowered into the water and continuously scoop up krill shoals for weeks at a time, sending them straight to onboard processing plants. These krill will end up being eaten by domesticated animals. Most are mashed and turned into feed for salmon farms or into pet food.

Of all the krill shoaling around Antarctica, fisheries currently capture less than 1 per cent. People in favour of the industry consider this amount to be far too small to be of any ecological concern. The devil is in the granular details. If fishing vessels were to spread themselves out and gather their catches from across the entire range of krill, then these fisheries would likely have little impact. But that's not what they do. Factory ships focus their attention on the peninsula, a krill hot spot that is the easiest and most profitable place to operate. Since 2000, the krill catch around the peninsula has tripled from 88,800 to 289,500 metric tons. By concentrating their effort, the ships may be competing with local wildlife trying to fill their bellies. For now, it's difficult to disentangle the combined impacts of climate change and krill fishing because they're happening in the same time and space. Indeed, as the ice is retreating south, the factory ships are also motoring farther south to access newly exposed regions of previously untouched sea.

Rather than industrial fisheries exploiting those waters, another option is to leave them alone. The organisation that regulates fishing around Antarctica, the Commission for the Conservation of Antarctic Marine Living Resources, has pledged to set up marine reserves to protect key parts of the Southern Ocean. At the time of writing, two such reserves exist. One is around the South Orkney Islands, which lie hundreds of miles north of the peninsula, and a second is on the other side of the continent, in the Ross Sea, where Apsley Cherry-Garrard went to find emperor penguin eggs. Since 2018, experts from Argentina and Chile have been leading a proposal to set up a third protected zone in the seas along the western coast of the Antarctic Peninsula. The safeguarding of these waters from exploitation would give krill and all the wildlife that depend on them as good a chance as possible of weathering the climate crisis. It would prioritise the Southern Ocean's biodiversity over directing profits to the pet-food and fishmeal industries. So far, through several rounds of negotiations at the commission, plans to protect the peninsula's waters have been rejected.

Even as sea ice and krill populations continue to rapidly decline, not all Antarctic species will suffer right away or to the same extent. Some will cope more easily than others. Gentoo penguins are already doing much better than their close relatives the Adélies and chinstraps. Similar in appearance to their sister species, except with a red beak, black head, and white band between the eyes, gentoo penguins live on the Antarctic Peninsula and on offshore islands, although not around the perimeter of the Antarctic continent. Their entire population is increasing, especially along the peninsula, where they're moving south and claiming new territories as the ice retreats. The gentoos' success most likely comes down to their flexible diet— they don't rely solely on krill—and they seem to prefer it when there is not so much ice around. Thanks to the gentoos' more resilient and, one might say, less refined nature, Antarctica in a warming world should still be home to large numbers of at least one species of penguin.

Drawing up lists of the likely winners and losers is perhaps a pragmatic way of dealing with the climate crisis. Some people argue that conservation efforts should be focused on the likely winners, leaving us to search for ways to grieve for the species that won't make it through the Anthropocene. It may come as some comfort to know that survivors will exist even in the most imperilled places, including in Antarctica and the Arctic, where other species depend, to differing extents, on the swiftly shrinking ice. Among the survivors will be plenty of generalists, the species best equipped to make do and carry on. They will take the place of the specialists that carve out exquisite niches, that depend on predictable seasonal timings or rely exclusively on another species that may also soon be gone. The Anthropocene will have less and less room for great evolutionary phenomena, the likes of crabeater seals with their unique, krill-straining teeth and emperor penguins with their bubble-making feather suits.

But still, it is too soon to consign those sensitive, more specialised species to the loser list. As the planet rushes past one degree of anthropogenic heating, there are locked-in changes that we can do very little to stop. But we do still have a chance to decide how much we will continue to heat the planet, and that very much matters. From this point forwards, every half degree of heating that can be avoided will make a critical difference for the future of all sorts of species and their endangered habitats.

If corporations and governments do nothing to decelerate the climate crisis, emperor penguins will dwindle within the lifetime of human babies now being born. Not long after 2100, the species will most likely be extinct—if not sooner. But this is not an unstoppable fate for these giant, ice-walking birds. There is still a chance to prevent them from becoming little more than memories of a species that people knowingly allowed to disappear.

Simulations of the future of Antarctica run by Stéphanie Jenouvrier and colleagues explore two alternative possible climate scenarios. If emissions can be reduced enough to keep global temperature rise this century to two degrees Celsius above preindustrial levels, then the outlook for emperor penguins will be distinctly improved. Instead of losing 80 per cent of emperor colonies, as would likely happen if humans carry on with business as usual, we can expect only around 31 per cent to collapse. Limit temperature rise to 1.5 degrees Celsius, and the number of lost colonies is even smaller, around 19 per cent. In that scenario, by century's end the entire population would stabilise at a new, lower level. Emperor penguins would be a great deal rarer than they are today, and they would persist in only a few climate refuges in Antarctica where enough sea ice remains, but the species would still exist.

There is also a more nuanced story that emperor penguins will tell. They will become a visible, incremental barometer of the climate crisis. A lot of the world's most endangered species will fade out without anyone tracking their decline or watching for the point in time when they are gone for good. Like the dodo, those ones will slip away before anyone realises they are no longer around. Extinctions in the ocean will be especially hard to prove and easy to overlook— given the vast nature of this liquid habitat, which contains plenty of places to hide—so that people can continue to wonder if certain species might still be out there, somewhere. Emperor penguins would be different because of their habit of hauling out onto the ice to rear their young. The entire breeding population leaves the sea at the same time and stands on the white ice, making it possible to count them year on year. The more that humans successfully limit carbon emissions and minimise future global heating, the more intact sea ice will remain, and the more emperor penguins there will still be. Scientists will be keeping an eye on them via spaceborne satellites and hoping to see that when another winter ends and the sun illuminates Antarctica once again, the emperors will still be there with their new chicks, waiting until they grow new feathers and can return to the sea and slip back out of sight.

Chapter 4
Missing Angels

In the sixteenth century, when European explorers set sail for the Americas, many of them encountered big sharks for the first time. When they returned home, they brought with them new words for the huge, unfamiliar animals they had seen.

"Above all there is an infinite number of some very large fish that they call *tiburones*," wrote Spanish monk and traveller Juan Gonzáles de Mendoza in 1585. The word *tiburón* originated in the indigenous language of the Kalina people from the coasts of South America, and it's still in use in Spanish today. The English adopted a term that has hazier origins and more multiplicitous meanings. It seems nobody can quite decide on the true origins of the word shark.

Both words originally applied to large sharks, distinguishing them from the smaller *cazón*, or dogfish, which Europeans in medieval times knew from fishing in waters closer to shore. Venturing beyond the horizon, sailors came across various pelagic sharks—those that roam across open seas—and no doubt included plenty of oceanic whitetip sharks. These bold, inquisitive sharks swim at the surface but only over water that's more than five hundred feet deep, and they have a strong habit of following ships. Anyone watching over the side of those medieval vessels would have spotted this shark's tall, rounded dorsal and tail fins, and long pectorals, all speckled in white at the ends as if they had been clumsily dipped in bleach. Even in those early days of European exploration, it was obvious that the ocean was teeming with oceanic whitetip sharks.

Shift forwards to the twentieth century, and there were still huge populations of this species cruising across the planet, through every ocean basin except the Arctic Ocean and the Southern Ocean, where the waters are too cold for them. A 1969 book about sharks described oceanic whitetips as "extraordinarily abundant, perhaps the most abundant large animal, large being over 100 pounds, on the face of the earth." The 1971 documentary *Blue Water, White Death* set out to capture great white sharks for the first time on underwater movie cameras. The bait was a dead sperm whale, shot with an explosive harpoon by a whaling ship off the coast of South Africa. Divers climbed inside a metal cage and had themselves lowered into the sea to see what animals showed up to scavenge the floating whale carcass. There were no great whites, but almost immediately, dozens of oceanic whitetip sharks appeared, swimming in circles, lunging in and biting off chunks of blubber. "There must be twenty tons of sharks down there," one of the divers said after making his way back to the ship.

A decade later, oceanic whitetip sharks were still reported to be superabundant. A 1984 report named them as one of the world's most numerous large marine animals. Since then, however, their situation has taken a dramatic turn for the worse.

For every hundred oceanic whitetip sharks that roamed the Pacific Ocean in the 1980s, fewer than five are alive today.* In some places, young whitetips have become vanishingly rare, and over time mature individuals have been shrinking in size, which could mean females are having trouble reproducing; the smaller a mother shark, the smaller the energy reserves she can draw on, and the fewer off-spring she produces. Data on the whitetips' status aren't available

---

*That's a 95 per cent decline.

throughout their global range; the situation in the Indian Ocean is especially vague. But wherever there is good information, a similar story is being told. These large sharks that were once so plentiful are disappearing from the ocean. In 2019, experts at the International Union for the Conservation of Nature (IUCN) considered all the available facts and declared the oceanic whitetip shark to be Critically Endangered—the most imperilled category in the IUCN's Red List of Threatened Species, a go-to guide to species endangerment.[*] Whitetips face a high chance of going extinct globally, and they're not the only ones. In total, more than one-third of all known shark species and their close relatives the skates and rays, collectively known as elasmobranchs, are threatened with extinction. They are the second most endangered group of animals on the planet after amphibians. Close to four hundred species of elasmobranchs face an uncertain future in the Anthropocene ocean.[†]

Cautionary tales tell of once superabundant species that humans nevertheless managed to extirpate. Passenger pigeons are a classic example. When Europeans began to settle in North America in the sixteenth and seventeenth centuries, somewhere between three and five billion of these graceful pigeons were living in mixed hardwood forests in the east. Settlers told stories of enormous flocks blotting out the sun for hours and days as they passed overhead, of tree branches breaking off from the sheer weight of birds roosting in them, and of their droppings lying inches thick on the ground. That all came to an end when people cut down forests and hunted the pigeons as

---

[*] The IUCN's Red List of Threatened Species, commonly known as the Red List, has the following categories of threat: Least Concern, Near Threatened, Vulnerable, Endangered, Critically Endangered, Extinct in the Wild, and Extinct. Experts periodically assess the status of species and assign them to these threat categories.

[†] There are also four threatened species of chimeras, sometimes known as ghost sharks. Together with sharks, skates, and rays, they belong to the class Chondrichthyes.

a source of cheap meat. By the turn of the twentieth century, there were no more passenger pigeons in the wild. On September 1, 1914, the very last passenger pigeon, named Martha after First Lady Martha Washington, died in the Cincinnati Zoo.

The lesson of the passenger pigeon is proving difficult to transfer underwater because the myth lingers on that the inexhaustible seas are too big and animals living there far too abundant for humans to put a dent in their populations. But as the oceanic whitetip sharks show, existing in huge numbers over vast tracts of ocean is not enough to make a species immune to human destruction.

The chief explanation for the whitetip shark's precipitous decline is linked to the very same habit that first brought the species to the attention of European sailors. As the seas have filled up with fishing boats, more whitetips have been swimming up to investigate and getting hooked and killed on fishing lines. The same goes for dozens of other ocean-roaming shark species. Great hammerhead sharks, up to twenty feet long, with their distinctive tool-shaped headgear, and their slightly smaller relatives the scalloped hammerheads are both now Critically Endangered. Great white sharks are classified as Vulnerable to extinction globally and as Critically Endangered in European seas. Pelagic thresher sharks, which stun fish in schools by whipping their immensely long tails over their heads, are Endangered. So are shortfin and longfin mako sharks, which race through the ocean faster than any other sharks. In all, since the 1970s, the global abundance of oceanic sharks and rays has declined by 71 per cent.

To wipe out so many animals that used to occupy hundreds of millions of square miles of ocean might seem like an improbable feat for fishing vessels alone to achieve. And yet, mounting evidence shows that fishing pressure is easily high enough to explain these multiple vanishings. In the past few decades, humans have massively expanded and intensified industrial fishing to the point that the collapse of once-abundant shark populations became inevitable.

A series of technological innovations made this possible, beginning with the switch from wind-powered to fossil-fuelled ships. In
the late nineteenth century, steam-powered trawlers began plying
the ocean, to be replaced in the twentieth century by diesel ships,
which were even faster, more powerful, and capable of hauling
larger fishing gear through the water and up on deck. At-sea freezing facilities allowed fishers to preserve their catches, stay out longer,
and venture farther from shore. Wartime technologies heightened
industrial fishing powers, with advances in sonar, radar, and nav-
igational tools making it safer to be at sea and easier to locate fish
schools. And in the 1950s, the American chemical company DuPont
invented a new type of fishing line made from a single, long nylon
fibre that was strong, lightweight, and difficult for fish to see in
the water. Monofilament lines swiftly became a favourite of fishers around the world and since the 1980s have been used to make
longlines, the gear used most widely through the ocean and that
catches the most sharks.

The principle behind longline fishing is straightforward. A vessel
pays out a single line, often using a mechanical line shooter that
propels it into the water faster than the boat speed so it has a chance
to sink down. Fixed on the longline at regular intervals are shorter
branch lines, or snoods. At the end of each snood is a palm-size metal
hook with a chunk of fish or squid attached as bait. The line can
be set at a chosen depth, for instance, to catch fish near the seabed,
such as cod and hake. More commonly, floats are attached so that the
line drifts near the surface and catches tuna, marlin, and swordfish.
Radio beacons are attached so fishers can find the ends of the lines
after they have soaked in the sea for anywhere from a few hours to
as long as a day. Then a hydraulic winch pulls the longline back in,
and crew on deck unhook the catch by hand.

The hauling-in process alone can take between ten and twenty
hours, which gives an idea of the scale of these operations. In the

US pelagic fleet, the average length of longline set by an individual vessel is twenty-eight miles. Many other fleets use lines more than twice as long.

Sharks snagged on longlines are often referred to as by-catch, because the prime targets of these fishing vessels are other animals such as tuna. Even so, sharks make up a major part of catches and are economically important for fishers, who commonly keep the sharks' meat and cut off their fins to sell in the trade for shark-fin soup. The precise number of sharks killed this way is not well known because most catches go unreported, and fewer than one in twenty tuna longliners have independent observers on board monitoring the catches. When observers are stationed on longliners, they witness just how intensive the shark slaughter can be. In 2018, observers on a Spanish longliner operating south of the Cape Verde Islands saw each longline catching an average of 7.6 oceanic whitetip sharks and as many as 54. During three months of fishing, that single vessel caught 416 whitetips, half of them dead by the time they were hauled in. Together all these living and dead sharks weighed more than twenty metric tons, an order of magnitude higher than the official reports for all the longliners operating that year across the entire Atlantic.

Until recently, it's been nigh on impossible to calculate the world-wide impact of longlining on sharks. The global fleet of longliners is an unwieldy mix of vessels, some big, some smaller, most operating far from shore way out of sight from land. Now, though, thanks to another technological advance, the full extent of longlining is coming into view, and with it a clearer idea of just how deadly this form of fishing is for sharks.

International maritime law requires all large vessels to carry an identification system that broadcasts their position via satellite every few seconds, so vessels can avoid crashing into each other. Now researchers are using the publicly available data to map fishing activity. Computer algorithms recognise the characteristic patterns made by different types of fishing vessels as they move across the ocean.

Trawlers take a wandering path. Purse seiners stay for longer in one spot while they gather in their circular curtain of nets, like a giant's drawstring purse. And longliners tend to draw narrow V shapes as they motor slowly in one direction when setting out their fishing line, then turn around and trace another straight course while hauling it back in.

One year's worth of satellite positioning data from seventy thousand vessels* showed they collectively fished for forty million hours and covered more than 285 million miles—the same distance one would cover travelling to the moon and back six hundred times. In that year, 2016, more than half of the world's ocean was industrially fished.† That's over four times the global area of agricultural land.

Longliners alone operate over at least 45 per cent of the ocean. They lace lethal lines throughout the territories of pelagic sharks, as revealed by thousands of sharks with their own identification systems in the form of satellite transmitter tags that scientists clip onto their dorsal fins. Pelagic sharks cruise immense distances through the high seas; one tagged oceanic whitetip shark swam four thousand miles in three months, all the way across the Indian Ocean. These species tend to occupy particular parts of the ocean where they feed and breed, such as a hot spot off the coast of California where great white sharks congregate, and many of these places are intensively fished. Combining satellite data from fishing vessels and tagged sharks, researchers have calculated how much the two overlap in space and time. Overall, pelagic sharks are forced to share one-quarter of their ocean space with industrial longliners. For some species the intrusion is much higher. During an average month in the North Atlantic, 63 per cent of the shortfin mako shark's domain falls under the footprint of longliners.

---

*This is a fraction of the world's estimated 2.9 million motorised fishing boats.

†This is certainly an underestimate, as many vessels either don't carry the automatic identification system or deliberately switch it off while fishing.

There are no accurate figures for the total number of sharks that industrial fisheries kill every year. The best available estimate for the annual global death toll ranges between 63 and 273 million sharks. Many more sharks are dying off the record. Still, the devastation that longlines cause is plain to see from the slaughter that a single vessel can inflict—and from the global dominance of the longlining industry. Unchecked industrial fishing undoubtedly has the power to empty the ocean of pelagic sharks. These magnificent animals that were once so abundant now have very few places left to hide.

Many other types of sharks are at risk of going extinct, not just the sleek, torpedo-shaped animals sliding across the wide, open ocean that are getting hammered by industrial fisheries. These others, often less well known and hidden away, face threats from smaller-scale coastal fisheries and loss of their habitats.

Daggernose sharks weave their way through mangrove forests at the mouth of the Amazon River and along the South American coast. They have tiny eyes and rely on electrosensory perception in their flattened, triangular snouts to detect twitching prey in the murk. They don't see the fine-mesh gill nets fishers set to catch mackerel until it's too late. In recent years, the number of daggernose sharks has collapsed.

There are endangered zebra sharks and catsharks, weasel sharks and nurse sharks. Night sharks have big eyes, all the better for seeing in the dark depths, two thousand feet down, where they spend their days before swimming to the surface in shoals at night, when fisheries most commonly catch them.

The puffadder shyshark lives on coasts around the tip of South Africa. They are small and slender, brown with rusty orange saddles resembling the markings on their namesake, the puffadder snake. When disturbed, these sharks curl up in a tight circle and hide their eyes with their tails. They're at risk partly due to their small native range, which is getting even smaller as the ocean warms and the shysharks are being forced southwards, but for this coastal species, the Cape of Good Hope is a dead end. They're getting stuck in a climate trap.

Many skates and rays, the sharks' close relatives, are also highly endangered. Giant butterfly rays look as if they've been flattened by a steamroller until they are eight feet across, making them all too easy to catch in fishing nets. Diamond-shaped flapper skates, nicknamed the manta rays of the North Atlantic, likewise suffer for their size; from the moment they hatch from their foot-long egg cases, the newborns are at risk of getting snagged in fishing nets. Wedgefish are sharklike rays that look as if they were made by stitching the tail of a regular shark onto the body of a stingray. Like sharks, wedgefish have fins that are highly valued in the soup-fin trade and command some of the highest prices; as a consequence of intensive fishing, they are now Critically Endangered.

All these elasmobranchs are struggling in the Anthropocene because the ocean is so intensively fished, a situation made worse by the fact that they tend to share a certain pace of life that puts them in jeopardy. Before humans came along, elasmobranchs were used to living in an ocean where they were rarely hunted and eaten. Usually, they were the ones doing the eating, and they evolved to be predators playing the long game. Sharks don't sprint through life at a hectic biological pace, unlike sardines or mackerel, which hurry to grow up fast and produce copious numbers of offspring because at any moment they could be eaten by something else. Many fast-living fish can have their whole lives done and dusted while sharks are still taking their sweet time to reach maturity. Female oceanic whitetip sharks start pupping in their teens, flapper skates in their twenties. Greenland sharks take it to an extreme and don't start reproducing until way past their hundredth birthday.

When sharks and rays are finally ready to begin reproducing, things still happen at a slow pace. Female sharks are typically pregnant for a year or more; shortfin makos give birth after a year and a half, basking sharks after two and a half. Female greeneye spurdogs, which gaze through the deep waters off Australia with dazzling emerald eyes, are pregnant for between thirty-one and thirty-four months, one of the longest recorded gestations of any animal.

Egg-laying elasmobranchs also have a leisurely start in life. Small spotted catsharks from the coasts of Europe entwine tendrils of their egg cases among seaweeds and seagrasses, leaving the embryonic pups to feed off yolk for up to eleven months before they hatch. In 2019, an angler off Scotland caught a female flapper skate, and before there was time to put her back in the sea alive, the shock caused her to prematurely lay an egg on the boat's deck. Luckily, the pup inside was at a late enough stage of development that it survived, and scientists at a nearby marine research station took good care of the egg case. Eventually, after 534 days, the eleven-inch male hatchling finally wriggled out of his egg case, wrapped up in his wings like a burrito. He was the first flapper skate born in captivity, and after swimming test laps of his aquarium tank, he was released into the sea.

Elasmobranchs generally pour a lot of time and energy into producing a small number of big babies, bestowing each one with as good a chance as possible of surviving in the wild. Oceanic whitetip sharks give birth to six pups, on average, only once every other year. After nearly three years of pregnancy, greeneye spurdog females have between four and fifteen pups. Blue sharks push the boat out and give birth annually to fifty and sometimes more than a hundred pups, but generally, sharks produce no more than a few dozen offspring in a year.

The least fecund are sand tiger sharks, which commonly give birth to twins, the winners of a cannibalistic battle that goes on inside their mother. Before they're born, fertilised eggs hatch into a shoal of tiny sharks, which proceed to eat each other until there are just two left, one in each branch of the pregnant female's two-pronged uterus. By the time the surviving pups emerge into the ocean, they are so big, between three and four feet long, they have few natural predators. Except now, of course: humans are changing the rules, and sharks are born into an ocean where being big and living a long, slow life is no longer an advantage.

Long before endangered shark species finally blink out and go extinct, their gradual diminishing leaves marks on the environment. Take them away, and it potentially changes the way whole ecosystems work, which is one major reason the future ocean needs more sharks.

The idea that sharks are important for a healthy, functioning ocean generally comes from their position at the top of food chains. A lot of shark species, especially the big ones, are apex predators, primed to have a disproportionate influence over other species—not only the animals they eat but also those further down on the food chain. The disappearance of sharks could set off ripples of change through the rest of the ecosystem.

Keystone predators, the ones that keep entire ecosystems in balance, were first identified in a pioneering experiment carried out in the 1960s. The keystone in question was *Pisaster ochraceus*, a stout, purple starfish that has a healthy appetite for shellfish. Marine biologist Robert Paine cordoned off areas of shoreline along the rocky northwest coast of Washington State, picked up all the starfish, and moved them elsewhere. Within a few months, in places that were missing the five-armed predators, the local mussel population exploded. Paine watched as the mussels swiftly hogged all the space and outcompeted everything else, mostly other molluscs such as limpets and chitons. He showed that by eating so many mussels and keeping their numbers in check, the predatory starfish allowed a greater diversity of other species to coexist. Lose the predators, and the ecosystem loses its biodiversity. These are the keystones keeping the rest of the ecosystem from collapsing. Paine had picked a good study system to detect these effects, with animals that can be easily moved about and then generally stay put.

Doing a similar experiment with pelagic sharks is impossible; thus, identifying their keystone role is much harder. No scientists have tried excluding sharks from areas of habitat to see what happens. Instead, they've tracked the changes that unfold when fisheries deplete shark populations in an area. Some studies have linked a decline in sharks to increases in their prey, including stingrays, octopuses, and moray eels. Whether ripples of change continue all the way through ecosystems —and hence just how important sharks are for the ocean—remains a matter of much debate among shark biologists.

The most controversial investigation into the issue began in 2007, with a study of the shark fisheries off the coast of North Carolina in the United States, where large, predatory sharks, including bull sharks, tiger sharks, and scalloped hammerheads, had been overfished for decades. As populations of these apex predators declined, scientists spotted an uptick in the numbers of smaller sharks and rays. Doing especially well were the three-foot-wide cownose rays, named for their domed heads and straight-lipped mouths, which when they're crunching on clams bear a passing resemblance to their terrestrial namesake chewing its cud.

While making the most of their new-found freedom from the jaws of larger sharks, the cownose rays were munching their way through the local bay scallops. Here was a ripple of change, kicked off by the loss of apex sharks, cascading all the way down the food chain—just as the science of keystone predators predicts. Authors of that 2007 study made an explicit link between the proliferation of cownose rays and the collapse of a scallop fishery. They made no comment on what, if anything, should be done about this; their job was simply to investigate the ecological changes taking place. But when members of the public caught wind of the study, their reaction was perhaps predictable.

"Save the Bay, Eat a Ray" was the slogan for a campaign that launched after fishers in the Chesapeake Bay decided their oyster harvests were dwindling because cownose rays must be eating them as well. Cownose rays were renamed "Chesapeake rays" to persuade people to eat them; the state of Virginia gave away free ray meat to restaurants to stimulate an appetite for it, and recreational fishers held tournaments to kill as many rays as possible. Like the Florida lionfish, the cownose ray was branded as an invasive species, and people were all too willing to help get rid of it. The truth is, cownose rays are not invaders but are native to the region, and they had been unfairly blamed for changes that were already taking place.

All this was laid bare in a 2016 study that found flaws in the original sharks-eat-rays-eat-scallops story and pointed out some overlooked facts about the species involved. A drop in predation by large sharks couldn't have triggered a sudden proliferation in cownose rays because the rays reproduce far too slowly; female rays take eight years to reach maturity and thereafter give birth to a single pup each year. Cownose rays just don't have the same capacity for rapid growth as Robert Paine had seen among mussels on the rocky shore. More likely, rays increased off North Carolina because they swam in from elsewhere. Cownose rays are known for congregating in the tens of thousands and undertaking immense seasonal migrations. Also, the timing was off. A more careful look at the data showed that the scallop fishery had already been collapsing for a while before the cownose ray bonanza. And besides, cownose rays don't even eat that many scallops or oysters. Tragically, the legacy of the original research lingers, and cownose rays are still being heavily fished and targeted in fishing tournaments.

Moving on from that sorry study, scientists are still untangling the ways sharks influence their environment. No simple story is emerging of what happens when sharks are gone. The bottom line is that ecology is complicated, especially in the ocean, where water flows and animals restlessly migrate, forming connections that reach far and wide.

There are hints, though, that the largest, most fearsome sharks hold sway over their surroundings without even eating their prey. Fear alone can shape ecosystems. Prowling sharks scare other animals, which alter their behaviour to avoid getting caught. Then, when there aren't so many sharks around, they no longer need to hide.

This happened at Seal Island in False Bay, a short way east of the Cape of Good Hope in South Africa. Since 2000, marine biologists have been monitoring the great white sharks that come to the island to hunt a huge colony of Cape fur seals. Tourists and wildlife filmmakers would also flock to the bay to have close-up encounters with great whites and watch them leaping into the air as they ambushed seals from below. Then, in 2015, there were suddenly far fewer great whites visiting the bay and far fewer seal attacks. Evidently, life became a lot calmer for the seals. Their anxiety levels dropped, as measured by a drop in the fight-or-flight stress hormones in their faeces, and they began spending more time farther from shore and over deeper water, places that not so long before had been very dangerous.

When great whites left the bay, seven-gilled sharks started showing up at Seal Island for the first time. These smaller predatory sharks, with gummy smiles, used to lurk in the shadows of nearby kelp forests where the bigger, bulkier great white sharks couldn't easily manoeuvre and chase them.

Great white sharks had been scared out of False Bay by even bigger and more fearsome apex predators. At around the time when the sharks left, orcas began showing up along the South African coast. The marine mammals are not renowned for shark hunting, but these ones adopted a new habit of attacking great whites in packs and eating just their livers, the most nutritious part, leaving the rest of the body untouched. Facing this new lethal threat, many of the surviving great white sharks seem to have fled in fear for their lives, abandoning their former feeding grounds. The arrival of orcas to these coasts is another puzzle of the changing ocean, perhaps linked to fisheries depleting their other prey and forcing these intelligent cetaceans to find alternative sources of food.

The sequence of changes triggered by orcas and great whites in South Africa indicates the magnitude of influence predators can have. It's possible that these impacts also extend into the surrounding habitats and potentially make ocean ecosystems more resilient to climate change. Shark Bay in Western Australia is aptly named for its large population of tiger sharks, which roam vast seagrass meadows, hunting dugongs and spreading fear through the seascape. The placid, seagrass-munching mammals know they're in danger when tiger sharks are around and thus behave cautiously; they hold their heads up, keeping a watchful eye, and nibble on the ends of seagrass blades. When the dugongs feel safer, they dig their snouts down into the seabed and rip up whole plants from the roots—a much more destructive feeding pattern for the lawns of seagrasses. With this in mind, marine biologists took the chance to see what might happen to the bay if there were no more tiger sharks. In 2011, Shark Bay was struck by a massive marine heatwave, which caused catastrophic loss of seagrasses, and the dugongs temporarily moved out. In their place, a team of diving scientists, trowels in hand, impersonated dugongs at their most carefree. In some experimental plots, they dug up seagrasses from the roots, just as dugongs do when there are no sharks in the neighbourhood to watch out for. Other plots they left alone. In the following months, the heat-stricken seagrasses grew back much better in areas the scientists weren't digging up. This suggests that when heatwaves strike, a decent-size population of tiger sharks could give seagrass meadows the respite they need from overgrazing, by forcing dugongs to stay alert and not uproot the plants.

Even with so many odds stacked against them, elasmobranchs have yet to suffer from extensive recent extinctions, although there are several species that haven't been seen in a long time. The Red Sea torpedo, a species of ray that sends electric shocks through the water, was originally named in 1898 and hasn't been reported since, despite biologists making a concerted effort to find one. The lost shark was last found in the wild in 1934. Both species are classified on the Red List as Critically Endangered (Possibly Extinct). Meanwhile, the Java stingaree was a dinner-plate sized ray that was only recorded once, in 1862, in a fish market in Jakarta, Indonesia. Following more than twenty years of searching fish markets for another specimen, and studying the highly-industrialized and heavily-fished seas of the region, in 2023 a team of scientists declared the species extinct.

There are also cases of sharks and rays that were thought to be vanishingly rare and restricted to a minute part of the ocean, which have, with more careful examination, proven to be more widespread and certainly not beyond hope. One species recently pulled out of obscurity is the angelshark.* So named because of its outspread wings, it sits and waits, pressing its flat, six-foot-long body against the seabed and nestling in the sand, hiding from passing prey. But angelsharks haven't been able to hide from trawl nets dragged over the seabed, and consequently, they're one of the most endangered of all the sharks.

Overexploitation of angelsharks was well underway in the nineteenth century, when fisheries across the northeast Atlantic and the Mediterranean were catching them. The sharks were intentionally targeted for their meat, their oily livers, and their skin, used to make into leather. In southeast France, on the Mediterranean coast, La Baie des Anges (the Bay of Angels) was named after all the angelsharks that used to be caught there. Angelsharks were a common catch around UK coasts, although the British didn't know they were eating sharks because the meat was sold under an alternative ecclesiastical name, monkfish. And seafood consumers had no clue when angelsharks

---

* *Squatina squatina*, one of twenty-two species in the Squatinidae family.

became overfished and disappeared from the menu. Fishers swapped them for two species of shallow-water anglerfish,* which they used to throw away but then started keeping and selling under the same name, monkfish, as still happens today. Apparently, nobody eating monkfish noticed the switch. The demise of angelsharks didn't even show up in fishery records but was lost amid the species substitution, because catches under the generic category of monkfish didn't decline. By the 1980s, the once-common angelsharks had almost disappeared. On rare occasions when one was caught in a fishery, it was considered a novelty and if still alive placed on display in an aquarium.

For years after fisheries depleted them across much of their range, one place became renowned as the last stronghold for angelsharks. In the Canary Islands, the Spanish archipelago two hundred miles west of Morocco, divers were having regular encounters with the mottled, flattened sharks. Thanks to decades of a trawling ban and swirling, food-rich waters, the Canary Islands population was doing well. But this wasn't the only place where angelsharks were still living.

It took a groundswell of action and collaboration between scientists, fishers, anglers, divers, and other ocean-goers to raise the profile of these overlooked sharks and show they still exist elsewhere and are well worth protecting. Local knowledge has been pivotal in building accurate maps of angelshark distributions. Researchers met and spoke with people living along coastlines in Europe to hear their stories of catching or seeing angelsharks; newspaper archives have turned up photographs of anglers posing with this unusual-looking species; a network has been set up so members of the public can report angelshark sightings.

A 2020 study gathered all this information together and showed that the angelshark's range is not as restricted as people had feared. There are still some locations where its presence is highly uncertain.

---

* *Lophius piscatorius* and *L. budegassa*, members of the same family as deep-sea anglerfish.

It's possible the species has been lost from the North Sea, along the Iberian Peninsula, and south to the Moroccan coast. Elsewhere, angelsharks don't occur in large numbers, but they do live along the coasts of Algeria, Tunisia, Libya, and Israel; in the Adriatic Sea off the Italian and Croatian coasts; and off Corsica, Cyprus, Greece, and Turkey. In addition to the Canary Islands, other important strongholds for angelsharks are the Irish and Celtic Seas. Along the coast of Wales, scientists are now searching for genetic clues left behind by angelsharks. Seawater contains a soup of DNA fragments from sloughed-off skin cells, scraps of mucus, and faeces. It's now possible to take water samples, extract the DNA snippets, and work out which species they came from. This environmental DNA, or eDNA, doesn't last long and soon breaks down, so when angelshark DNA shows up in samples of Welsh seawater, it means one must have swum by in the past few days. In 2021, a diver filmed a young, live angelshark underwater, a first for British waters and a sure sign that female angelsharks are using the Welsh coast as pupping grounds. And in July 2023, an angelshark was spotted near the city of Brighton off the south coast of England.

Angelsharks remain highly endangered, but conservationists, now armed with a much better idea of where these animals live, are putting together plans to protect them. These plans also include two similar-looking relatives, the smoothback and sawback angelsharks,* which share a similar range along European and African coasts but have lost a lot of ground to fishing and habitat destruction.

It won't be an easy task bringing back more of these rare, flat sharks to an ocean that's still intensively fished. Angelsharks are protected in British and EU waters, where it's illegal to cause them deliberate harm or to keep them when they're caught in fisheries, but trawlers are indiscriminate and will keep catching them. Conservationists are working with fishers to help them find ways of safely handling

---

* *Squatina oculata* and *S. aculeata.*

angelsharks and carefully untangling them from nets and lines, to give them a better chance of surviving once they've been let go.

In the Canary Islands, Greece, and Turkey, recreational scuba divers are looking out for angelsharks and reporting when and where they see them. Their input is helping scientists to identify places that are especially important—the parts of the seabed where angelsharks go to feed, find mates, and give birth—and that need urgent protection from fishing. In this way, angelsharks are also acting as so-called umbrella species, helping to protect other species that share their habitats.

Angelsharks almost slipped away from the ocean decades ago, but now they are making a comeback, thanks in large part to the everyday people who are spotting them in the wild and becoming their champions. Most people will never catch sight of the ocean's wandering sharks, such as an oceanic whitetip, hammerhead, or thresher. Swimmers, divers, and anglers along the world's coasts have a much greater chance of an enchanting encounter with one of these serene angelsharks lying quietly on the seabed.

A lot is changing for elasmobranchs, and not all of it for the worse. At the turn of the twenty-first century, there was very little international attention on their plight. Fisheries were catching as many sharks as they wanted with no limits. The trade in shark fins was freewheeling without scrutiny. Popular Western culture was plagued by lingering fears of shark-infested waters, stirred decades earlier by the movie *Jaws*, and sharks still were not looked on kindly in the public eye.

Gradually, these stereotypical beliefs shifted, and alternative views of sharks started to become more mainstream. Scientific studies helped with this, uncovering new details of the nuanced, intelligent lives of sharks. Early breakthroughs in the field of shark intelligence were made in the 1950s by American biologist Eugenie Clark, who showed that these fish are not mindless killing machines but are capable of learning and have good memories. She kept lemon sharks in open sea pens and successfully trained them to push a target with their snout, which rang a bell and released a piece of food. The sharks stopped feeding through the colder winter months, but as soon as spring arrived and the water warmed, they remembered precisely what to do and swam up to the target to get their food.

More recently, scientists working at the Bimini Biological Field Station in the Bahamas tracked young lemon sharks marked with coloured tags. From atop a tall tower set in shallow lagoons of a mangrove inlet, researchers watched through binoculars and noted down the individual movements of each shark cruising around the shallows. Often, they saw the same two, three, or more sharks swimming together. Some sharks stayed in the same groups throughout the whole two years of the study, evidently preferring their mutual company to that of any other sharks in the area.

Young sharks also make close acquaintances under controlled laboratory conditions. Given the choice, they prefer to stay close to sharks they've met before rather than strangers. These social networks likely help sharks learn from each other, passing on knowledge on how to find food and avoid predators.

New ways of thinking about why sharks matter have also been coming to the fore. It's long been known that shark ancestry can be traced back at least four hundred million years. That evolutionary heritage has come into focus with the advent of new genetic techniques that allow scientists to decode their genomes and learn about how elasmobranchs have been evolving their own unique ways of doing things. Sequencing the DNA of great white sharks, for instance, identified the genes that allow their wounds to heal swiftly, an important attribute for a species whose courtship involves a lot of biting. If great white sharks, or any other species, went extinct, millions of years of their unique evolutionary information would be lost that could have all sorts of applications and uses in the human medical world.

More people than ever are embracing a new fondness and compassion for sharks, seeing them as graceful, efficient, and important animals. Members of the public are joining scientists in campaigns to make the ocean a less dangerous place for sharks. Even victims of shark attacks are advocating for their conservation and are convinced the ocean will be a better place with more sharks in it. This is arduous work because of the slow lives of elasmobranchs and the slow pace of international negotiations, but gradually the situation is improving, and there are hopeful signs that sharks and their kin can make a comeback.

Back in 2009, the Pacific island state of Palau banned targeted shark fishing from all its waters, an area of more than two hundred thousand square miles. This was the world's first shark sanctuary. It was followed by more than a dozen others. Several countries, including French Polynesia and Kiribati, have territories covering more than a million square miles of ocean, which they declared off-limits to shark fishing. Most of these countries have major tourism industries, and the income generated by visitors keen to encounter wild sharks was deemed to be more significant than revenues from fisheries catching sharks. Now, more than 3 per cent of the global ocean is technically a shark sanctuary, where it's illegal to deliberately catch and sell sharks and in some cases rays too.

More than a decade after many of these sanctuaries were declared, it isn't entirely clear how well they're helping shark populations to rebuild, chiefly because very little data have been generated. In most places, nobody knows how many sharks were there before the sanctuaries were set up or how many are there now. The best indication comes from a survey of scuba divers' opinions, which suggests countries with sanctuaries are seeing less drastic declines in sharks compared to elsewhere. In general, shark meat and fins are not often seen openly on sale in countries with shark sanctuaries. Sharks were already well protected in some of these countries before sanctuaries came into force. In the Bahamas, for instance, commercial longlining had been banned for years when the shark sanctuary was declared. The sanctuary did, however, prevent a new fishery from opening that would have begun exporting shark fins.

While these sanctuaries might seem like a shark utopia, only commercial fishing for sharks is prohibited within many of them, and other fisheries continue to catch a lot of sharks and then dump them over the side because it's illegal to keep them. A 2023 study used satellite data to track the operations of longline vessels and estimate how many sharks are caught and killed within the boundaries of eight shark sanctuaries in western and central parts of the Pacific Ocean. Close to three hundred thousand large pelagic sharks were likely caught in a single year (2019), and more than one hundred thousand of them died, including blue sharks, silky sharks, thresher sharks, and oceanic whitetips. Until the death toll from longliners can be reduced, these areas will offer sharks little sanctuary.

Other than the shark sanctuaries, most marine reserves have been set up without elasmobranchs in mind. Globally, the average size of an individual reserve is roughly the same as that of Central Park in New York, which is woefully small for protecting animals that can roam great distances and migrate across entire ocean basins. And when it comes to protecting sharks and rays, a lot of marine reserves are not at all well enforced. In the Mediterranean, catches of endangered elasmobranchs are higher inside reserves than in places with no official protections at all.

While poorly patrolled marine reserves are struggling to make a difference for sharks, more focused measures are helping to protect specific parts of the ocean that are important for endangered and rare species, including some spots that have been discovered rather by chance. In 2019, British marine conservationist Chris Rickard spotted on social media a photograph of a giant egg case, the size of a football, and he instantly knew it must be the egg case of a Critically

Endangered flapper skate. It had been pulled up by a scallop fishing boat off the west coast of Scotland, in cold waters of the Inner Sound of the Isle of Skye, and Rickard persuaded the skipper to take him back there to have a look. He dived down to the seabed and saw forty flapper egg cases, each one with a wriggling embryo inside. The following year Rickard went back again, accompanied by fellow marine conservationist Lauren Smith, and together they counted more than one hundred giant egg cases nestled on the seabed. They had found a flapper skate nursery.

It wasn't far from the spot where the female flapper skate had been hauled on the deck of a fishing boat and laid the egg that hatched a year and a half later. Maybe that pregnant skate had been caught on her way to the seabed nursery. Rickard and Smith instantly understood the importance of this egg-laying habitat. Very little is known about the breeding habits of these rare animals, making this a major finding for the species. And it was obvious the flapper skate egg cases were at tremendous risk of being scraped up by trawlers and dredgers while they gestate for eighteen months on the seabed.

Working with local fishers and conservation groups, Rickard and Smith spread the word and remarkably quickly got the response they hoped for from the Scottish government. Within six months, the Red Rocks and Longay Urgent Marine Protected Area was announced, banning all fishing from the area for an initial period of twelve months across the entire area where the egg cases had been found. It was a bold and swift move. The site was deemed to be so vulnerable, it was even made off-limits to scuba divers in order to leave the female skates and their eggs in peace. In February 2023, a larger, permanently protected area came into force.

Sharks are also beginning to gain protection while they're on the move. Advances in satellite-tracking technologies are showing that elasmobranchs don't wander the ocean at random, but they intelligently navigate along predictable routes, often through waters belonging to many nations and out into the high seas. This makes international cooperation critical for conservation plans. In November 2021, the presidents of Ecuador, Panama, Colombia, and Costa Rica announced they were joining up and expanding existing marine reserves to create a huge, protected corridor between their countries. For hundreds of miles through the eastern Pacific, from the Galápagos Islands along a chain of deep seamounts to Cocos Island and on to the mainland of Central and South America, multiple endangered species migrate back and forth in a wide stretch of ocean. Giant manta rays; tiger, silky, hammerhead, and whale sharks; and green and leatherback sea turtles all follow the same path. Now that those four countries have agreed to work together, the next big challenge will be keeping long-range industrial fisheries from operating in this wildlife superhighway.

Efforts are also being made to cut down the killing of endangered sharks by industrial fisheries. Since 2010, tuna fisheries in the Atlantic have been banned from keeping and selling any oceanic whitetip sharks they catch. In 2011, a zero-retention regulation was brought in that requires fishers to release oceanic whitetips that get caught on their lines or in their nets. Other endangered species are similarly required to be set free. But zero retention does not translate to zero deaths. Some sharks can survive relatively well after they've been released, including blue sharks, the species most commonly caught by longliners. However, many sharks don't survive the ordeal of an encounter with a longline because they suffocate. It's not true that all sharks need to keep swimming in order to breathe; there are those, angelsharks included, that lie on the seabed and actively suck in water to oxygenate their gills. But pelagic sharks, such as oceanic whitetips, typically breathe by opening their mouths as they swim and letting oxygen-rich seawater pass right over their gills, a process known as ram ventilation. They can't do that when they're caught and tangled on a fishing line.

Even if sharks survive the ordeal of being caught, how long they can live after they've been released from a longline is another question.

A 2021 study conducted in waters off Florida showed that some species are reasonably robust. Scientists tagged the sharks with accelerometers, a shark version of a digital fitness-tracking device, and monitored their movements following release. After being caught on a longline hook, only three out of every hundred tiger and sandbar sharks died within twelve hours of being set free. Other species didn't do as well. The accelerometers showed that many of the blacktip sharks and spinner sharks swam around erratically before sinking to the seabed and lying very still. For those sharks, the trauma and physiological stress of capture proved too much, and they soon died.

There are also proven ways of cutting down the number of sharks caught on longlines. The straightforward step of adjusting the depth where lines are set can make a big difference. For instance, in the Indian Ocean, fisheries that target marlin catch most sharks on lines set below five hundred feet. When lines are set in the top three hundred feet of the sea, the same number of marlin tend to be caught, but far fewer sharks end up getting snagged. Switching the type of bait can also be effective, as happened when a swordfish fishery in Hawai'i swapped squid bait for fish and started catching a third fewer blue sharks.

Much research has focused on developing technologies to deter sharks from biting lines and hooks. Pulsed electrical fields, emitted by small electronic devices fixed onto the snoods of longlines, seem to do the trick. Without causing any lasting harm, these seem to briefly overstimulate the electrical sensors on a shark's snout, so it swims away. Sea trials in a small-scale bluefin-tuna longline fishery in the Mediterranean reduced the already very low catches of blue sharks even further. Illuminating gill nets with LEDs also reduces the number of sharks being caught, presumably because it helps them to see the nets and avoid swimming into them. For now, it's debatable how well any of these measures will scale up to the large fisheries that catch the most sharks, chiefly because it will be expensive for fishers to buy the devices.

Making relatively minor adjustments to fishing gear, and legally requiring the release of endangered species, are pragmatic measures that can help ameliorate the death toll of sharks, but they deflect from a deeper question. Given that industrial fisheries dominate the ocean and intrude on the global territories of so many endangered sharks, should we really be longlining at all?

Most notoriously, sharks are exploited for their fins, for use as an ingredient in traditional Asian soups. The fins themselves have little taste, but when dried, shredded, and boiled, they give the broth a sinewy, chewy texture that is highly regarded among diners who pay top prices for this luxury food. The brutal practice of cutting off fins from sharks at sea, then dumping the bodies back in the ocean, has been widely outlawed. Known as finning, it's horrendously cruel when performed on live animals and encourages overexploitation of populations, because fishers keep the sharks' fins without taking up space in their holds with the bodies, which generally have a lower market value or no quota to legally bring them back to land; shark fins are also much easier to hide. Over the past twenty years, dozens of countries have introduced laws that require any landed shark bodies to be accompanied by a certain weight of the fins on the same vessel, or they must have their fins still naturally attached, as is the case in US waters, India, Colombia, Brazil, Taiwan, and elsewhere; while in Oman and South Africa, sharks can only be legally sold whole. Finning is now illegal on EU vessels operating anywhere in the ocean. Since 2019, Canada has banned the import and export of detached shark fins, and the UK's Shark Fins Act was passed into law in June 2023, banning the trade into and out of the country of shark fins and any product containing them, such as canned shark-fin soup.

There have also been advances in controlling the trade in shark meat and fins under the aegis of the Convention on International Trade in Endangered Species of Wild Fauna and Flora (CITES).

Known best for banning trade in wildlife products like elephant ivory and tiger bones, this global body also regulates trade in species that are not deemed to be on the very brink of extinction but are heading that way. In 2002, the basking shark and whale shark were the first elasmobranchs to be added to CITES, and they were joined by the great white shark in 2004. It took another decade of tireless work by campaigners before several more endangered elasmobranchs were listed, including the manta ray, great hammerhead shark, and oceanic whitetip shark. Except for the incredibly rare and endangered sawfish (a type of ray), in which trade is banned, all the other elasmobranchs were placed in Appendix II of the convention, which allows a certain level of trade. Permits required to engage in trade certify that consignments of these species are legal and traceable and do not threaten their survival in the wild.

This should, at least in theory, help to reduce impacts of shark fishing, because fins and meat can be legally traded only if they're proven to come from sustainable fisheries. Providing that proof is the big challenge—even knowing which species are being traded was a long-standing problem. Once a fin was detached (legally or otherwise), dried, processed, and trimmed, it was almost impossible to work out by eye which species it came from. Genetic tools have transformed the monitoring ability of the fin trade, allowing regulators to accurately identify shark species from the DNA in their dried fins. Scientists in Hong Kong, the main hub in the international fin trade, have been conducting routine surveys, visiting seafood vendors once a month and purchasing small bags of trimmings—the pieces snipped off fins to neaten them for sale. They found that many CITES-listed species were still being traded in huge numbers and not always accompanied by the necessary permits.

A turning point came in 2022 with the release of another study showing that species in the fin trade are inordinately threatened with extinction. The study identified eighty-six elasmobranch species in the trade, of which sixty-one were listed in the IUCN's Red List of Threatened Species. The study warned that most sharks in the trade are being caught in fisheries lacking good management, and that without better controls, a wave of species extinctions was likely.

That study was very well timed, and later in 2022 it proved highly influential at a landmark meeting of CITES in Panama, where the biggest-ever vote passed in favour of sharks. The entire guitarfish family, comprising thirty-seven species of sharklike rays whose fins are highly valued, was added to CITES Appendix II, as were several hammerhead shark species. Also listed was the entire family of requiem sharks: the fifty-four species, all close relatives of oceanic whitetips, of which include lemon, spinner, blue, and copper sharks, along with whitetip and blacktip reef sharks. These additions mean that around 90 per cent of all sharks in the fin trade are now CITES-listed.

The next step will be for countries to enforce these new trade regulations, which should be easier now that superfast DNA tests can identify illegal shipments that don't have the required permits. Results from DNA sequencing used to take a week or longer to come back from the lab, which is no use to customs officers in most countries, as they can impound suspected illegal consignments for only a day or two. Now a mobile shark DNA lab can be taken to a container of shark fins at a port, and customs officers can conduct a far simpler test and within a few hours identify the species.

For CITES to help conserve sharks depends on how well fisheries can be managed so populations don't continue to spiral into decline. On that score, there's still a lot of work to do. Less than 10 per cent of the global shark catch is currently well managed within sustainable limits. Some shark species, such as blue sharks, are abundant, reproduce relatively quickly, and are likely candidates for sustainable fisheries—that is, if resources can be devoted to proper monitoring and management. For the more endangered species, including oceanic whitetip sharks, sustainable fisheries will never be a good idea. Their populations are much too small, and even if they do recover substantially, these animals live such long, slow lives that a sustainable fishery would only be able to take incredibly low numbers. So why bother? Better to leave these magnificent animals alone after decades of maltreatment of their species.

A ray of hope recently shone onto the lives of endangered oceanic sharks. A 2023 study of shark fisheries in American waters provided the first compelling evidence that with time and effort, these sharks' troubles can be reversed, and that they are not doomed to disappear from the ocean. Several decades ago, leading up to the 1990s, fishers in US waters were actively encouraged to catch sharks because it was the general opinion that these wild animals were going to waste as they swam around the seas and could be put to better human use—they were classified as an underutilised resource. In that sense, the shark-catching campaign was a tremendous success. It didn't take long before this resource was thoroughly utilised and exhausted. In 1993, the US government backtracked and introduced a recovery plan to halt unchecked overexploitation of sharks in the Atlantic. New regulations were strictly imposed by the US Coast Guard and other law enforcement agencies. Limits were introduced on the number of sharks that can be caught. For the most imperilled species, quotas were set to zero. Fishing pressure was reined in. The plan was not just about preventing species extinctions but about reaching for a more ambitious goal of rebuilding populations.

Scientists have compared the situation in US Atlantic waters before and after this protection plan came into force. Using data from Sharkipedia, an open-source database of shark populations, they found that for nine species of large pelagic sharks—the *tiburones*—the grim, pre-1990s outlook has distinctly improved. Scalloped and smooth hammerheads pulled out of a nosedive and levelled off, and their populations have gradually begun to grow. Declines in tiger sharks and great whites have also stabilised, and their numbers are rising. Great hammerhead populations are steadily climbing as well.

The important message from the northwest Atlantic fisheries is that building a future ocean with more sharks in it is possible. There's no swift bouncing back for species that spend decades reaching maturity and devote years of pregnancy and egg development to producing a smattering of burly offspring. Even a few decades after shark fishing was restricted in the northwest Atlantic, most of the recovering shark species still have a long way to go to regain their former abundance. But now that they've been given a chance, these sharks are slowly, slowly coming back. The same could happen elsewhere, and for many other species, if decisions are made to give elasmobranchs more of their ocean back.

Chapter 5
Poisoned Hunters

There she lay on the beach not far from the cold Scottish waters she had called home, one of her flippers pointing at the sky. People had known this female orca for more than twenty years and recognised her by the shape of the white patches behind her eyes and the pale saddle across her black back. This was Lulu.

She was named in 1995 when she first appeared in a pod known as the West Coast Community, a distinct variety or ecotype comprising the last resident orcas in the seas around the British Isles. Around New Year's Day, 2016, somewhere near the small island of Tiree in the Inner Hebrides, Lulu became entangled in fishing lines. For several days, she dragged the heavy ropes behind her, as they made it exhausting for her to swim and hunt. In the end, Lulu drowned.

By the time she washed up on the beach in Tiree, the fishing ropes were gone, but the deep wounds they left in her skin remained. Entanglement is generally uncommon for these quick-witted, agile predators. A necropsy revealed a problem that likely contributed to Lulu's demise. Analysis of chemicals in her body revealed she had been carrying a huge toxic load. The concentration of polychlorinated biphenyls, the pollutants commonly called PCBs, was so high she was one of the most contaminated animals ever found. When they percolate into living bodies, these chemicals interfere with the immune system and brain function, so it's possible Lulu was too confused to avoid getting snarled in the fishing line and too weak to cope with the added weight once she was entrapped.

PCBs also disrupt hormones and cause infertility, which likely explains another finding of the postmortem. Even though she was at least twenty years old and sexually mature, Lulu had never given birth to a calf. When she died, she left behind eight other members of the West Coast Community, four mature females and four males. The Hebridean Whale and Dolphin Trust has been monitoring the pod since the 1990s, and in that time a calf has never been seen. Lulu's poisoned body provided evidence that accumulating toxins could be to blame. Since she died, the situation has become even more bleak. Only two orcas from the pod have been spotted recently—both males.

Measuring up to thirty-two feet long and weighing five or even ten metric tons, orcas, also known as killer whales, are the world's largest dolphins. They occupy every ocean and live long, intricate lives. Tight-knit pods are commonly led by a female, whose children and grandchildren stay with her throughout her life. A recent study found that grandmothers protect their sons from getting into fights with other orcas. The matriarch remains the head of the family into her old age, at eighty, ninety, even a hundred years old and way past her menopause; orcas are one of only five animal species in which females are known to outlive their fertility.* Grandmother orcas are the wise elders, keepers of expert knowledge of where to hunt, and they call other members of the pod to them with a splash of their tail.

Orcas are supreme hunters, the killers of whales and other marine predators. Distinct populations dispersed across the ocean have evolved to specialise in particular prey. In Antarctica, they hunt for

---

*The others are short-finned pilot whales, belugas, narwhals, and humans.

penguins, seals, and young minke and humpback whales; along the coastlines of Patagonia, orcas deliberately beach themselves to grab sea lions. Elsewhere, orcas prey on salmon, herring, and, as seen recently off South Africa, great white sharks.

As cosmopolitan apex predators, orcas are sentinels for the global health of the ocean. It's revolting but true that the ocean is a dilute mix of just about everything humans make, use, and throw away: raw sewage, farming effluent, spilled oil, pesticides and herbicides, chemical weapons, nuclear waste, mercury that rises from chimney stacks of coal-fired power stations and then rains down from the skies, and so much plastic. Orcas accumulate and concentrate pollutants in their bodies and are often hit the first and the worst as human-made contaminants percolate through the ocean.

The toxic compounds that ended up in Lulu's blubber were manufactured long before she was born. There are more than two hundred types of PCBs, all sharing a similar molecular structure.* None occur naturally. They were first synthesised in laboratories in the 1870s and went into mass production in the 1930s, first by the Monsanto Company in the United States, then by other manufacturers in other countries, in particular Russia, Germany, France, and the United Kingdom. These chemicals were widely used in refrigerators and television sets, in sealants, paints, pesticides, herbicides, glues, and lubricants. PCBs were added to coatings on electric cables to stop them from snapping and sprayed onto roads to prevent dust from being kicked up. They were used in carbon paper, floor polish, and false teeth.

From the start, manufacturers knew there were health risks when people working in PCB factories broke out in disfiguring skin conditions. Later studies recognised PCBs as carcinogens and endocrine disruptors and linked them to a plethora of debilitating health

---

*PCB compounds contain two rings of carbon atoms with multiple chlorine atoms attached.

conditions. In 1968, in the journal *Nature*, scientists reported that PCBs were contaminating wildlife and were already widely dispersed in the global ecosystem. Amid spiralling concerns about their impacts on human health and the environment, PCB manufacture was phased out in the United States in the 1970s, and a European ban followed in 1987. But that was already far too late.

Decades have gone by since the last PCBs were made, and still they're poisoning the planet. The very same properties that made them so appealing for industrial uses now make them especially dangerous. They belong to a larger group of toxic synthetic substances, generally known as persistent organic pollutants,* among them the insecticide toxaphene, which was used on American cotton crops in the 1960s; chlordane, which was sprayed over termite-infested houses; and the insecticide DDT, which American author Rachel Carson alerted the world to in her 1962 book *Silent Spring*. All these chemicals are toxic to humans and wildlife, and they're all tough molecules that don't easily break down.

More than a million metric tons of PCBs were manufactured between 1930 and 1993, and roughly 80 per cent of them still exist today. While it is possible to safely destroy PCBs by incineration at very high temperatures, there are massive stockpiles of them in old buildings, electrical equipment, bridges, ships, and landfill sites. As infrastructure crumbles and poorly managed rubbish dumps leach contaminants, more PCBs get into soils and waterways and eventually end up in the ocean. Another route to the ocean is through the air. The toxic molecules evaporate and get blown around the atmosphere before raining down on land and sea.

Once in the ocean, PCBs make their way into ecosystems by sticking in thin layers to the outside of phytoplankton and zooplankton, which then bestow their toxins to plankton-eating animals and

---

* Organic in the chemical sense, meaning these are molecules that contain carbon atoms bonded to each other and to hydrogen atoms.

on through the food web. PCBs are not readily shed back into the ocean but stay stored inside living cells and tissues, accumulating over an animal's lifetime, until they're passed on to the next predator or scavenger that comes along.

Even the deepest parts of the ocean are turning into a toxic soup. PCBs bind to organic particles of marine snow that drift downwards and feed multitudes of animals in the water column and on the deep seabed. The toxins are showing up in dangerous levels in the bodies of deep-sea shrimp and fish, in vampire squid that float in the twilight zone, in anemones and sea lilies, and in sea cucumbers that roam the abyssal seafloor. In the extreme depths of the Mariana Trench, between five and six miles down, sandhopper-like crustaceans called amphipods have levels of PCBs in their bodies fifty times higher than crabs living in paddy fields fed by the Liao River, one of the most polluted waterways in China.

PCBs and other organic pollutants are highly soluble in fats, which is why aquatic mammals with thick layers of blubber are at especially high risk. Seals, porpoises, beluga whales, narwhals, and polar bears have all been found with highly contaminated blubber, often way above thresholds that are known to suppress the immune system and interfere with reproduction.

Dolphins around the coasts of Europe live in small and declining populations that are producing few calves or none at all, a likely upshot of the toxins the adults are carrying in their bodies. In a study of male harbour porpoises around Britain, the more PCBs they've absorbed into their bodies, the smaller their testes and the lower their fertility. For decades, California sea lions have been dying of cancer at one of the highest rates found in any wild species. The disease is triggered by a herpes virus and made much worse by chronic exposure to organic pollutants, including DDT that was dumped in the ocean off California in the 1960s and PCBs that washed from the urbanised and industrialised coastline. Pollutants from industry and agriculture play their parts in the demise of endangered Yangtze finless porpoises in China and Ganges River dolphins in Nepal, India, and Bangladesh.

Even before they're born, seals and cetaceans inherit a toxic load from their mothers via the placenta. Newborns then suckle on rich, fatty milk, which delivers yet more of their mother's toxins. This is one likely reason Lulu the orca became so very contaminated—she wasn't getting pregnant, giving birth, and feeding her calves. Normally, reproductive female orcas become less contaminated over time because they repeatedly pass on the pollutants to their offspring. Lulu just kept accumulating toxins.

A trio of traits makes orcas some of the most contaminated animals of all: they live a long time, they have a lot of fat, and they're top-level predators. Orcas that feed the highest up the food chain are especially at risk from the magnified toxins. Around Iceland, orcas that hunt for seals and porpoises have been found to have PCB levels in their blubber almost ten times higher than orcas that eat only fish.

To get a handle on just how much of a threat PCBs are for orcas globally, a group of scientists simulated the species' possible future in a toxic ocean. They compiled available data on the PCB concentrations in the blubber of orcas around the world and compared these to levels that are known to impact their immunity and reproduction. The team then built a computer model to predict how each population might change over the next hundred years, whether it would likely increase, stay roughly the same, or decline.

The model predicted that within a century, more than half of the world's orca populations could collapse. Orcas suffer from such chronic exposure to PCBs that their immunity is weakened and reproduction impaired to the point where they may struggle to maintain their numbers. If adult orcas fail to rear offspring year after year, their populations will gradually dwindle and blink out, as already seems to be happening to Lulu's West Coast Community off Scotland.

At greatest risk and most contaminated today are orcas living offshore from the industrialised regions that produced and used the most PCBs, including Japan, North America, and Europe. PCBs have also blown far and wide in the atmosphere, contaminating orcas in places where the chemicals were never used, from Greenland and the Faeroe Islands to the Ross Sea in Antarctica. No place is out of reach of these toxins.

Decades-old PCBs are not the only toxic threat to orcas and other marine life. A new chapter is opening in the chemical pollution of the planet and its ocean. When PCBs were phased out, the chemical industry, overseen by negligible regulation, developed new substances to take their place. Just like PCBs, these tend to be large, complex organic molecules that don't occur in nature. Many are clustered in groups sharing similar chemical formulas, which have tough, waterproof properties; long, unpronounceable names; and horrible acronyms. One group that's causing huge concern comprises the polyfluoroalkyl and perfluoroalkyl substances, or PFASs, which—just like PCBs—persist and accumulate in human bodies and the environment. They've been widely dubbed "forever chemicals"* because they're practically indestructible. It will take centuries for them to break down,† and they're everywhere, in fire extinguishers, smeared on non-stick cookware, sprayed on waterproof hiking jackets and snowsuits, added to stain guards for armchairs and school uniforms, and used as grease-proof coatings in pizza boxes, carry-out containers, and sandwich wrappers.

It's no surprise at all that forever chemicals already pervade human lives. We breathe them in, absorb them through our skin, eat and drink them. A study in the United States revealed they contaminate the drinking-water supplies of at least two hundred million people.

---

*In December 2023 the phrase "forever chemical" was added to the Oxford English Dictionary, a historical record of the English language that notes first use and meanings of words.

†One reason PFASs are so tough is because they contain carbon-fluorine bonds, one of the strongest chemical bonds in existence.

Experts suspect that forever chemicals are likely in the blood of every human on the planet, even unborn babies. And these chemicals are incredibly dangerous. Even tiny amounts increase the risk of cancer and are linked to a growing list of other serious health problems including birth defects, kidney disease, and liver damage.

Of course, these chemicals are also showing up everywhere in nature. They're spraying into the atmosphere when waves crash on beaches and melting out of Arctic sea ice. They've been found in plankton, manatees, sea otters, and polar bears.

Truly daunting is the fact that forever chemicals are a messy mix of unregulated, unmonitored substances. There are at least fourteen thousand different types. The majority remain untested for their precise toxic thresholds, and for some, no method is available to detect their presence in the environment. So far, only two have been widely restricted for their dangerous toxicity. One of them, known as C8,* was the subject of a long legal battle by US lawyer Robert Bilott, who unearthed evidence that chemical giant DuPont had continued to produce the chemical and contaminate water supplies long after knowing its toxic effects. Hundreds of millions of dollars in compensation have been paid out to people in contaminated communities, although the payouts apparently are not steep enough to persuade major players in the chemical industry to behave any differently. Like a stuck record, DuPont and another chemical manufacturer, Daikin, have known since 2010 about the dangers of another forever chemical† used in food packaging, but hid the findings of their studies from the public and regulators, as revealed in an investigation by the *Guardian*.

There are, however, signs that the flow of forever chemicals into our bodies and the environment could be diminishing. In the United States, numerous state laws have banned forever chemicals in food

---

*C8 refers to the chain of carbon atoms in the structure of this chemical, perfluorooctanoic acid, or PFOA.

†This one is called 6:2 fluorotelomer alcohol, or 6:2 FTOH.

containers and cookware. In California, forever chemicals aren't allowed in clothing or cosmetics. Firefighting foams, which badly pollute local watercourses, are banned across much of the United States and Australia. Other countries, including Aotearoa (New Zealand), are considering similar restrictions on certain uses. Companies are also stepping up. One of the world's biggest producers, 3M, has pledged to end manufacturing forever chemicals by the end of 2025. At a federal level, however, the US is not taking such bold moves. Regulators at the Environmental Protection Agency keep on changing their definition of what constitutes a forever chemical. In 2023, their view narrowed even further, excluding thousands of substances that won't be regulated and instead the industry will be allowed to continue manufacturing and profiting from them.

What's needed most urgently is a decisive ban on all forever chemicals, all in one go. This avoids the same loophole that's been used many times before, when manufacturers replace one chemical from this dangerous group with a slightly different one that's likely just as damaging, if not worse. And there's a chance the European Union could lead the way in this bold move. In February 2023, the influential European Chemicals Agency proposed a ban on the production, sale, and use of the entire group of chemicals.

Meanwhile, the story of PCBs is still being told, and how it ends is going to depend on how nations deal with the legacy of these toxins. The Stockholm Convention on Persistent Organic Pollutants, which came into effect in 2004, bans their production globally and sets targets for phasing out their use by 2025 and cleaning up stockpiles by 2028. Many countries signed on to the convention but are likely to miss those targets. The United States has produced and used more PCBs than any other country (on average, more than four pounds per person), and billions of dollars have been spent on clean-up efforts. In 2001, General Electric was forced to pay to dredge New York's

Hudson River and remove PCB-laced toxic wastes the company had dumped over decades. But the United States isn't party to the Stockholm Convention and has set no binding national deadlines for finishing the clean-up. Canada and the Czech Republic, showing it can be done, have already safely disposed of most of their stocks of pure PCBs and dealt with PCB-contaminated materials by actions like stripping out sealants and transistors from old apartment blocks and skyscrapers.

In the ocean, the phasing out of PCBs has been taking time to show an effect. Animal populations, such as the beluga whales of the Beaufort Sea on the fringes of the Arctic Ocean, are just as contaminated as they were decades ago. Pollutants in the bodies of striped dolphins in the Mediterranean dropped but then levelled off, and they remain worryingly high. And some species are gradually improving, as more of the chemicals already in the environment have settled into seabed sediments and new pollution is subsiding. The Franciscana dolphin, small and rare with a long, slender snout, lives along the coast of Brazil and regularly gets caught and dies in gill nets. Scientists have been measuring the persistent organic pollutants in the bodies of these dead dolphins and since 2000 have tracked a fall in their contamination.

It's not often the case that reducing pollution is the single action that saves a species or a population in the ocean, because multiple threats exist. The more immediate problems may be overhunting or habitat destruction, but chronic exposure to pollutants weakens an ecosystem already stressed and depleted. Undoing the problem of pollution can give wildlife a much better chance of recovering and replenishing, allowing more young to survive and numbers to grow.

That is happening in the Baltic, a sea notorious for its troubled environmental history. For decades, this brackish sea that winds around the Scandinavian peninsula had suffered from overfishing, overhunting, and the pollutants pouring in from the nine surrounding industrialised countries. In the early twentieth century, a swift collapse of a whole suite of top marine predators occurred. Grey, ringed, and harbour seals and harbour porpoises were all vanishing and headed towards local extinction, as were cormorants and white-tailed sea eagles. The fish these birds hunt were depleted, and their bodies were tainted with DDT and PCBs. Very few large animals remained swimming in and flying above the Baltic. But the eco-system was not too far gone. With hunting controlled, overfishing reined in, and chemicals banned, a dramatic revival began. Levels of PCBs in ringed and grey seals, as well as in the eggs of white-tailed sea eagles, have been steadily dropping since the 1970s, and now far more chicks and pups are surviving, raising the populations of birds and seals.

The fishing nets and ropes that tangled around the tail of Lulu the Scottish orca are the kinds of large plastic debris in the ocean that have gained a great deal of public attention and concern, and for good reasons. It's heartbreaking to see animals harmed by the trash that ends up in the seas, whether it's a seal with a plastic ring cutting into its neck, a sea turtle with bundles of plastic bags stuffed in its stomach, or dolphins drowned in ghost fishing nets that break away and drift by themselves, still pointlessly catching and killing wildlife. But there's mounting evidence that an even greater danger is posed by an invisible smog of minute plastic particles that contaminate every part of the global ocean.

Recent estimates indicate there are between 82 and 358 trillion microplastic particles afloat in the ocean, each measuring less than one-twentieth of an inch across and cumulatively weighing as much as 4.9 million metric tons—roughly twice the weight of all the Afri-can elephants alive today. This plastic burden will get worse in the future, not just because plastics will keep getting dumped into the ocean but from the breakdown of the larger plastics already there, creating a toxicity debt that will linger for decades to come.

The global impact this is having on ocean life is complex and poorly understood, but already it's obvious that the smaller the plastic particle, the greater the harm it can cause. Microplastics enter ocean food webs when they are eaten by zooplankton and small fish. Copepods, flea-size crustaceans, are among the most abundant zooplankton. They create water currents with their flickering legs and antennae that draw particles towards their mouths. If they taste an inert plastic particle, they will sometimes spit it out, but not if it's mixed in with their phytoplankton food, in which case they swallow the whole lot together. Once in the guts of these tiny animals, microplastics can build up and stop them from feeding. Microplastics also interfere with the gut microbiome, the mix of microbes that are essential for an animal's healthy immune function and nutrition; even their behaviour can be affected by plastic-induced changes in their microbiome.

Laboratory studies suggest that much of the microplastic fish swallow is excreted in their faeces within a week, which should limit the harm they do. However, microplastics break down and get even tinier, entering the size range of nanoparticles* and raising the likelihood they will stay in the body and accumulate in tissues. Nanoparticles can get inside living cells and pass from the gut into the blood system and then distribute all around the body and into the brain. They can alter expression of genes and elicit inflammatory immune responses.

In addition to their direct impacts, plastic particles also act like Trojan horses, bringing other dangerous substances inside living bodies. Chemical additives are used to manufacture plastics that are tough, flexible, and flame-retardant, and many are known to be toxic, such as bisphenol A (BPA), commonly used in water bottles and food cans. Plastic debris also picks up toxic molecules from

---

*Nanoparticles are between one and one thousand nanometres in size; there are more than twenty-five million nanometres in one inch.

the ocean, including PCBs and other persistent organic pollutants, adding to the flow of these chemicals into food webs. Another concern is that microplastics can carry pathogenic bacteria and viruses.

Thousands of ocean species have been found with microplastics inside their bodies, either eaten directly or passed to them from their prey. Plastic-contaminated animals are entering the human food chain, creating potential health risks, especially for coastal communities reliant on seafood for their nutrition. In the wild, the animals likely at greatest risk from microplastic pollution are baleen whales, which filter and strain small prey from seawater using bristles inside their enormous mouths. A 2022 study calculated the microplastic load picked up by whales when they visit the California coast each year to feed. Data from tags fixed onto diving whales showed they mainly forage between around 160 and 820 feet down, which overlaps with a zone containing ten times more microplastics than the surface. The whales don't filter microplastics directly from seawater but mostly consume them via their diet of krill and fish, such as anchovies, which they eat in colossal quantities. A fin whale can take in close to six million plastic particles every day. A blue whale consumes more than ten million particles per day, cumulatively weighing as much as ninety-six pounds. Over the course of the four-month feeding season, each blue whale likely consumes more than a billion plastic particles. Owing to its krill-rich diet, the biggest animal that ever existed is being contaminated by infinitesimal flecks of synthetic materials because krill crush the microplastics into even smaller nanoparticles when they feed. And the Pacific waters off California where this study was conducted are by no means the most contaminated in the world ocean. Baleen whales elsewhere are likely consuming even more plastic, and they will continue to do so as long as plastic debris keeps entering the ocean.

For decades, humans have been transforming the ocean homes of whales across the globe, introducing a potent mix of chemical pollution and many other threats. One of the most endangered populations of orcas, known as the Southern Resident Community and made up of three distinct pods, lives along the Pacific coast of the United States and Canada, where fewer than eighty individuals remain. Its members are expert fish hunters and depend on Chinook salmon as their main source of food. Declines in Chinook, especially the fattiest spring migrants heading inland to spawn, are making it harder for the orcas to find enough food. The orcas' bodies are contaminated with pollutants, including PCBs and 4-nonylphenol, a chemical used in paper, textile, and detergent processing, and commonly found in toilet paper, that escapes into the environment via sewage treatment plants. Furthermore, the habitat of these orcas has become increasingly noisy. Southern Residents spend the summer months in the Salish Sea, a busy inland waterway bordered by major Canadian and US port cities, including Seattle, Vancouver, and Victoria, and crisscrossed by international shipping lanes and ferry routes. The underwater roar of engines masks the orcas' repertoire of pulse calls, jaw clacks, and bellows. Whirling propellors create streams of cavitation bubbles that collapse and pop at the same frequency as the echolocation sounds that orcas use to hunt. These highly sonic animals have trouble communicating with each other and hearing echoes bouncing off their prey while subjected to a din roughly equivalent to a lawnmower thundering past.

A ship passing within a few hundred yards will commonly cause orcas to end their foraging dives. Presumably, they intuitively understand that when so much other noise is raging around them, trying to hunt with intricate beams of sound is pointless. Females are especially sensitive and halt their hunts more often than males, likely because they have offspring to look out for. Nonstop disturbances while they're trying to forage could mean females go hungry and struggle to produce enough milk for their young.

Compared to the lingering legacy of toxic chemicals, a much simpler solution for noise pollution can be implemented. When ships slow down, they immediately quieten down. Trials of voluntary reduced speeds in parts of the Salish Sea have successfully reduced the background volume in orcas' foraging grounds. When ships passing through are slower and quieter, orcas spend more time hunting and feeding.

A few Southern Resident orcas haven't experienced the growing volume and toxicity in the ocean because they were taken away from it. In 1964, a young male from the community was the first orca to survive in captivity for more than a few days. Collectors had planned to kill him and use his carcass as a mould to sculpt a replica for the Vancouver Aquarium, but amazingly the orca survived, even after the harpoon fractured his skull and damaged his brain. Mistaken for a female, he was given the name Moby Doll and put on public display in a sea pen off a beach in Vancouver for just one day, and thousands of people came to see him. From then on, out of the public eye, his keepers struggled to work out what to feed him, and after three months in captivity, Moby Doll died. His short life was enough to demonstrate that it was possible to keep orcas in captivity and, more importantly, that the public was keen to watch them.

After that, around one-third of the Southern Resident community was captured and sold to aquariums and theme parks, including a young female originally known as Tokitae. She was around four years old when she was taken from her family in 1970 and sent to Miami Seaquarium in Florida. Tokitae was trained to leap and do stunts. For performances she was renamed Lolita and paired up with an older male from the same community called Hugo. For a decade, Tokitae and Hugo were kept together and performed tricks for the crowds twice a day in the smallest orca aquarium tank in the United States.* They mated many times, but Tokitae never gave birth to a live calf. Hugo died in 1980 after incessantly ramming his head against the side of the tank. Thereafter, Tokitae was kept in isolation from her species. She was the last Southern Resident orca in captivity.†

During the time of Tokitae's confinement in the Florida aquarium, the tide turned against keeping orcas in captivity. A watershed moment came in 2013 with the release of the feature-length documentary *Blackfish*. It told the tragic story of Tilikum, an orca captured in Iceland and then sent to SeaWorld in Orlando, Florida, where he killed several trainers, his aggression symptomatic of post-traumatic stress disorder induced by a captive life. The film triggered public outcry, attendance at SeaWorld slumped, and the American public became disenchanted with the unethical spectacle of confined, performing animals.

For decades, campaigners pleaded for Tokitae to be released from captivity and returned to her native waters. Among the most passionate advocates for her return were members of Washington State's indigenous Lummi nation, who have cultural and spiritual ties to the Southern Resident orcas, known to them as *qwe'lhol'mechen*, the people beneath the waves.

In March 2022, Tokitae was retired from public shows. A year later, Miami Seaquarium finally agreed to release her. The plan was for Tokitae, or *Sk'aliCh'elh-tenaut*, as the Lummi people know her, to be flown to the Pacific and transferred to an open-water enclosure in the Salish Sea, then perhaps one day allowed to swim free. There she would have found out how much her home waters had

---

* Their concrete tank was eighty by thirty-five feet and twenty feet deep; Tokitae measured twenty feet long.

† At time of writing, fifty-four orcas from other communities were kept elsewhere in captive conditions.

changed since she was taken away. She would have sensed the tang of unfamiliar chemicals in the seawater and in the fish she ate. She would have heard how noisy and crowded these seas had become. She might have heard calls she remembered from more than fifty years ago and known that her community was somewhere nearby. She may have even recognised the sounds of the elder female orca who is still alive in the wild and likely is her mother. And it's possible Tokitae would have mourned the orcas from her community who are no longer there, the ones who like her were sold into captivity. But Tokitae never made it home. On August 18, 2023, she died while still in the same concrete tank she had been held in for fifty-three years at Miami Seaquarium. She was fifty-seven years old.

A few days later, hundreds of people gathered at Jackson Beach Park on San Juan Island, in the heart of the home waters of the Southern Resident orcas. Mourners laid flowers on a totem that in 2018 had been taken from the Salish Sea to the Seaquarium and back, and they listened to some of Tokitae's last calls recorded shortly before she died. Lummi dignitaries and elders asked those present to remember not just Tokitae but the rest of her family, the seventy-five remaining members of the community who are struggling to survive in the wild.

While humans have turned them into captives and spoiled their world, orcas have shown they are capable of great madness and also great sadness. In July 2018, an orca known as Tahlequah was the first member of the Southern Resident Community to give birth to a live calf in three years. But the newborn lived for only a half hour. Why it died so soon, nobody knows for sure, but polluted waters were likely at least partly to blame. Neonate orcas have washed up on beaches in other places, and scientists have tested their bodies and found them loaded with PCBs and other dangerous chemicals. After her baby died, and for the next seventeen days, Tahlequah carried the small body with her as she followed her pod on what became a thousand-mile funeral cortege. Each time the dead calf began to slide into the deep, Tahlequah swam down and brought it back to the surface, balancing it on her nose. She was grieving, orca experts widely agree, and wasn't ready to let her calf go.

It's not too anthropomorphic to imagine that orcas can feel sorrow for their changing ocean, as they watch their calves dying far more frequently than before and grieve the lost ones. And some orcas, maybe, are witnessing their ocean changing around them and getting angry about it.

Off the coasts of Spain and Portugal, orcas have been behaving strangely of late. This is another highly endangered group, made up of at most thirty-nine animals. They visit the Strait of Gibraltar each year to feed on Atlantic bluefin tuna that swim into the Mediterranean to spawn. The orcas give chase until the exhausted tuna can swim no more. Some orcas have also learned to save their energy and pick off tuna from fishing lines in a local fishery. Then, in 2020, some of these tuna-hunting orcas began deliberately ramming into boats. Dozens of sailors have reported seeing groups of orcas swimming up behind their yachts and then slamming their bodies against the vessel repeatedly, for up to two hours at a time. The orcas bring the boats to a sudden halt and turn them in circles. Often their final act is to snap off the rudder, leaving the boat without steering. In most instances, the skipper and crew have radioed for assistance and a tow back to shore, but on several occasions, boats were rammed so badly they sank, although with no harm to the people on board.

This previously unseen behaviour has continued in Iberian waters, and scientists remain mystified as to why it's happening. Many experts are keen to avoid labelling these as calculated attacks or projecting human-centric motivations on the orcas. Some think it could have been started by a few curious and boisterous orcas, and then others joined in until the situation got rather out of hand. The plot thickened in June 2023, when orcas from a different group, two thousand miles to the north of Gibraltar, repeatedly rammed into a yacht off the Shetland Islands of Scotland. How and why they developed a similar habit is yet another mystery. It's possible highly mobile orca pods have been swimming long distances and passing on the idea of messing with boats, or the Scottish orcas could have started doing it all by themselves. And it's possible one day they will all just stop. Orcas are known to pick up new habits, then drop them just as quickly. In the 1990s, one orca pod began killing fish and carrying them around on their noses; after a while, they stopped. Boat bumping could just be the latest vogue that started among the Gibraltar orcas and is catching on elsewhere.

But it's not out of the question that something more complicated is going on. Several of the orcas involved in this unusual behaviour, the unruly ringleaders, were found to have recent injuries, likely from collisions with boats travelling at speed. These orcas may have finally grown fed up with living in a busy shipping lane and figured out how to deliberately slow boats down, targeting yachts because they're easier to take on than larger craft.

PART THREE

OCEAN REVIVAL

Chapter 6
Restoring Seas

In the Caribbean Sea, roughly halfway between Havana, Cuba, and Kingston, Jamaica, lies the island of Little Cayman. At ten miles long and a mile wide, it's the smallest of the three Cayman Islands. Known best, perhaps, as a tax haven, these islands are also a haven for fish. During the winter months, when the moon is full, the sea off the western end of Little Cayman fills up with Nassau groupers. For most of the year these large predatory fish, one to two feet long, live solitary lives on the coral reef that fringes the island. But they know, when the time comes, to gather—maybe they sense the strengthening pull of the spring tide, or they notice the moon shining down—and they set off, intently swimming towards the same destination. On the outer shelf of the reef, in an area roughly the size of London's Trafalgar Square, thousands of groupers congregate. The milling shoal can become so dense no water can be seen between fish. Then, a secret signal goes out, and a dozen or more groupers at a time pinch off from the group and rush towards the surface, aiming for a spot in the water above their heads. Their bodies form a brief, shivering huddle, and a second later they split apart, leaving behind a cloud of eggs mixing with sperm. This is how new groupers are made.

Flocking together in large shoals most likely boosts each grouper's chances of reproducing successfully. Fish and their fertilised eggs are generally safer in numbers and less vulnerable to predators, which can't possibly eat every last one of them. Timing is key for these events, coinciding with the strongest tides so the fertilised eggs are swept offshore, away from the reef and the many hungry animals that live there. After a month spent afloat at sea as tiny larvae, growing and learning to swim, juvenile groupers are ready to return to the reef.

Aggregations like this are now a rare spectacle, but they used to occur across the Caribbean. The first scientist to publish an eyewitness account of an enormous Nassau grouper spawning aggregation was C. Lavett "Smitty" Smith, curator of ichthyology at the American Museum of Natural History. In 1972, he visited Cat Bay in the Bahamas and reported seeing at least thirty thousand and perhaps as many as one hundred thousand groupers coming together to spawn.

On reefs and atolls in many Caribbean countries, Nassau groupers would periodically migrate to their spawning grounds, at the same places and times year after year, some of them swimming for hundreds of miles to get there. However, the predictable timing of these events made them easy targets for fishers. Nassau groupers used to be the mainstay of fisheries in the region year-round, but the biggest catches were taken from aggregation sites during the brief spawning seasons. As a result, breeding populations were run down until their numbers were so low the adult fish no longer showed up to spawn. Nassau grouper aggregations shrank, then one by one, they blinked out.

That's what happened in the Cayman Islands. Several historic spawning grounds were wiped out, including one at the eastern end of Little Cayman that formed until 1993; then the fish stopped coming, and so did the fishers. But the Nassau groupers were not entirely gone. They have long lifespans, up to at least thirty years, and they can wait out many seasons without spawning, and then come together again when conditions suit them.

In 2001, fishers discovered the new aggregation forming at Little Cayman's western end, where none had been seen previously. That year, around seven thousand groupers gathered, and fishers caught some two thousand of them in one week of fishing. The following year, when the remaining groupers came back to spawn, fishers caught another two thousand. At that point, local authorities stepped in and introduced strict regulations on fishing. Initially, a year-on, year-off rule was brought in for fishing the aggregation site, with a catch limit of twelve Nassau groupers per boat per day. The aggregation continued to shrink in size, and in 2003, the regulations were strengthened to a blanket ban on fishing throughout the winter spawning months. Now it's illegal to catch, own, or sell a Nassau grouper between December and April anywhere in the Cayman Islands. The rest of the year, people are still allowed to catch them, although not using spearguns, and with a daily catch limit of five fish per boat.

As Nassau grouper populations began to collapse throughout the Caribbean, other countries introduced protection measures, but so far only in the Cayman Islands is their recovery obviously underway. The aggregation at Little Cayman is the largest known spawning site for the entire species, and it's growing.

Diving scientists have been conducting yearly surveys, measuring individual fish with laser dots projected onto the sides of their bodies and tagging them to see how often they come back to spawn and to estimate the total size of the population. Over the course of fifteen years, the numbers of Nassau groupers at Little Cayman has gradually increased—not a smooth and consistent recovery, but over time the population has tripled in size, returning to an abundance approaching that before the fishing spree began at the start of the century. There are also signs of recovery at a spawning site on the nearby island Cayman Brac.

The Nassau grouper is one of many coral-reef fish species that congregate in huge numbers to spawn and have historically been targeted, overfished, and extirpated. The message from the Cayman Islands is that recovery of these endangered populations is possible, but it takes commitment, patience, and time.

A lot of ocean animals are in trouble because humans are overexploiting them to the point that the survivors can't replace the lost ones fast enough. Without human interference, wild species are killed and eaten by other animals, and while populations naturally fluctuate, in general a balance is struck between predators and prey so that neither explodes nor collapses. Humans add to the predation pressure, and as long as they are not too greedy, prey populations can keep pace and maintain themselves. And if the numbers of targeted prey animals begin to dwindle, there are simple steps to take to avoid their extirpation. Reduce the number that are hunted, fished, and extracted, and populations should recover and restore.

At times, this has happened rather by chance. A little over a century ago, on beaches along the Pacific coast of California and Mexico, commercial sealers crept up on northern elephant seals as they were lined up like so many giant, furry sardines, the titanic, fifteen-foot-long males fighting each other, raising their bulbous-snouted heads and bellowing at the sky. While the seals were trying to mate and rear their young, sealers killed them for their blubber to render down and burn in oil lamps. The slaughter only stopped when there seemed to be no more seals to kill, and the species was presumed to be extinct. Then, in 1892, scientists from the Smithsonian Institution visiting Guadalupe Island, 150 miles off the coast of Mexico, found nine elephant seals alive and well. The species wasn't extinct after all—but the scientists didn't help the situation. Presuming the seals were on their way out anyway, they killed seven to take back to the museum.

In the following decades, more scientific expeditions went to Guadalupe Island and found the elephant seals were still not quite gone, and they carried on catching them. Some seals were kept alive and displayed at public aquariums, where generally they died after a year or two. More were killed and stuffed for museum exhibits. Fortunately for the seals, the commercial trade in blubber was moving on as fossil fuels were replacing animal fats and oils, so pressure from sealers was reduced. Despite scientists showing up now and then to grab more seals, their numbers gradually began to increase. In July 1922, when a survey counted 264 elephant seals on Guadalupe Island, the species was finally deemed worthy of protection. That same year, it became illegal to hunt elephant seals in Mexico, and soon after in the United States.

An American zoologist from the San Diego Natural History Museum, Laurence M. Huey, went on several trips to Guadalupe and witnessed the early days of the seals' recovery. In 1930 he wrote: "Let us trust that it may continue, that again this largest of all seals may inhabit its former hauling grounds and prevent at least one black deed from entering the annals of man's wanton destruction."

Huey would surely have been happy to know that elephant seals have continued to make a good recovery. All that was needed to save the species was for people to stop hunting them. Now, to see a northern elephant seal no longer requires a boat trip to Guadalupe Island. At certain times of year, along California State Route 1, the highway that skirts the Pacific Ocean, drivers can call in at several beaches and watch elephant seals snoozing on the sand. The total number of northern elephant seals, ranging from Castle Rock in Washington State to Isla Natividad off Baja California Sur,* is now estimated to be in the region of two hundred thousand.

---

*Midway along this range, seals at Año Nuevo State Park, a short way south of San Francisco, were fitted with sensors, which revealed their deep-diving, spiralling snoozes.

Helping ocean life to recover is relatively effortless when commercial industries have given up hunting threatened species and moved on to something else, as the sealers did. It's much harder to find ways of killing fewer animals when they're still in high demand, but it can be done. In October 2020, off the coast of Cornwall, where England dips its foot into the North Atlantic, surfers witnessed, for a few brief, implausible moments, a massive fish leaping from the sea. The giant bluefin tuna jumped again and then a third time, as if to say, "I am here. We are back." For decades, the spectacle of bluefin tuna had been missing from British waters. They had been gone for so long, most people had no idea they were ever there.

Commonly growing to between six and ten feet long, Atlantic bluefins are the biggest of the three bluefin-tuna species. The other two live in the Pacific Ocean. They all look like they've been cast from polished steel into a teardrop shape, painted indigo along their back, and given an elegant, crescent tail, and pectoral fins that fold away into slots in the sides of the body to improve streamlining while cruising at high speed. As they swim, bluefin tuna keep their body stiff and push their tails from side to side, in the classic thunniform style.* To breathe, they open their mouths and let water flow over their gills, supplying oxygen to the ruby-coloured muscles that power their long-distance endurance swimming.

Bluefin tuna in the Atlantic were being fished as long ago as the Stone Age. In a cave on the Rock of Gibraltar, archaeologists have found prehistoric remains of bluefin-tuna bones dating back more than twenty-two thousand years, which could have been left there by Neanderthals. Perhaps early hominids didn't fish for bluefins but scavenged them from beaches after pods of orcas chased them onto shore. Farther to the east and thousands of years later, during the Mesolithic, on the small island of Levanzo near Sicily, people painted images in a cave that look a lot like bluefin tuna. Dated to around

---

*The word *thunniform* comes from their Latin name, *Thunnus thynnus*.

ninety-two hundred years ago, this is the earliest reliable evidence that people had started fishing for bluefins in the Mediterranean. To go to the trouble of painting them, people must have thought these fish were important.

Commercial fisheries for bluefin tuna got underway across the Mediterranean during the time of the Phoenician civilization and the Roman Empire.* People caught bluefins in traps and beach-seine nets, preserved them in salting factories, and traded them in earthenware amphorae. Bluefins were one of the species that ancient Romans processed into the flavour-enhancing condiment *garum*, by laying out leftover trimmings, intestines, and blood to ferment in the sun. In fishing settlements from Turkey to Morocco, coins were minted with bluefin-tuna designs.

Archaeological remains show that bluefin tuna were also caught for millennia in the waters of northern Europe, and there, during the early part of the twentieth century, fishing effort increased. Fishers had known about the enormous tuna that swam into the region each year as they chased after smaller forage fish, like herring and mackerel, the same shoals that fishers themselves were after. In the early 1900s, in Øresund, the narrow strait between Denmark and Sweden, Danish fishers used bluefin tuna as scouts, following them to find and catch shoals of needle-shaped garfish. In the 1920s, Norwegian fishers complained about bluefin tuna ruining their nets by grabbing for any stray fish while the catches were being hauled in.

Herring fishers occasionally caught bluefins in their nets and traps and soon realised they could sell the huge fish for a good price. A photograph from 1910 of a German fish auction hall shows a dozen bluefins lined up on the floor waiting to be sold. Around the same time, fish markets in the northern French town of Boulogne sold bluefins that fishers caught over Dogger Bank in the North Sea.

---

* 1200 BCE to 470 CE.

Canning factories began opening in Denmark and Norway to process the growing catches of bluefins.

While commercial fishers looked to profit from bluefin tuna, sport fishers also turned their attention to these giants. A Danish sport fishery for bluefins opened in the 1920s. In 1928, one fisher single-handedly caught sixty-two tuna in the Kattegat sea.

The Tunny Club opened in 1930 in the coastal town of Scarborough in northern England. Members of the aristocracy and movie stars, including John Wayne and Errol Flynn, motored offshore in search of bluefins in the oceanic equivalent of big-game hunting parties in Kenya and India. Men and women strapped themselves into reinforced harnesses and hooked bluefins on enormous rods, often with a team of professional fishers on hand to help reel in the catches.

A silent film from 1933 documents one such trip as people wrestled with the wildly thrashing fish. "And so closes a perfect day," the caption card reads on-screen, followed by a shot of at least eight enormous tuna lying dead on deck, outsizing and outnumbering the smiling people on board. That same year, a UK record-breaking bluefin tuna was caught, weighing 851 pounds, almost twice as heavy as a mature male Bengal tiger.

Sport fishing for bluefin tuna also became popular in the western Atlantic along the US coast. Small bluefins were being caught along the coast as early as the 1850s. When stronger tackle was developed in the 1900s, anglers began battling larger animals. American author Ernest Hemingway was a big fan of hunting bluefins in the Bahamas.

Meanwhile, industrial fisheries in northern Europe were inventing more efficient ways of catching bluefins on an industrial scale. People started shooting them one by one at the surface with harpoon rifles. In Norway, fishers experimented with a new type of fishing gear, laying out a great loop of net to engulf an entire shoal of tuna in one go. At first, these early purse seines didn't work well because the muscular fish shredded the nets when they were trapped. By the 1950s, Norwegians had developed sturdier nets and mechanical winches to drag them back on deck, and the new industry snowballed. In 1949, there were forty-three boats in the Norwegian tuna fishery. A year later there were two hundred, making it Europe's biggest bluefin-tuna fishery.

As technologies advanced and fishing intensity increased, so did catches of bluefin tuna—but only to a point. By the early 1970s, bluefin fisheries in northern Europe had collapsed, and the species disappeared from Skagerrak, Kattegat, and Øresund, from the Norwegian and North Seas.

Elsewhere, fishing for bluefins continued. Purse-seine fisheries opened along the US eastern seaboard. Japanese longliners entered the Atlantic, taking bluefins while targeting yellowfin and albacore tuna for canning.

A major turning point in the Atlantic came in the 1970s, when a new appetite for bluefins took off. American anglers were catching bluefins but mostly not eating them, because the meaty flavour didn't appeal. Often the giant fish were thrown away or sold to pet-food factories. However, Japanese businessmen spotted an opportunity. The market in electronic devices, like cameras and personal radios, was booming with major exports from Japan to the United States. Rather than returning to Tokyo with empty cargo planes, Japanese airlines began filling up on cheap frozen tuna. This wasn't a traditional ingredient in Japanese cuisine, but tastes were changing. During the Second World War, American imports of meat to the Pacific, including processed Spam, had introduced Japanese people to meatier flavours, priming them for bluefin tuna.

A trend for bluefin sashimi caught on in Japan, and it became embedded within the food culture. Today, at showcase fish auctions each New Year, sushi magnates bid millions of dollars for individual bluefin tuna. This is mostly a marketing stunt aimed at stirring interest among consumers, and prices are less extortionate the rest of the year, but still, there's enormous demand.

The 1990s saw a swift rise in bluefin fishing across the Atlantic. In the Mediterranean, fisheries started using small aircraft to spot tuna shoals from the air and send in fishing vessels to scoop them up in giant purse-seine nets. A new technique emerged of catching younger tuna to rear in giant cages at sea, fattening them up before shipping them to Japan. Within a few decades, the wild populations of Atlantic bluefins had shrunk by at least half, and as the fishing frenzy continued, the species urgently needed protecting.

By then, an organisation responsible for regulating bluefin-tuna fishing already existed, the International Convention for the Conservation of Atlantic Tunas (ICCAT).* Its remit was to assess the tuna populations and set quotas that would prevent the species from being overfished. But amid the bluefin crisis, ICCAT soon earned itself an appalling reputation. A panel of expert scientists reviewed the organisation's performance and declared it to be an international disgrace. Environmental campaigners called it the International Conspiracy to Catch All Tunas.

In 2006, a recovery plan was introduced aimed at making the fishery sustainable by 2022. Scientists at ICCAT advised that the only way the population could recover was to limit the catch to no more than 15,000 metric tons of bluefins per year. But as happened repeatedly, ICCAT ignored the recommendations and set the catch limit at 29,500 metric tons. The actual catch, including estimates of illegal and unreported fishing, was more than double that.

In 2009, the stakes were raised. Environmentalists were piling on the pressure to protect the Atlantic bluefin tuna. A campaign was launched to add the species to the Convention on International Trade in Endangered Species (CITES). An Appendix I listing would prohibit all international trade, placing bluefin tuna alongside such

---

*ICCAT is one of around seventeen regional fisheries management organisations (RFMOs), which regulate fishing activities in the high seas. They are set up by international agreements and treaties and take different forms: some focus on particular species; others have a broader mandate. There are five RFMOs around the world focused on tuna.

Gannets diving for fish,
Shetland, Scotland

A lionfish, an introduced
species now stirring
troubles in the
western Atlantic
and Mediterranean

In 2017 in Atka Bay, Antarctica, an adult emperor penguin (above) makes a desperate l
into the sea after being trapped on a high ice shelf when the sea ice melted earlier tha
normal. Without a full coat of adult feathers, a lone chick (below) won't survive the ju

Critically endangered
oceanic whitetip shark

Species seen in a cubic foot of coral reef during a 24-hour period, Moʻorea

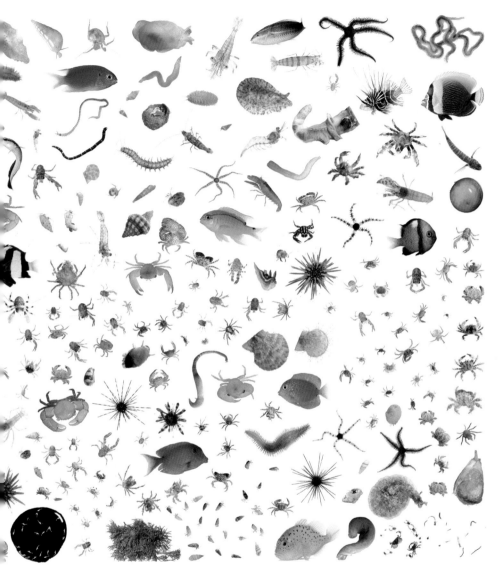

Endangered Nassau groupers gather to spawn

Mangroves and seagrasses nurture life and protect coastlines

Almaco jacks hunt in a floating sargassum forest, Sargasso Sea

At 130 feet, rebreather divers explore a mesophotic coral reef in Tahiti

Black rockfish shelter in a Pacific giant kelp forest

Octopus seen by the author, Brittany, Fra[

Critically endangered
sunflower sea star

famously endangered species as the giant panda, Asian elephant, and tiger.

Despite meeting the necessary criteria for a CITES listing, the proposal was rejected—but the message of bluefin endangerment had finally got through. Decision-makers at ICCAT listened at last to their scientific advisers and late in 2009 agreed to cut the quota to 13,500 metric tons.

A little over a decade later, there are signs that the tuna recovery plan is working. Atlantic bluefin tuna are no longer vanishing in droves from the seas; their numbers seem to be tentatively increasing, and they are beginning to show up again in their former haunts.

Off the west coast of Ireland in the Celtic Sea, and in the English Channel, fishers, scientists, surfers, and wildlife tour operators have started witnessing spectacular giant fish leaping from the sea. They've seen the water boiling where shoals of bluefins were swimming near the surface. Divers and underwater photographers have seen bluefins hunting tight, swirling bait balls of silvery fish.

Bluefin tuna are also coming back to Nordic seas. Animals of a similar size to ones seen and caught in the 1960s are once again migrating along the Norwegian coast. But there have been no signs of tuna returning to the English coasts of the North Sea. It's possible the 1930s sport fisheries took out all the biggest fish, the ones that put up the best fight. These older animals—bluefins can live for forty or fifty years—would have passed on their knowledge to other tuna of the best feeding grounds. But without those ocean elders, new generations of bluefins may have no way of knowing that the waters of the North Sea are worth visiting.

There's no practical way to count exactly how many bluefins are swimming around the Atlantic, and it's hard to know for sure how the species is doing. Fisheries scientists base their quota recommendations on stock assessments, which estimate a population size based on various available data, including how many tuna the fisheries are catching. There's a lot of uncertainty in models like this. For instance, ICCAT scientists manage bluefins as two separate stocks, on the eastern and western sides of the Atlantic, although satellite tagging studies show that some tuna swim all the way across the ocean, and there is some mixing between eastern and western populations. Nevertheless, there are good signs that compared to past decades of crisis, these are now relatively good times for Atlantic bluefin tuna. In 2021, the species was moved off the Red List of Threatened Species. Even though experts don't have a clear idea of just how the entire population is changing, they cautiously think there's no immediate risk of Atlantic bluefin tuna going extinct.

It's not all good news for tuna, though. While eastern Atlantic bluefins appear to be on the rise, the western population that spawns in the Gulf of Mexico has been in continual decline for the past forty years. But because those western tuna constitute only a small part of the total population, the species as a whole is still considered to be out of trouble.

The warming ocean adds another layer of complexity to the picture of recovering tuna. There are natural fluctuations year to year in tuna abundance and their prey, likely linked to the climate. One theory for the return of tuna to Scandinavian waters is that a 2003 heatwave in the Mediterranean allowed a large portion of tuna larvae to survive. When these young tuna matured in the 2010s, they started showing up as adults in feeding grounds off Norway.

Bluefin tuna are also going much farther north than they used to, some crossing the Arctic Circle and reaching as far as Svalbard, only five hundred miles from the North Pole. They've also recently been seen for the first time in the seas around Greenland. Bluefins are likely following shoals of mackerel, which are expanding their range north as the ocean warms. Big, old tuna can survive in these cold waters by virtue of their size; this biological feat, known as gigantothermy, allows the tuna's large muscles to generate a lot of heat, which is held in their bodies via a network of blood vessels around their gills, keeping their vital organs warm and their vision sharp in their golf ball–size eyes.

Other tuna species also seem to be doing better than they have been in recent times. The southern bluefin tuna, previously classified on the Red List as Critically Endangered, was upgraded to merely Endangered in 2021. Albacore tuna is now thought to be out of jeopardy. Likewise, the bluefins' sister species, the yellowfin tuna, is on a path to recovery, although it is still being badly overfished in the Indian Ocean. In early 2023, the Indian Ocean Tuna Commission (the region's equivalent of ICCAT) voted to phase down a controversial technique used for catching tuna. Fish aggregating devices (FADs) are clumps of plastic netting and lines that fishers set adrift in the ocean to attract sea life that come in to seek shelter. Tuna then show up to hunt the smaller fish. Fishing vessels encircle the whole lot in huge seine nets, catching everything there, including juvenile tuna, sea turtles, sharks, and dolphins. New measures proposed by a dozen Asian and African nations include a reduction in the number of FADs each vessel can deploy and a seventy-two-day period each year when the devices are banned, all in the hope of allowing yellowfins and other ocean life forms to recover. A short while after the vote went through, the European Union, which runs the largest tuna fisheries in the Indian Ocean, announced it was exempting itself and would not comply with the new ruling.

The future of many species that roam the open ocean depends on the precarious balance of international diplomacy. Disagreements are raging over bluefin tuna too. Turkey has repeatedly lodged objections to the catch limits set by ICCAT and has decided it is allowed far higher bluefin quotas in the Mediterranean, claiming they represent the country's historic share of the catch. If other countries decide to follow suit and adopt similar tactics, the scientific advice could become powerless, and Atlantic bluefin populations could once again be in danger of collapse.

Even with such ups and downs, it's not too soon to celebrate the recovery of bluefin tuna or Nassau grouper or any of the other species that still exist in the ocean when they could so easily have already disappeared. To pull any species back from the brink of extinction, rather than carelessly or deliberately push it over, is a promising step in the right direction.

Such victories may yet be only a slight return to healthier, more abundant ocean life, compared to what it once was, and recent progress must be maintained. We also need to determine where to set our sights next. What can we aim and hope for? How many tuna, or grouper, is the right number? How many is enough?

Commonly, the people who ultimately have the most influence in deciding how many fish there should be in the ocean are industrialists who run the fisheries that profit from these species and the lobbyists working for them. The question they're asking is a slightly different one: How large do fish populations need to be before they can push quotas back up and start catching more?

The reality is that bluefin tuna are being carefully managed not just so they can continue to exist for their own sake but mainly so they can continue to be hunted. There is an underlying presumption that the ocean provides animals for humans to hunt and eat and, perhaps most importantly, make money from. It's why organisations like ICCAT exist. In the years since Atlantic bluefin numbers have begun to climb, ICCAT already has been raising the catch limit back upwards, bowing to pressure from industrial fishing nations. Sport fisheries for bluefins, likewise, have reopened in Scandinavia, although with the strict requirement that animals are not to be killed but let go alive—and hopefully that they can survive after their battle on a fishing line. Sport fishers in the UK can now buy licenses to catch bluefin tuna, as long as they fix marker tags on the fish and then set them free, to help assess the size of the stock. In August

2023, the UK government took advantage of its post-Brexit freedom from European Union regulations and unilaterally decided there were already enough bluefin tuna swimming into British waters to justify restarting a commercial fishery.

People are always going to fish and hunt in the ocean, but the future will look very different depending on who gets to make decisions about fishing. Well-run, sustainable fisheries are certainly a better option than allowing industrial vessels to do as they please. The problem is that there is no single definition of sustainability.

The mainstream view of commercial fishing is to run operations to catch as much as possible and maximise profits without causing fish populations to decline. That's currently the situation with roughly two-thirds of the world's fisheries. Catches are reasonably stable and could continue that way for years to come. In that sense, these fisheries are sustainable. But those fish are far less abundant than they would be without people catching them. In most species, fished populations are roughly half the size they were before intensive fishing began. That means the ocean could and should contain a whole lot more life than it does today. An alternative view is to think of fish and other sea life not as a resource to profit from but as animals that have their own right to exist.

The notion of sustainability can easily be pulled in different directions and co-opted by those wanting to exploit the seas for profit. Call it the "blue economy" or "blue growth," stick an eco-label on it, and it's easy to fall back on the idea that the only true value of the ocean is the money it can generate. That's one reason talk had begun of lifting the global ban on industrial whaling, a hard-won triumph for the ocean that's been in place since the 1980s. Since then, many species of great whales have been slowly showing signs of recovery from centuries of intensive exploitation. More humpback whales are returning to the Southern Ocean to gorge on Antarctic krill. Blue whales are swimming around the subantarctic island of South Georgia again. During the commercial whaling heyday in the early twentieth century, as many as four thousand blue whales were killed in South Georgian waters every year. Then, for decades, nobody saw any of these animals there at all. Eventually, blue whale numbers gradually began to climb, and in 2020 scientists celebrated when they spotted fifty-eight of these giants in the area. Nations that were involved in industrial whaling have been let off the hook from causing tragic extinctions. But the current glimmers of recovery are convincing some that the time has come to resume commercial whaling, as if that's all they can think of to do with these magnificent animals.

Imagine what the ocean could be like if, instead of siphoning off profits to a handful of conglomerates and industry leaders, ambitions for sustainable fishing focused on two things: first, on providing food and livelihoods for people whose income and food security most depend on the ocean and who are most at risk from the climate crisis; and second, on running fisheries and looking after the ocean with the ambition of keeping wild species diverse and abundant, keeping whole ecosystems intact and functioning, and maintaining the countless benefits this brings to all of us alive now and for generations to come.

Chapter 7
Rebalancing Seas

The sea was calm, wrinkled just a little by a westerly breeze, and a pair of swans serenely drifted by as I tiptoed into the water, testing the cold. A few fin strokes from the shore, and I was floating on six feet of sea, a garden of seaweeds beneath me—filamentous browns, mossy greens, red tufts, long ruffles of sugar kelp, giant palms of flopped-over oarweed. Crabs raised their pincers as I dived down to look; white, spiny starfish lay still. A shoal of young cod hung among blades of eelgrass. I swam between threads of bootlace seaweed, also known as mermaid's fishing line, which connected the seabed and the surface, and I carefully watched the tangled tentacles of lion's mane jellyfish wafting past. A scallop the size of a tea plate sensed my shadow fall across it with a hundred tiny, blue-green eyes, and it squeezed its shells together, leaving a fringe of tentacles sticking out like whiskers.

Sea life thrives in Lamlash Bay because no fishing has been allowed here for years. The bay lies on the eastern side of Arran, a Scottish isle of a little over ten by twenty miles, which packs in mountaintops, rivers, forests, moorland, and sandy beaches. It lies in the Firth of Clyde, a fjordic inlet off the west coast of Scotland that was historically a rich fishing ground. Before the onset of industrialisation, sailing boats used lines and nets to take huge catches of herring, haddock, turbot, and cod. Then, in the nineteenth century, demand soared when railways arrived, and fresh fish could be delivered across the country. More intensive methods of fishing were introduced, including steam-powered trawlers that dragged huge, heavy nets over the seabed. Predictably, the ecosystem was soon overfished, and catches plummeted. In 1889, in a progressive move prompted by scientists and local fishers, the Firth of Clyde was closed to trawlers. The ban stayed in place until 1962, when bottom trawlers and dredgers, now diesel-powered, were allowed into the firth and started catching a species of small orange lobster, known variously as langoustine, Dublin Bay prawn, or scampi. For some time, trawling had been banned within three miles of coastlines, but that restriction was lifted in the mid-1980s, and once again fishing boats could go, more or less, where they wanted. After that, fish catches were heading for terminal decline. Scientists from the University of York, Ruth Thurstan and Callum Roberts, later described the Firth of Clyde as a marine ecosystem nearing the end point of overfishing. Soon there would not be enough animals left for any commercial fishing to be worth the effort.

In the middle of all this lay the Isle of Arran, where the stage was set for a revolution to take place, though the narrative began decades earlier on the other side of the world. In 1962, the same year the Firth of Clyde was opened again to trawling, a marine research station opened in Aotearoa (New Zealand), fifty miles north of Auckland, overlooking the cold waters of Tīkapa Moana (Hauraki Gulf). Valentine Chapman, a seaweed expert from the University of Auckland, suggested the waters bordering the station should be protected so that scientific work could be conducted in peace without fear of fisheries damaging research equipment or catching the study species. The site could be safeguarded from human pressures, allowing scientists to study the sea in a state as untouched as possible and giving them a reference point to compare to other areas. But at the time, Aotearoa had no legislation to allow such a thing to happen.

Reluctant to let the idea drop, Chapman and the research station's inaugural director, Bill Ballantine, spent six years lobbying politicians, gathering public support, and generating data to support their plans, until finally parliament approved the new Marine Reserves Act. Another six years were needed to protect the coastline on either side of the research station. The Cape Rodney–Okakari Point Marine Reserve, off Te Hāwere-a-Maki, or Goat Island, is modest in size, at two square miles. One of the world's first no-take marine reserves, it was the first piece of Aotearoa's coastline to be fully protected, and it paved the way for dozens more that are now dotted around the country and its outlying territories, from the subtropical Rangitāhua (Kermadec Islands) in the South Pacific to Moutere Ihupuku (Campbell Island) in the subantarctic.

Many of Aotearoa's marine reserves attract scuba divers from around the world, who come to see spectacular underwater life flourishing in the seclusion of protected waters. I visited Tawhiti Rahi (Poor Knights Islands) almost forty years after a marine reserve was established and learned what it feels like to hover in the water and see nothing but faces of countless fish turned to watch me. I saw shoals of demoiselles, small, steely-blue fish flowing through the water as if they had been poured from a jug. A convoy of short-tailed stingrays passed by, each one wider than the space between my outstretched arms and quite obviously one of the world's biggest species of stingrays. There were sunshine-yellow moray eels poking their heads from between kelp-covered rocks, and finger-length blennies hiding on steep walls blooming with sea anemones. And as if to demonstrate to me that this was a healthy, functioning ecosystem, swift packs of hunting yellowtail amberjacks chased a glinting shoal of koheru, a type of horse mackerel indigenous to Aotearoa waters.

It was scenes like this that a scuba diver from the Isle of Arran, Dan MacNeish, witnessed when he visited Aotearoa in 1989. He saw for himself what the benefits of strictly protected marine reserves can be, and he met with Bill Ballantine, who inspired him to do something similar. MacNeish's family goes back generations on Arran, and he had been diving around the island since the 1970s and in that time had seen how dredgers and trawlers were wiping out life on the seabed, leaving behind empty barrens of nothing but gravel and sand. Returning from his Aotearoa trip, MacNeish visited his friend and fellow diver Howard Wood and suggested they could do something to help protect Arran's waters.

Neither of the pair was a scientist or professional conservationist, and they had no campaigning experience between them, but they set about a tireless crusade similar to the one Chapman and Ballantine launched to establish that first reserve in Aotearoa. For years, Mac-Neish and Wood worked to garner support in the local community. They understood the power of images to persuade people to care, so they learned how to shoot underwater photographs and videos of the wildlife around Arran, and they visited other, healthier parts of the Scottish seas to document what could be. They found pictures from the recent past of Arran's anglers and other fishers with huge catches, showing how much more abundant sea life had been just a decade or so earlier. Gradually, more locals came on board as they realised their seas were worth protecting.

All the while, MacNeish and Wood were frustrated that the Scottish government was focused solely on supporting the livelihoods of prawn trawlers in the firth, while ignoring the needs of other people who benefit from the sea—the anglers, tourism operators, shellfish divers, crabbers, swimmers, and snorkellers.

In 1995, the pair set up the Community of Arran Seabed Trust (COAST), bringing on board many other islanders, including members of the fishing community, who were determined to push for better protection of their local waters. The focus for the campaign became plans for a small marine reserve in Lamlash Bay and protecting a critical habitat that grows there. Divers volunteering with COAST found living carpets of pink and purple maerl, a type of seaweed that looks like little coral colonies lying in loose clusters on the seabed. The naturally pulverised remains of these algae, which accumulate limestone in their cells, is what makes the tropical-looking fine white sands on many of Scotland's beaches. Maerl is legally recognised as a priority for conservation in Scottish seas,* and it's known to be easily smashed by fishing gear. This meant that COAST could make a case to the government that the maerl beds of Lamlash Bay needed sheltering inside a marine reserve. But the path to protection wasn't smooth.

Hurdles were constantly thrown up, and members of COAST found ways around them. When the local water board announced plans to build a sewage-outflow pipe into Lamlash Bay directly over the maerl beds, COAST successfully campaigned to have it moved. When a multinational aquaculture corporation planned to open what would have been Scotland's largest salmon farm right next to the bay, COAST worked hard to have it stopped. When the government dismissed the group's proposals for a reserve because the surveying divers were amateurs, the team members got themselves fully trained as citizen scientists with the organisation Seasearch and started collaborating with academics.

After thirteen years of forging alliances, gathering data, and drawing and redrawing lines on maps, COAST reached its initial goal, and at midnight on September 19, 2008, Lamlash Bay was closed to fishing, and the marine reserve was designated.

The Lamlash Bay No Take Zone is Scotland's first highly protected marine reserve, an area where no forms of fishing are allowed. And it's small, a little over one square mile, roughly the same size as the financial district of the City of London. The idea all along had been to use Lamlash Bay to demonstrate what's possible and to show how the seabed can recover when it's left alone, even in small areas. In the years since protection came into force and the dredgers and

---

*Maerl is one of Scotland's eighty-one Priority Marine Features, a list of habitats and species that legally need protecting in Scottish seas. Other listed habitats are seagrass meadows, oyster reefs, and cold-water coral reefs.

trawlers have been kept out, biodiversity has increased, and healthy habitats are thriving and covering more of the seabed inside the reserve. There's now more maerl, as well as more seagrasses, sponges, seaweeds, hydroids, sea squirts, and feather stars, all of which provide shelter for young fish. Lamlash Bay has become a safe haven for bright blue lobsters and king and queen scallops, which are all much bigger and longer-lived inside than outside the reserve. These grand old animals are highly fecund and produce copious offspring that are replenishing populations both in Lamlash and beyond.

In a similar way, Lamlash Bay itself has spawned change beyond its boundaries. In 2016, COAST's proposal to protect more of Arran's coastal waters was adopted. Now the Lamlash Bay No Take Zone sits within the boundaries of a larger protected area, which prohibits dredging in almost one hundred square miles of sea around the southern part of the island. Trawling is allowed in only a few places around the periphery. This roughly puts back the protections that had been in place until the Victorian-era three-mile trawling ban was overturned in the 1980s.

Farther afield, COAST's work has empowered other coastal communities to demand a better future for their own parts of the coasts and seas. COAST is showing that the ocean is a public good and should be safeguarded for everyone's benefit. Any coastal community has the right to healthier seas on its doorstep and can be part of a powerful push for change.

As I made my way back towards the shore of Lamlash Bay, I felt invigorated not just by the cold water and the intricate sea life I had encountered but also by knowing this small piece of sea is being watched and cared for by the people who live on Arran.

On a signboard at the water's edge, a map marks the no-take zone's boundaries, starting on either side of Holy Island, a short way offshore, and leading to two points on Arran's shoreline on either side of the spot where I stood. Since the no-take zone was established in 2008, there have been only a handful of known incursions by fishers into this narrow stretch of sea, all of them seen and reported by local residents. There's a telephone number on the noticeboard by the bay for anyone to call if they spot suspicious activities. That day, I had no reason to call.

The ability of sea life to heal itself is a powerful and hopeful phenomenon, and sits at the heart of many efforts to undo the troubles humans have let loose in the ocean. More pieces of sea around the world are being cordoned off, and high-profile campaigns are pushing to protect 30 per cent of the ocean by 2030.

The discipline of ocean protection comes with a baffling mix of terminology. There are *no-take zones*, like the ones at Lamlash Bay, which are also referred to as *highly protected marine areas*. They are the most stringent, where all damaging activities are prohibited: no coastal developments, no sewage outflow pipes, no fishing, no fish farms, no mining, no aggregate dredging, and no oil drilling or any other form of extraction.

More loosely defined areas include *marine parks*, *marine reserves*, *marine protected areas*, and *ocean sanctuaries*. These generally carry less strict regulations and often encompass a mix of protection levels. One of the biggest and most complex is the Great Barrier Reef Marine Park in Australia, which is divided into a patchwork of zones covering some 130,000 square miles of coastline, reefs, and islands. Around a third of the park's zones allow traditional uses by indigenous people as well as scientific research and tourism. Preservation zones, covering less than 1 per cent of the park, are off-limits to members of the public, and only researchers with special permission can gain access. In the general-use zones, fishing is allowed.

Another approach, which is popular in Europe, is to protect parts of the sea to safeguard particular vulnerable habitats or species and to prohibit only the specific activities that impact them. For instance, in parts of Scotland, maerl beds are protected from trawling and dredging. However, if the protections safeguard a species that lives up in the water column, such as the bottlenose dolphin or basking shark, then trawling is often allowed in the protected area, under the misguided assumption that the seabed and the water column above it are ecologically separate, when in fact everything is connected.

All these various protected areas share a similar ethos of trying to help ocean life to be generally healthier and more abundant. Protecting the seabed from physical damage, most importantly by heavy fishing gear such as trawlers and dredgers, can keep habitats in good condition and stop more from being destroyed. And parts of the ocean that are already degraded and depleted can be safeguarded to give sea life a chance to recover, as is happening in Lamlash Bay.

In some cases, the same protected area encompasses both healthy and degraded habitats, with the aim that local regeneration will occur. A hundred miles off Cape Wrath, the most northwesterly point of the United Kingdom, and around three thousand feet down, lie hundreds of thickets of cold-water corals that have been growing there since the end of the last ice age, around ten thousand years ago. Individual corals are estimated to be at least forty-five hundred years old, and unusually for deep-water corals, they're growing not on firm, rocky ground but on soft humps, known as sand volcanoes, where seawater bubbles up through the seabed. First discovered by scientists in 1998 and named the Darwin Mounds after their research vessel, the RRS *Charles Darwin*, these coral ecosystems are also rich in many other life forms, including fish, crabs, sea urchins, and single-celled organisms called xenophyophores, which look like basketball-size chunks of honeycomb.

By the time scientists knew about the Darwin Mounds, parts of them had been damaged already by trawling nets dragged over the seabed to catch fish such as orange roughy. A protected area prohibiting trawling was set up in 2003. In 2019, scientists sent an autonomous underwater robot to survey the mounds and found that areas that had been heavily trawled were not yet showing any obvious signs of recovery after sixteen years of protection. The good news is that parts of the Darwin Mounds that weren't too badly trawled are looking healthy. Coral larvae have settled and are growing into new colonies. For long-lived, slow-growing species such as deep-sea corals, recovery is obviously going to take a long time—all the more reason to protect them before damage occurs.

Regulations are gradually being put in place to protect the most vulnerable parts of the deep ocean. Bottom trawling on seabed deeper than a half mile has been banned in European Union waters of the northeast Atlantic since 2016 to safeguard fragile coral and sponge reefs growing on underwater mountains. An additional six thousand square miles of habitat was protected in 2022, when that lower limit for trawling was raised up to thirteen hundred feet. Much damage has already been done by decades of unrestricted deep-sea trawling, but these measures should begin to turn things around.

Elsewhere, pre-emptive steps are being taken to protect parts of the ocean from future impacts. Among the biggest marine protected areas is the Ross Sea in Antarctica, one of the most significant areas of largely intact ocean ecosystems left on the planet. Despite being incredibly remote, more than two thousand miles south of Aotearoa and reaching within two hundred miles of the geographical South Pole, this sea has faced growing pressure from industrial fishing fleets pushing into its icy waters to catch krill and Antarctic toothfish. Between them, krill and toothfish are staple foods for many other Ross Sea animals, including emperor penguins, Antarctic petrels, and Weddell seals. The Ross Sea is also the exclusive home to the world's smallest orcas, known as type C, which grow to only twenty feet long. Until recently, scientists weren't sure what this population of orcas feeds on. Then, when marine-mammal expert Regina Eisert was working at the ice edge in the Ross Sea, an orca swam right up and head-butted the waterproof camera she had lowered into the water on a pole. The orca opened its mouth and revealed a large, chewed tail of an Antarctic toothfish. Eisert was convinced the orca had done this on purpose, like a cat presenting a dead mouse to their owner. It proved that type C orcas eat toothfish, and further studies have shown these fish constitute more than a third of their diet. This means the Ross Sea region Marine Protected Area is critical for protecting the food source of this unique population of marine mammals.

Setting up the protected area in 2017 had taken years of difficult negotiations among all the nations that are part of the Antarctic Treaty, since no single nation can lay claim to Antarctica and its surrounding seas, and all members must agree on regulations. Several countries with major fishing interests supported the protected area only when the original plans were reduced in size by almost half, down to 420,000 square miles, and when concessions were made to allow fishing in some areas. Holding out until the end were Russian officials, who agreed to the plans after a sunset clause was introduced. The Ross Sea was given an initial period of thirty-five years of protection.

The boundaries of marine protected areas drawn on maps are chiefly there to show the people running fisheries where they can and can't legally operate, but obviously those lines don't exist out in the ocean, and marine organisms are oblivious to the designations. This leads to another of the potential benefits of ocean protection. Within protected waters, animals have a chance to live longer, grow bigger, and produce more offspring, as is happening among the scallops and lobsters of Lamlash Bay. But they don't all stay inside the no-fishing zone. Mature animals may have home ranges bigger than or straddling boundaries of protected areas, or they may embark on seasonal migrations that lead them into more distant waters. What's more, their young likely drift and swim away to start their own lives elsewhere, replenishing surrounding seas.

Conservationists and fisheries scientists refer to this as spillover* and generally see it as a good thing, using it as a major argument for protecting more of the ocean. Stop fishing in some places, and catches overall should improve because fish populations will be healthier and more productive. Even if fishers lose out in the short term when they're denied access to parts of their normal fishing grounds, the theory suggests that catches in nearby areas could soon outweigh the losses. Several studies confirm that protected areas work beautifully within their boundaries, boosting the abundance and diversity of species inside compared to outside. It's much trickier to detect the spillover effect, in part because the ocean is so endlessly complex and dynamic. It also takes time for depleted populations to recover enough for spillover to be noticeable, and many parts of the sea haven't been protected for long enough. In the United States, for instance, most marine protected areas are less than twenty years old.

While scientists are still busy debating whether spillover is a general effect that will occur more widely in the coming years as protected areas mature, some hints of it are occurring. In the northern Channel Islands off the California coast, there are now more spiny lobsters hunkered on the seabed both inside and a short distance outside a series of ten-year-old no-take zones. In Aotearoa, the effect of one small no-take zone was measurable much farther away. One in every ten juvenile sea bream occurring in waters up to thirty-five miles away is born within the protected waters of the reserve.

Even highly mobile species that head off on long migrations across ocean basins are beginning to show signs that marine reserves can work for them too, although the areas they need to cover are truly vast. In 2016, US president Barack Obama expanded the

---

*Bob Ballantine called it "the thistledown effect."

Papahānaumokuākea Marine National Monument* to encompass all the waters surrounding the northwestern Hawai'ian Islands, so that it now covers an area almost half as big again as the Ross Sea region Marine Protected Area in the Antarctic. To determine whether this enormous no-take zone is having any effect on tuna populations, scientists analysed catch data from the Hawai'ian longline fishery going back to 2010. Since the reserve was expanded, longliners have seen the catch rates of yellowfin and bigeye tuna increase up to a hundred nautical miles outside the boundaries.

Details within the data suggest this is a genuine spillover effect. Longliners working closest to reserve boundaries have seen their catches increase the most, suggesting they're snagging the tuna as they swim out of the protected waters where their spawning grounds lie. The apparent spillover is, as expected, gradually building over time as more tuna mature. And the species that had been hardest hit by overfishing, the yellowfin tuna, has shown the most pronounced increase. Its catches have seen a dramatic uptick, with the number on each longline increasing by over half compared to earlier catches. It makes sense that the depleted yellowfins are benefiting most, and the reserve is helping their population recover.

Papahānaumokuākea is a phenomenally large marine reserve, quite likely still the world's largest by the time you read this, and it seems to be of the necessary magnitude to help protect these fish that swim so fast and far. Still, it may not be big enough or in the right place to continue safeguarding tuna as the ocean around them changes. Tuna will keep responding to the shifting conditions as their seas warm and lose oxygen and their prey moves too. Where tuna spawn and feed today will likely not be where they do so in ten, twenty, or fifty years.

---

*The name combines Papahānaumoku, a mother figure in Hawai'ian tradition who is personified by the earth, and Wākea, a father figure personified by the sky. Native Hawai'ian people recognise these figures as their ancestors, whose union resulted in the creation of the entire Hawai'ian archipelago.

The same fluidity that helps marine reserves to restore ocean life beyond their boundaries may also be their undoing. Their watery borders can't hold back warming, acidifying waters any more than they can hold back the climate migrants that swim through them. Conservationists are grappling with the difficult, unanswered question of how the ocean's protected areas will fare in the climate crisis.

Species are moving, habitats are shifting, and new ecosystems are assembling, and soon it will no longer be enough to decide where to install a marine reserve and then step back and leave that part of the sea alone. As the ocean changes, ideas of what protected areas can be, how they are run, and what they can do will have to change.

There's an inherent contradiction in trying to establish reserve boundaries around species and ecosystems that are responding and shifting with the changing climate. The way reserves are set up will have to become a lot more responsive, with plans and regulations that can change and adapt as the environment changes. For that to happen, necessary legislation will need to be already in place. Our intentions won't be of any use if it takes years or decades of legal wrangling for new types of reserves to be established.

Uncertainty of what exactly lies ahead is no excuse to do nothing but sit back and watch as the present generation of marine reserves gradually stops working. Pre-emptive actions will be critical. One idea is to create stepping stones through the seas and protect areas not only where species exist now but where they will likely move to in the future as the ocean continues to warm. Another approach involves combining the fixed reserve approach with more dynamic measures. Methods exist now for tracking vulnerable species and diverting threats away from them in near real time, as has happened with North Atlantic right whales. Fewer than three hundred and fifty of these docile giants are left, and many of them recently moved into the Gulf of Saint Lawrence in Canada, the body of water through which the North American Great Lakes drain into the Atlantic. The whales followed the climate migration of their staple food, small

swimming crustaceans called copepods. This brought the whales
into the busy waters of the gulf, where many of them were killed
when ships ran into them or they got tangled in fishing gear and
drowned. In 2017 alone, thirty-one right whales were found dead,
and likely twice that number died and were never found. In response
to this crisis, the Canadian government introduced a system to track
the right whales based on reported sightings as well as detection of
their underwater calls through hydrophones. Daily updates then
determine, depending on the whales' whereabouts, where fisheries
need to be closed and ships told to slow down. This kind of effort
requires considerable expense and coordination, but it's helping to
save more of these critically endangered animals.

A paradigm ingrained in marine science is that marine protected
areas could boost the ocean's resilience to climate change. If this
turns out to be true, they could simultaneously protect against local
and global threats.

The idea behind this concept is that protecting species and habitats
helps them to be more resistant to change and better able to recover
from crisis. Protected areas should contain more biodiversity, which
acts as insurance against disaster; if some species are lost, others are
available to take their place and keep the ecosystem functioning.
There may also be greater genetic diversity, making populations
more likely to adapt to changes in the environment. Protected
areas should also contain bigger animals with more substantial food
reserves in their bodies, which can help them survive tough times.

Though not enough evidence exists to show these things happening inside marine reserves and confidently turn this concept
into reality, there are some hints. Wild winter storms in 2013 and
2014 pummelled the rocky reefs in a protected area off Britain's
south coast, which is home to lacy, bubblegum-pink sea fan corals.
The seabed in Lyme Bay was scoured by waves and sediments, and

habitats inside and outside the reserve ended up in a similar state of devastation. And yet, by 2016, the pink corals were growing again inside the reserve. The corals were recovering much faster than they had when the reserve was originally set up and scallop dredging was first banned, suggesting that protection is boosting the ecosystem's resilience.

Evidence is also emerging that marine reserves have a role to play in helping ecosystems mitigate climate change. A 2022 review of more than twenty thousand studies found that where protected areas keep habitats such as mangroves and tidal marshes intact, they can help protect coastlines from sea-level rise. Protected areas help lock up more carbon from the atmosphere in green habitats like seagrass meadows. Seabed sediments also sequester more carbon when they're not being dragged over by trawl nets and dredges.

The big picture from across all these studies backs up the theory that protected areas can boost biodiversity and increase food security and income for people living along coastlines. At a broad scale, increased fish catches from areas adjacent to protected areas can more than offset the losses when fishers are excluded from fishing grounds.

Even so, protected areas are not always welcome. In 2022, plans were scrapped for a no-take zone around Lindisfarne, a tiny tidal island off the northeast coast of England that's home to an ancient monastery and a small fishing community. Fishers were up in arms over the potential loss of their livelihoods. The vicar of Lindisfarne warned that the fishing ban would rip the heart out of the community. In 2023, marine protection became a hot-button topic in Scotland as rows broke out in fishing communities over the government's plans to introduce more no-take zones. Fishers in various parts of the country feel these measures are being imposed on them, and they're convinced the zones would ruin their industry. The response is a far cry from that of the Isle of Arran community, which worked towards safeguarding its waters for everyone's benefit, showing why successful planning for the future ocean must involve everybody who has a major stake, right from the start.

Making certain parts of the ocean off-limits to exploitation comes with other potential drawbacks and can lead to a false sense of security and risky decisions about how the rest of the ocean is used. Plans are accelerating to open the world's first deep-sea mines and extract metal-rich rocks from the seabed several miles underwater. Fevered mining interest is gathering pace in the Clarion Clipperton Zone (CCZ), a twenty-five-hundred-mile-wide tract of the central Pacific Ocean between Mexico and Hawai'i, where the undulating abyssal seascape is covered in fine sediments and rocks. Since 2001, more than a dozen mining companies have been buying up prospecting permits for plots of seabed in the CCZ, each one around thirty thousand square miles in area, which is slightly larger than the island of Sri Lanka. The companies are eager to get their hands on black, potato-size rocks scattered across the seabed, generally referred to as polymetallic nodules, which contain valuable elements like cobalt, nickel, and rare-earth metals. The nodules also create vital habitat for a diverse ecosystem, which scientists are only just beginning to know and understand. Biological surveys of the CCZ so far have found more than five thousand species, including delicate sponges made of glass, intricate brittle stars and feather stars, octopuses, corals, and worms. Nine out of ten of these species haven't been seen anywhere else, and scientists haven't yet had a chance to name them. It's likely that at least eight thousand unique species live in the CCZ, making it a critical hot spot of the earth's biodiversity.

Some parts of the CCZ have not been sold off to prospective miners but instead have been designated as no-mining zones, to try to limit the impacts of the industry. The problem is, those protected zones were selected after mining companies had first pick of the seabed. The protected areas were pushed to the periphery of the CCZ, in places that mining companies weren't interested in mining anyway because the nodules there are far less abundant. And where there are fewer nodules, fewer species exist because the rocks themselves are the basis for the ecosystem. Nodules provide the solid foundation for corals and sponges to grow on and habitats for all sorts of tiny creatures that live on and inside them. The protected zones in the CCZ are not ecologically equivalent to the areas that may be mined. It's like protecting only the edges of a forest and not its dense heart. Parts of the seabed with greater abundance and diversity of life undoubtedly will be damaged and destroyed if mining of the CCZ goes ahead.

As part of their licensing deal, mining companies would also be required to leave some portions of their leased CCZ plots unmined. However, the environmental gains this could have are based on some dubious assumptions. A study modelling the impacts of noise pollution from seabed mining has indicated that nowhere within an entire thirty-thousand-square-mile plot will be left in peace. Massive, remotely operated mining machinery would thunder across the seabed, scooping up rocks and shooting them, clattering along riser pipes, to the surface, sending waves of sound for hundreds of miles through the ocean. This would interfere with the richly acoustic lives of the whales that migrate through the CCZ. Very little is understood about how important sound is for many of the delicate organisms of the deep, but some are thought to use subtle vibrations in the water to find their way around and detect prey. This means that even the animals that aren't directly killed by mining or choked in sediment plumes would still have their lives transformed if their quiet world is turned into a noisy industrial zone. The so-called protected areas in the CCZ will not protect the overall ecosystem.

There are plans to mine deep-sea metals from other parts of the deep ocean, including the tall chimney stacks of hydrothermal vents known as black smokers. These ecosystems, some of the most extreme and diverse in the deep sea, flourish in the dark by tapping into the energy of toxic chemicals pouring out of the seabed. Black smokers are home to their own entourage of phenomenal organisms, the likes of which are seen nowhere else on earth. There are Yeti crabs that farm bacteria in their fur, golden-coloured snails with their shell made partly from iron (no other animals we know of do that), and worms clad in glittering sequin-like scales that protect them during fearsome worm-on-worm battles.* All these creatures have the misfortune of living on and around hydrothermal-vent chimneys that mining companies are hankering to exploit.

Along parts of the ten-thousand-mile north–south underwater mountain chain of the Mid-Atlantic Ridge, mining companies from Russia, Poland, and France have bought licences to prospect hydrothermal vents. Just as parts of the CCZ would be off-limits, the vent mines could be interspersed with strips of no-mining zones that, theoretically, could help the mined sites regenerate once the machinery has moved on. Regeneration would depend on those protected areas remaining intact and healthy, but they could easily be harmed by the noise and toxic sediment clouds generated by mines on either side. What's more, any recovery of mined sites will require animal larvae to drift in, something they naturally do, riding currents and colonising vent fields that are dotted along the linear mountain chain. For now, it's not at all well understood how far different species can disperse or how well they would cope with crossing over mined sites and passing through contaminated seawater. Mining might well leave behind nothing but a series of dissected, diminished patches of vent habitat that stand little chance of persisting in the long term.

A far safer option would be to protect whole hydrothermal vent systems from mining, a preventative measure that has already been achieved in a few parts of the ocean. In Antarctic waters, a protected

---

*These are the Elvis worms, named after the King of Rock and Roll and the sparkling costumes he wore later in his singing career.

area surrounding the South Georgia and South Sandwich Islands prohibits any future mining activities on the entire deep hydrothermal vent fields there and safeguards their inhabitants, including Yeti crabs with chests covered in auburn hairs.

Many hydrothermal vents elsewhere in the ocean remain unprotected. Iron-shelled, scaly-foot snails live on only three remote black smokers in the Indian Ocean; prospecting permits for two of those sites have already been sold to German and Chinese mining companies. Because of the future threat of deep-sea mining, scientists have listed this snail species as Endangered on the IUCN's Red List. A full survey of all the snails, clams, and other molluscs living on deep-sea vents reveals the peril facing the entire group. Out of 189 species of vent molluscs worldwide, only 25 are considered safe from deep-sea mining. All these nonthreatened species live inside protected areas where mining won't be allowed. They include *Gigantopelta* snails with smoothly spiralling, golf ball–size shells, and *Provanna* snails with delicately ridged, turret-shaped shells, both of which live alongside the hairy-chested Yeti crabs on the protected vents of Antarctica. All the other vent-living mollusc species face varying degrees of extinction risk, their Red List rankings ranging from Vulnerable to Critically Endangered. When a similar analysis for other animals living on vents is produced, no doubt the same story will emerge of species endangerment driven by the threat of mining.

Done well, ocean protection holds great promise for helping sea life and people thrive together, although what protection actually means remains alarmingly ambiguous. Numerous studies have shown that ocean protection is most effective in no-take zones, where no fishing or any other extractive activities are allowed, at least when regulations are properly enforced. The reality is that today, many so-called protected areas are only partially protected—if at all.

France, for instance, has declared that, as of 2022, it has exceeded its target of protecting 30 per cent of its seas. Second only to the United States, France has a vast oceanic territory covering almost four million square miles. Most of it is made up of overseas territories, holdovers from the colonial era, including French Polynesia and New Caledonia in the Pacific, French Guiana in the Atlantic, and a collection of obscure islands in the southern Indian Ocean. Across all the ocean that France claims, less than 2 per cent lie in highly protected no-take zones, and most of those strictly protected areas lie around the uninhabited subantarctic Crozet, Kerguelen, and Saint Paul and Amsterdam Islands. In contrast, only a minute fraction of the waters around Metropolitan France are well protected. Similar numbers play out elsewhere. In the Mediterranean, 0.06 per cent of the ocean basin is highly protected. Across the northeast Atlantic, the figure is half that.

What is actually happening inside many of these designated protected areas is even more alarming. In waters of the European Union, more than half of all so-called protected areas are commercially trawled. Data from tracking systems on vessels operating in Europe indicate that the intensity of trawling is higher inside protected areas than outside. Some is illegal fishing, which obviously needs dealing with, but much of it is fishing activity that is perfectly legal; often regulations allow fishing within protected areas. Consequently, ocean life is often worse off inside than outside reserves. European protected areas are home to smaller populations of endangered species of sharks and rays than occur elsewhere, even though they're precisely the kinds of animals these areas are supposed to safeguard.

The situation is barely any better in Britain following its departure from the European Union. Despite the chanted chorus of taking back control and pledges to protect British seas, the UK government is still making feeble progress. Proud announcements have been made that nearly a quarter of British territorial waters are already protected, and yet almost all the protected areas are being legally dredged and bottom-trawled. In the years after Brexit, the already-absurd levels of trawling inside protected areas tripled in some places, rather than being reduced, and there have been only tentative steps towards establishing more no-take zones.

In the scramble to meet international targets, political expediency is taking precedence over the real needs of the environment. Quantity is coming before quality. The more of the ocean that is declared protected and then is left unguarded or is assigned regulations that are so weak as to be meaningless, the greater the risk that global leaders will lose sight of what actually matters in the ocean. The more ocean protection is pushed to the distant, unseen, and largely unfished parts of the ocean, the less relevant it will become. And when these marine unprotected areas fail to deliver the benefits that were promised—of better fishing, improved livelihoods, and greater abundance and diversity of ocean life—then it's possible those in charge will give up entirely on protection.

Instead, we must embrace and celebrate the incredible power of ocean life to regenerate, and thoughtfully and effectively push for more. Wherever possible, the protections need to be driven by the people who live and work in and around the affected areas. Plans will need to adapt to the changing climate, and efforts to enforce protections will need to be coordinated internationally, between nations across whose jurisdictions the same wild species roam.

In 2015, the year he died, Bill Ballantine wrote that "conservation needs places where nature is left wild." The pioneer of marine protection remained a lifelong advocate for identifying significant parts of the ocean where no fishing of any kind should be allowed. He never argued that these highly protected areas were all that ocean life needs in order to survive or even thrive in the Anthropocene. Ballantine always made it clear that no-take zones should be additional to other established means of managing human activities and impacts in the ocean, such as regulating fishing gear and controlling pollution.

Chapter 8
Future Forests

In the ocean there are forests—great, verdant, important places—that mirror their counterparts on land. Pay a visit to an underwater forest with a mask, snorkel, and thick wet suit (underwater forests grow only in cold places), and this version of a sylvan stroll will take you drifting through the canopy. Watch out, though. These aquatic realms are constantly in motion in ways that can be disorienting. Many times, a switch has flipped in my mind, and all at once the undulating foliage fixes in place, and the rocks beneath begin sliding to and fro. I've learned to relish the dizzy feeling, knowing that it won't last long before my mind reorients, the world once more behaves as expected, and the seabed holds still.

The wildlife of underwater forests is unlike that anywhere else. Within one, I've watched minute white sea slugs stream gently by, like horizontal snowflakes, and had one land on my fingertip and explore my hand. I've seen tall piles of red-mottled, mouse-size sea hares stacked one on top of another, each of these shell-less hermaphrodite molluscs mating with the one below it; the lowest in the pile acts solely as a female, the topmost as a male, and all the others in between as both male and female, a highly efficient way to go about things when you're a sea hare. Countless endemic species are found only in underwater forests. This is where sea dragons, giant cuttlefish, and whiskery flat sharks called wobbegongs live, as well as fish that walk on the seabed on fins like splayed-out fingers—fish that are so rare now and difficult to spot in the forest shadows that nobody is quite sure they still exist at all.

At least a quarter of the world's coasts are fringed in underwater forests, which collectively occupy more than five hundred thousand square miles of the ocean, five times the area occupied by the world's tropical coral reefs. The forests grow in regions bathed in waters rich in dissolved nutrients often delivered from below by deep, upwelling currents. Their foundations are not ocean-growing trees but varieties of large brown seaweeds known as kelp, which belong to an entirely separate assemblage of living things to other algae and plants.*

More than 140 kelp species inhabit different coasts. Offshore from California's coastal redwood forests, the Pacific Ocean grows its own giants—the biggest kelp of all, *Macrocystis pyrifera*. These tangled towers can reach well over 150 feet, not quite as tall as the tallest redwoods but much faster growing. Given enough food and light, giant kelp can put on two feet a day, or around an inch an hour, placing them among the fastest-growing organisms on earth. Giant kelp hold themselves upright, oriented skywards, with gas-filled orbs and form a floating canopy at the surface.

Bullwhip kelp (*Nereocystis luetkeana*) is another imposing species at up to 115 feet long, with a slender stipe (the equivalent of a tree's trunk) and a lollipop mop of fronds on top.† Other kelp species are not quite as huge, five or ten feet tall, but are no less intricate. There are forests of golden kelp (species of *Ecklonia*) with ragged-edged fronds that look as if they've been torn from larger sheets of kelp. *Undaria* species resemble ferns with deeply divided blades. Across

---

*Brown seaweeds are included within the proposed kingdom Chromista, and they are a taxonomic class, Phaeophyceae, within which is the kelp order, Laminariales.

†I think it looks like the lollipop-shaped Truffula tree from Dr. Seuss's book *The Lorax*.

the Northern Hemisphere grow feathery *Alaria*; huge, hand-shaped *Laminaria*; and long, crinkled strands of *Saccharina*.

It's possible to explore the life of kelp forests without getting wet. After storms off temperate and cold coastlines, beaches are often strewn in pieces of kelp that were torn away and expelled from the sea. Hold a kelp blade up and see if it's taller than you are (quite possibly). Feel the smooth and pliable material, slippery but not slimy, which may feel like manufactured plastic but is entirely natural. Kelp stipes lie like fallen sapling trunks or twisted ochre bones poking through the sand. Other seaweeds, many of them red and wispy,* use the stipes as a firm habitat to settle on, a miniature forest within the forest. Look for holdfasts, like balled-up fists, that grow at the base of kelp. These aren't roots, and don't absorb water or nutrients as roots of land plants do, but are simply there for holding tightly to rocks. They serve the incidental purpose of creating habitat for the many other small creatures that burrow among their fingers—sponges, bryozoans, bivalves, gastropods, amphipods, copepods, and worms, all adding to the biodiversity of a kelp forest.

Piles of storm-stirred kelp on the beach make up only a small portion of the organic matter lost from underwater forests. As it grows, kelp absorbs carbon dioxide that has dissolved in seawater from the atmosphere above. Fragments of kelp that break off and drift away from the forest end up sinking, taking that harnessed carbon with them, sometimes into the deep ocean, where it can no longer act as a greenhouse gas. Calculating exactly how much carbon kelp forests sequester in the deep is not easy, certainly compared to terrestrial forests, in which carbon is stored within the standing biomass of trees, the roots, and the surrounding soil, making it relatively straightforward to measure. Underwater, carbon is not locked

---

*Red seaweeds, or rhodophytes, belong to a separate kingdom and are more closely related to land-based plants than kelp are.

up within forests themselves, and so it's much harder to gauge the magnitude of the long-distance carbon highways streaming from kelp, especially because this varies greatly depending on ocean currents and storms. The latest estimates suggest kelp forests globally remove eighteen megatons of carbon dioxide from the atmosphere each year, thereby soaking up the equivalent of the emissions from approximately one million North Americans.

The value of kelp forests goes far beyond the carbon they can banish from the atmosphere. They generate at least $500 billion yearly, mostly from fisheries. Kelp forests create important habitat for many commercial species, such as lobsters, abalone, and the kelp itself. In Australia, kelp forests are the summertime home for young bluefin tuna, which later in life are caught and sold for huge sums.

Kelp forests help protect coastlines because water flow slows as it passes through the canopy, baffling wave energy and reducing the impacts of erosion and storm surges. Crucially, they also improve water quality in coastal seas by absorbing nutrient pollution that pours off the land. Agricultural fertilisers, as well as sewage from humans and livestock, contain high concentrations of nitrogen and phosphorus, which are key nutrients for stimulating plants and seaweeds to grow, but too much can be highly problematic. Excess nutrients washing into the sea cause other seaweeds and phytoplankton to grow so fast they swamp ecosystems, choke waterways, and trigger toxic blooms that contaminate fisheries, kill wildlife, and make drinking and bathing water unsafe. When blooms die and decompose, they rob the water of oxygen and create dead zones where little life survives. With its naturally fast growth, kelp removes enough nitrogen from the surrounding water to substantially reduce the chances of problematic blooms, saving tens of thousands of dollars annually in clean-up costs for every acre of intact, healthy forest.

Kelp forests also have many other, incalculable values. They are hot spots of biodiversity, home to unique species that live nowhere else on earth. Kelp forests take their place in healthy, functioning seas and extend their influence far beyond the forest boundaries. Fast-growing kelp are enormously productive and generate huge amounts of energy for food webs around them. Broken chunks of kelp drift off and forge connections to distant ecosystems where animals pick over the forest's remains. This is similar to terrestrial trees dropping their leaves and earthworms dragging them into their burrows, only instead of feeding animals on the forest floor, much of the food from kelp forests ends up hundreds of miles away.

Nevertheless, compared to many other wild places, kelp forests remain largely overlooked, understudied, and underappreciated. And just like forests on land, they're vanishing at alarming rates because of habitat destruction and climate change combined—although rather than burning down, kelp forests melt away.

In 2011, when the coast of Western Australia was hit by a record-breaking marine heatwave, kelp forests there began to collapse in a matter of weeks. High temperatures were killing them outright. Prior to the heatwave, roughly three-quarters of the rocky reefs along the coast north of the city of Perth had been covered in thick stands of kelp. By the time temperatures fell back down, long stretches of coast were left deforested. This is the westernmost end of Australia's Great Southern Reef, a five-thousand-mile-long inter-connected fringe of rocky reefs dominated by kelp forests that wrap all the way along the southern coast of the continent, around the island of *lutruwita* (Tasmania), and north along the coasts of Western Australia and New South Wales. In that one heatwave, this enormous biome became at least seventy-five miles shorter.

Five years later, diving scientists resurveyed the Western Australian coastline and found a major shift had taken place at that short-ened end of the Great Southern Reef. Where golden kelp had only recently been flourishing, tropical seaweeds now grew in its place.

Instead of complex, lush forests, the seabed was covered in low-lying seaweed turfs, where animals have no place to hide and have far less food to eat. These new habitats contained a small portion of the rich biodiversity in the forests they had replaced.

Aiding this transformation were shoals of tropical fish that moved south with the heatwave and stayed. The pin-spotted spinefoot, a type of rabbitfish, is covered in white spots and has a gold stripe along its back; like all rabbitfish, it is a herbivore. Large shoals of these spinefoots are nibbling away at kelp spores as soon as they settle, thus preventing the forests from regenerating. As the influx of rabbitfish continues to sweep south, beyond the limits of the original heatwave, the seaweed turfs are expanding and pushing the kelp forests even farther back. The spreading of these simplified ecosystems diminishes the ocean environment in species and structural complexity, leaving coastlines more vulnerable to waves and storms, and fisheries stripped of critical habitat.

Turf wars are playing out across many kelp forests around the world. It's one reason why around half of kelp forests are in decline globally. A mix of troubles is triggering these transitions, including declining water quality and the loss of key species. The changes can be abrupt, or they can unfold more gradually.

Sometimes, when the initial cause of kelp loss is halted and undone, the forests can regrow. That has been happening along the south coast of England, where a successful campaign led to a ban on trawling in 2021, and the kelp ecosystems began recovering.

In many cases, though, as happened in the wake of the 2011 Western Australian heatwave, kelp forests don't spontaneously return. Too much is changing in these ecosystems, and they're shifting into alternative states that are stubborn and difficult to reverse. Among many of the kelp forests that have been depleted and rubbed out in recent decades, it's uncommon to see natural recovery taking place. Leaving lost forests alone to regrow by themselves will not be enough to bring them back.

Rewilding is becoming increasingly popular for terrestrial ecosystems. At the heart of rewilding lies the idea of putting back, and sometimes taking away, certain important species. Their presence or absence can help restore balance and kick-start the recovery of vanished ecosystems. These are keystone species, a concept that originated in Robert Paine's 1960s studies of starfish on rocky shores. Rewilding efforts tend to focus on bigger animals and most often mammals, species like European beavers, which were hunted to extinction in the British Isles and are now, tentatively, being reintroduced from remnant populations on the continent. The beavers' role is not merely to reacquaint people with a native species that's been missing for centuries but to get busy using their huge buckteeth to chew down trees, dam rivers, and construct their lodges. Beavers create wetlands, which become homes for other animals such as water voles and fish. Their constructions slow the flow of water, reducing flooding downstream, which will become ever more important as the climate crisis delivers wilder, more frequent rainstorms.

In North America, wolves have become the most prominent rewilded species, following their reintroduction to Yellowstone National Park in the mid-1990s. The job for these apex predators is to hunt, and also simply to scare, the large populations of grazing elk, which in turn gives aspen and willow trees and the rest of the woodland ecosystem a chance to thrive.

For decades, rewilding has also been happening in the ocean, although it has rarely been called that. Some of the earliest efforts didn't originally intend to create more resilient, biodiverse ecosystems but were meant to save one particular species from extinction.

Sea otters used to live along all the coasts of the North Pacific, from Hokkaido, Japan, to Baja California, Mexico. Each of the three subspecies—Asian, northern, and southern sea otters—has a distinct range. Their story pivots on the relatively recent return of their ancestors to the ocean, in the past three million years. Other marine mammals have been swimming for much longer—the whales and sea cows for around fifty million years, seals and sea lions for around twenty million years—and they've all evolved a thick layer of fat to keep them warm and to serve as an energy source when they dive. Perhaps in time, sea otters too will transition to blubber, but for now they insulate themselves just with fur.

And what incredible fur it is. With up to one million hairs per square inch of skin, otter fur is the thickest and most luxuriant of any animal. An outer layer of waterproof guard hairs keeps the under-fur dry, holding a layer of insulating air next to the skin, akin to emperor penguin feathers. To survive in the cold Pacific, sea otters must keep their fur in good condition, which is why they spend so much time grooming. For hours every day, sea otters float on their backs and rub themselves all over with their paws, fluffing up their fuzzy cheeks and reaching every point on their bodies thanks to their unusually flexible skeleton. With retractable claws they comb their fur and squeeze out water; then with their mouths they blow in air. Sea otter pups have such fluffy fur it acts as a life jacket, keeping them bobbing at the surface while their mothers dive down for food.

Indigenous peoples have long made use of the sea otters' super-dense fur to make clothing. But a commercial trade in their fur did not begin until Russian and European explorers encountered sea otters in the mid-eighteenth century, and hunters began to system-atically wipe them out. Sea otters gather in single-sex groups known as rafts, where they groom and rest. Trappers would kill every otter in a raft before moving on to the next, leaving no animals behind to rebuild their numbers. The exploitation was more akin to strip mining than to any form of vaguely sustainable hunting.

By the end of the nineteenth century, the fur trade had collapsed, not through regulation but because otters had become so rare that hunting was no longer profitable. Across the Pacific, the population had crashed by 99 per cent. At most one or two thousand otters were left. Along thousands of miles of previous otter territory, there were none at all. In California, they were all gone except for a single group of around fifty otters, spotted off the coast of Big Sur in the 1930s, that had somehow gone unnoticed and uncaught. They were the last remaining members of the southern sea otter subspecies.

With the mass slaughter finally over, remnant populations of the three otter subspecies began to increase by themselves, slowly. People made attempts to speed up the process by moving sea otters from place to place. The Russians were the first to try this, in 1937, when they sent nine otters by ship and train from the Pacific Ocean to the Barents Sea in the Arctic Ocean, thousands of miles from their native range, planning to establish a new fur trade. Only two otters survived the journey, and commerce in their pelts never emerged.

Americans were more successful in their otter-moving efforts. They were driven by a different ambition, not to carry on killing them but to rescue the species from extinction. Initial attempts had mixed results, and many otters died in transit, especially before handlers worked out what to feed them. Frequently, as soon as otters were released in new environs, they would swim off, never to be seen again. Some swam all the way back to their original territories.

The first translocation that really worked was in 1965. In Prince William Sound, Alaska, forty-one otters were loaded into an amphibious aircraft and flown 450 miles to Shee Kaax (or Chichagof Island) in southeast Alaska. Roughly half of the otters survived the flight, and several were seen alive in the wild the following year. Numerous other translocations continued intermittently until 1990, and some have paid off. Sea otters once again roam parts of the coasts of Washington and British Columbia. In southeast Alaska, an initial population of 412 relocated otters has grown to around 25,000. It hasn't worked everywhere: there are still no otters along the coasts of Oregon or Mexico. But overall, sea otters have been pushed back from the brink of extinction. Roughly 50,000 otters—a third of the current global population—are alive today thanks to these translocations.

Now, at various spots along the Pacific coast of North America, you can stand on the shore at dusk and watch a raft of sea otters twirl in the floating canopy of a giant kelp forest, anchoring themselves so they don't drift away while they sleep, holding their four paws aloft to conserve body heat. And otters have been entwining their lives deeper into ocean forest ecosystems. Only when they were brought back did it become obvious how important otters are for keeping balance in the ocean. Their return inspired scientists to construct a new ecological paradigm around them. North Pacific kelp forests, as it turns out, need otters.

The otter-kelp connection comes down, once again, to this mammal's relatively recent return to an aquatic life and its reliance on its fur. A fur coat is not enough to keep a sea otter warm in the cold Pacific. In addition, it relies on its incredibly high metabolic rate, which runs around three times faster than the metabolism of other warm-blooded mammals of a similar size. Leaky mitochondria, the energy-producing structures inside every cell, churn out heat from an otter's muscles without any need for them to move or shiver, but this requires a lot of energy. To supply it, sea otters must do a lot of eating. Each day, they consume around a quarter of their body weight, and they've evolved to be highly skilled hunters. They're the only marine mammals that catch prey with their paws and not their teeth, and they use stones to smash open mussels and clams and to whack abalones off rocks. They carry their favourite stone tools with them in pockets of loose skin in their armpits. Depending on what's available, sea otters eat all sorts of fish and invertebrates, and they're especially fond of purple sea urchins. They carefully pick them up with their tough paw pads and bite into the underside, where there are fewer spines, then slurp out the insides. Otters can eat so many urchins, their bones and teeth turn purple.*

---

*This is described as echinochromicity, after the echinochrome pigments found in sea urchins, which happen to have antiviral and antibacterial properties and have been investigated as potential therapeutic drugs against Covid-19.

Otters eat urchins, and urchins eat kelp—lots of kelp. At first glance, a sea urchin is deceptively simple, little more than a spine-covered sphere gently squeezed and flattened top to bottom. On closer inspection, an elegant, pentaradial symmetry is revealed, showing these animals are obviously close relatives of starfish.* Turn over an urchin, and there's a star-shaped mouth with what look like five little bird beaks pinching together. This is the tip of a complex apparatus called Aristotle's lantern, which is controlled by dozens of muscles that move the teeth in any direction the urchin chooses. This beautiful piece of biological engineering is the secret to an urchin's tremendous eating abilities, allowing it to rasp at seaweeds lodged in nooks on rocky reefs.

The enormous appetites of otters and urchins tie both animals to the future of the ocean. When the fur trade demolished sea otter populations, urchin numbers exploded. Spiky armadas marched across the seabed, chewing through kelp stipes and swiftly converting former forests into devastated expanses known as urchin barrens. Anywhere from five to seventy-five urchins per square yard of seabed can flip an ecosystem from forest to barren.

When sea otters were gradually restored to their former territories, they helped drive urchin numbers back down, giving kelp spores a better chance of settling, allowing the forests to rise again. In Alaska and British Columbia, when otters came back, so did kelp. This is the kind of ecological cascade that people have been searching for among sharks and largely failing to detect. Sea otters, in contrast, have thoroughly proven their abilities as keystone predators. And their influence reaches even further. They are not only playing their part in bringing back lost ecosystems but also helping to make them more resilient to the changing ocean.

---

*Sea urchins, starfish, sand dollars, brittle stars, feather stars, and sea cucumbers are all echinoderms, a phylum of animals named for their spiny skin (from the Greek word *echino*, meaning "spiny," and the Latin word *derm*, meaning "skin"). Within the echinoderms, sea urchins belong to the echinoid class.

In central California, otters are boosting the resilience of eelgrass. Green blades ten to twenty inches long grow in dense meadows across Elkhorn Slough, a sheltered estuary that flows into Monterey Bay and lies at the heart of a watershed dominated by farmland where many of California's orange groves and almond orchards grow. Over past decades, sales of artificial fertilisers have exploded, and the estuary has become overloaded with nitrogen and phosphorous. This has been causing algae to proliferate and grow all over the eelgrass, blocking sunlight from reaching the photosynthesising blades and causing the grassy meadows to die off.

When a few young male sea otters made their own way to Elkhorn Slough from the recovering wild population, they were joined by foundling otters that had been rescued and reared at the Monterey Bay Aquarium. Mother otters will abandon their pups if they can't find enough food, or they sometimes get separated by storms or shark attacks. Young pups that wind up stranded and alone will soon die—unless concerned humans watch out for them and place them in the arms of captive female sea otters. Since 2002, surrogate mothers among the sea otters at the Monterey Bay Aquarium have cared for dozens of stranded pups, teaching them essential life skills, including how to groom their fur coats and use rocks as tools to crack open shellfish. (People watching wear amorphous black capes and welder's masks to make sure the pups don't grow accustomed to human presence.) More than thirty rehabilitated otters have been released into Elkhorn Slough where, rather by chance, they're proving yet again their ability to help ecosystems recover after years of decline.

The otters' influence on eelgrass ecosystems is more complex than their impact in kelp forests, involving more steps in the food web. Since sea otters have arrived in Elkhorn Slough, they've been eating a lot of crabs. A drop in crab numbers favoured the crabs' prey, in particular eelgrass sea slugs, which crawl around eelgrass blades, slurping and chewing on the smothering algae. With more otters, there are fewer crabs and thus more sea slugs and less algae, and the eelgrass meadows are flourishing, even though the estuary's waters are still burdened with farmland runoff.

To the north, off British Columbia, sea otters are encouraging eelgrass meadows to burst into bloom. Eelgrass and other types of seagrasses may look like seaweeds, but they are in fact types of flowering plants, as are terrestrial grasses and trees. As otters dig into the seabed searching for clams, they disturb the plants and stimulate them to produce flowers, release pollen, and set seed. The disturbed eelgrass is thus hedging its bets, sending its offspring into the ocean to find somewhere to settle and grow or to lie dormant as seeds in the seabed waiting for favourable conditions to return. In the process, parent eelgrass plants are mixing their genes and boosting the genetic diversity of their offspring.

When they're left in peace, eelgrass and other seagrass species tend to reproduce by cloning. They split off copies of themselves and create perennial meadows that can spread for miles. These stands of genetically identical plants have in some regions survived for millennia, but their lack of diversity renders them vulnerable. As Charles Darwin figured out long ago, variation is the raw material that enables populations to adapt, evolve, and keep pace with their shifting environment. In parts of British Columbia where sea otters have been back the longest, more flowering has been taking place, and the eelgrass meadows are more genetically diverse—and where there's more diversity, there's more resilience to change.

Elsewhere in the world, from Iceland to Ireland, Japan to Australia, many kelp forests that never had any sea otters have also collapsed, and urchin barrens have taken their place. Other urchin predators have been overfished and overhunted, and warming seas are allowing urchins to expand their range and spread their influence. Urchin barrens can be relatively small, a few hundred yards across, and exist in ephemeral mosaics interspersed with patches of kelp forest. They can also be huge and persistent. Entire forests along thousands of miles of coastline have disappeared without a trace. Witnessing this, kelp restorationists are on the rise, and many of them have decided the best way to bring kelp forests back is to get rid of urchins.

A mix of conflicting ideas has come to surround these humble echinoderms. For millennia, humans knew about them from star-crossed rocks buried in earth that could so easily have fallen from the night sky. These were the fossilised remains of ancient urchin species that have existed in the ocean for hundreds of millions of years. Neanderthals collected fossil urchins and carved them into stone tools. Neolithic people buried them with loved ones, sometimes a single urchin clasped in the deceased's hands, other times hundreds decorating a grave. Across Europe and North Africa, fossil urchins have been pierced to wear as necklaces, used as protective amulets, and lined up on window ledges or buried beneath the thresholds of houses to keep out the devil.

Many people today still think of urchins as animals to treasure. For Māori people in Aotearoa (New Zealand), kina urchins are *taongo*, a sacred species, as well as *kaimoana*, a traditional food. A delicacy in Japan, *uni* is either the testes of male urchins or the ovaries of females. Five in each shell are carefully scooped out and savoured for the creamy texture and the sweet, briny flavour. Orange and yellow *uni* apparently taste subtly different depending on where in the ocean they came from, similar to the terroirs of French wines.

However, the plight of kelp forests is transforming sea urchins from magical creatures and cherished foods into what many see as little more than spiny pests. There are roughly a thousand living species of urchins, which range from the tideline all the way down into oceanic trenches. Of those thousand, twenty are known to be powerful controllers of kelp growth, including purple urchins in California, black urchins in Chile, green urchins in the North Atlantic, and long-spined urchins in Australia. They can proliferate into swarms and bring down entire forests, and restorationists have tried various ways of wiping them out.

Caustic quicklime spread across the seabed is an effective means of killing urchins. This method was tested in California in the 1970s, but it also obliterates a lot of other marine wildlife. A more selective option is urchin smashing. Often this involves divers swimming down with hammers and bashing urchins to pieces. Stabbing them with knives also works. The fastest reported crushing rate for a diver is more than seventy urchins per minute.

It's a crude technique, but it does seem to work. In one study off the coast of Hokkaido, Japan, a team of twenty volunteer divers spent two days clearing away urchins from about a half acre of seabed. Eight months later, *Saccharina* and *Undaria* kelp were beginning to grow again. Off Vega Island in northern Norway, after scuba divers meticulously picked off urchins around a small, rocky islet, *Laminaria* kelp came back. But a diver can collect or smash only so many sea urchins. Most urchin-removal programmes have worked over small, experimental areas. To scale up efforts, a tech start-up company based in Atlanta, Georgia, plans to replace hammer-wielding divers with automated underwater robots equipped with artificial intelligence to detect and dispatch urchins.

Rather than wasting all these urchins and smashing them in the name of reforestation, another possibility is to eat them. If there's one sure-fire method humans have implemented for effectively removing animals from the ocean, it's to catch, sell, and eat them. The problem is that sea urchins roaming empty barrens are generally not good to eat. Once all the kelp has gone, these starved animals have shrivelled, unappetising gonads.

One workaround is to gather live urchins from barrens, then fatten them up until their gourmet body parts are ready to eat. An urchin ranch was opened in 2020 in Stavanger, Norway, followed by another in 2022 in Nagato, Japan. The urchins are kept in water tanks out of the ocean and fed on sustainably grown seaweeds; their gonads are destined for high-end sushi restaurants.

Sushi lovers will need to eat a huge amount of *uni* if they're going to help keep the kelp forests intact. There are billions of urchins in barrens worldwide. And studies show that kelp forests are likely to return only if almost all the urchins are removed from the area. The urchin population needs to be pushed far below the number that stripped the seabed bare in the first place; the two tipping points, forwards and backwards, are not the same. This is partly because urchins can survive for a long time with nothing to eat. Nicknamed zombie urchins, they hang around ready to nibble any young kelp as soon as it starts to grow. And just like zombies in the movies, urchins in barrens just keep on coming. To maintain a regrowing kelp forest, it's usually not enough to clear away urchins just once; restorationists need to keep smashing or removing new arrivals over and over.

Killing thousands upon thousands of urchins is undoubtedly a desperate measure and a dismal sign of how drastically ocean ecosystems have shifted out of balance. Urchins have been vilified as an invading scourge, but they're guilty of nothing more than surviving in the Anthropocene and coping with everything humanity has thrown at them. Wiping out urchins en masse does nothing about the underlying problems of rising temperatures and predator loss, which are worsening and complicating each other.

Humans can kick-start the kelp recovery process by clearing away an urchin swarm—as carefully as possible—to pave the way for wild predators to take over and maintain the longer-term balance. For that to happen, there need to be healthy populations of animals that eat urchins, such as triggerfish, wrasse, crabs, and lobsters, which do much better inside well-protected marine reserves. A study of two of Aotearoa's no-take zones, including the original one set up at Cape Rodney–Okakari Point by Valentine Chapman and Bill Ballantine in the 1970s, showed that urchins are much more likely to get eaten by predators inside reserves than outside. The marine reserves contain blooming forests of kelp and other seaweeds thanks to the large, abundant silver seabream, blue cod, and spiny lobsters that are keeping urchin numbers in check and discouraging the spread of barrens. Highly protecting more of the ocean from fishing and hunting will give more kelp forests a chance to thrive.

Now that sea otters have proven their abilities to engineer more resilient kelp forests, various conservation groups along the coast of the Pacific Northwest region of North America have started thinking about a new wave of otter reintroductions. In 2021, the US Congress officially recognised sea otters as critical for ocean ecosystems and instructed the Fish and Wildlife Service to investigate the feasibility of bringing back otters to more parts of the coast where they're still missing more than a century after fur hunting ended.

One proposal is to move otters into the biggest remaining gap in their historical range, reaching north from San Francisco Bay into Oregon. California otters are not moving north into these areas by themselves, maybe because they would have to run the gauntlet of great white sharks that are shifting northwards as coastal waters warm. Great whites don't normally prey on sea otters. They're not nearly fatty enough to be worth eating. But one investigative chomp is easily lethal for a small marine mammal. Dead otters with shark bites have been washing up on California beaches in increasing numbers. What's more, otters are more likely to be picked off by sharks when they leave the shadowy canopy of kelp forests. In areas where kelp is dwindling, shark-bitten otters are far more common than they are in places where forests are still intact. As the ocean changes around them, otters may well need kelp forests just as much as the forests need otters.

If otters were returned to more of their former North American range, they would play a part in the fight against the climate crisis by helping underwater seagrass meadows and kelp forests flourish, and in the process harness more carbon dioxide from the atmosphere. These otter-renewed habitats would have the added benefit of nurturing local fisheries by welcoming in new generations of young fish.

People living near coastlines where otters could be reintroduced are generally in favour and want to see the species back in their neighbourhoods. Among the indigenous peoples who have shared their views on the matter, many are enthusiastic and hope the otter reintroductions will help restore balance to the ocean. The Confederated Tribes of the Coos, Lower Umpqua, and Siuslaw Indians in Oregon describe feeling a kinship with otters, which were once an important part of the ocean environment.

By contrast, voices of concern are coming from some communities involved in fishing for species that sea otters like to eat, including crabs, sea urchins, and abalone. Conflict has raged on and off for decades between environmentalists and fishers over whether sea otters should be encouraged or even allowed at all in California waters. Though fishers today generally appreciate the critical role otters play in ecosystems, in the past some claimed otters have an unfair advantage because they don't have to abide by seasonal restrictions or catch limits and can help themselves to as much precious shellfish as they want.

The future of kelp forests is not all about otters and urchins. Up until a couple hundred years ago, enormous Steller's sea cows lived in the kelp forests of the North Pacific and may well have boosted the ecosystem's resilience. These thirty-foot-long giants had so much blubber they couldn't dive down, and so they spent their time floating near the surface browsing on kelp. This would have opened up the canopy and allowed more light to pass through to the understory, likely allowing the seabed to flourish with a garden of colourful seaweeds. Today, in darker, denser forests, where there are no more floating megaherbivores thinning out the canopy, seaweeds struggle to grow on the seabed.

A speculative idea, based on mathematical models, hints that these sea cow–enhanced forests may have coped better with heatwaves compared to modern kelp forests; the understory seaweeds could have helped feed urchins and dampened their tendency to fell whole forests. Nobody is seriously considering genetically engineering massive manatees or dugongs to replace the absent Steller's sea cows. But one group of scientists is suggesting it might be worth trying to mimic the sea-cow effect in some other way, perhaps by selectively cutting away the upper fronds in kelp forests.

More realistic is the return of a lost species that has been missing from kelp forests for only a few years. Sunflower sea stars are the size of bicycle wheels, among the biggest of all the sea stars.* They have velvety-looking skin and dozens of golden, red, or purple arms. Draped across the seabed, they don't look like formidable hunters, but when they sense food, they can show a turn of speed, using thousands of tube feet to glide along by a body length per minute—fast for an echinoderm.

Fellow native species of the North American Pacific coast, sea otters and sunflower sea stars used to work together to keep sea urchins in check. The furry mammals generally bother catching only the most nutritious urchins, those larger than a baseball. These are too big for sunflower sea stars, which instead go for urchins a finger's width across or smaller. The sea stars are such effective predators, little urchins learned to hide under the spines of bigger urchins, presumably where they won't be noticed. By devouring urchins of different sizes, the otters and sea stars effectively prevented kelp forests from being overgrazed.

But in 2013, sunflower sea stars, along with dozens of other sea star species, were afflicted by a horrifying plague. Sea star wasting disease, as it was later named, caused a stricken sea star to break out

---

*Or starfish, as they are interchangeably called by people (like me) who aren't too bothered by the ichthyological overtones.

in skin lesions, its internal organs spilling out of its body and its arms falling off, with no chance of regrowing new ones. Millions of sea stars wasted away, leaving behind smears of sickly slime and piles of white bony ossicles, the structures that form their spiny exoskeletons.

No one has yet figured out what exactly makes sea stars so suddenly fall apart. Some studies point towards bacteria and viruses, while others have found no such link. It's possible sea stars are wasting away for various reasons that show up as a similar set of symptoms. The mass die-off of sea stars in the eastern Pacific has been linked to warming seas and could have been a stress response to fast environmental change.

It was further inflamed by what was arguably the biggest ocean heatwave on record. Nicknamed the Blob, it occurred when a persistent high-pressure zone pinned a thousand-mile-wide body of unusually warm water against North America's west coast from Alaska to California and stayed there from 2014 to 2016. Sea temperatures were as much as five degrees Fahrenheit higher than average. Subsequent analysis confirmed the Blob was not related to natural climatic variations but was a direct result of the climate crisis. The heated sea unleashed chaos in oceanic ecosystems, causing food webs to collapse; starving millions of fish, seabirds, sea lions, and whales; and killing off kelp forests. The heatwave also made sea star wasting disease worse, and by the time the Blob dispersed, there were very few sunflower sea stars left.

For now, the sea star wasting disease has eased in the Pacific,* but there are no signs of sunflower sea stars recovering in the wild. Fearful for the future of the species, conservationists have stepped in. Staff at the Nature Conservancy teamed up with echinoderm expert Jason Hodin at the University of Washington, who they hoped could figure out how to rear sunflower sea stars in captivity. In 2019, they located one of the last known populations of the species

---

*At the time of writing.

in the Salish Sea, gathered up a few dozen healthy-looking adults, and took them to the Friday Harbor Laboratories on the shores of San Juan Island off the coast of Washington State.

Almost nothing was known about the biology of the species. Hodin had a lot of experience rearing and studying other echinoderms, but with sunflower sea stars he was starting more or less from scratch. Much of the information in existing scientific literature turned out to be wrong. For instance, it assumed these sea stars spawn in summer months. But when Hodin brought them into his laboratory in the summer of 2019, nothing happened. Not until the following winter were the adult sea stars ready to spawn. Hodin's team carefully collected the sea stars' sperm and eggs, mixed them together, then filled beakers and jars with the resulting larvae, which look nothing like sea stars and more like odd-shaped sea slugs.

For two months, Hodin waited patiently for the sea star larvae to reach the most dramatic moment in their lives, metamorphosis. He watched as star shapes began to assemble inside the transparent bodies of the larvae. Then came the time when the larvae sank to the bottom, cast off their younger incarnation, and transformed into five-armed sea stars, two one-hundredths of an inch across.

Still, Hodin and his team faced one of their biggest challenges. They had to work out what to feed the juvenile sea stars. It's common for young sea stars to graze on microscopic algae, but not sunflower sea stars. After a lot of trial and error, and uneaten food offerings, the tiny sea stars finally started nibbling on even tinier baby sea urchins. As it turns out, sunflower sea stars have a good appetite for urchins throughout much of their lives.

Now the aquarium tanks at the Friday Harbor Labs contain dozens of enormous sunflower sea stars. They've answered another important question about their biology: to reach maturity takes them three years. The next step is to see how these captive-reared animals fare in more natural conditions. Hodin's team will deploy cages in select spots off the coast and place sea stars inside, giving them their first taste of wild waters.

The story of sunflower sea stars warns of a frightening new reality for the ocean. Changes can sweep in so quickly that a species could be lost before biologists have a chance to learn about its life and work out a plan to save it. Hodin and the Nature Conservancy may have got to sunflower sea stars just in time, but the future of the species remains uncertain. There's no telling if or when the wasting disease might return. But there is at least an inkling of good news coming from Hodin's laboratory studies. Preliminary research is showing that captive-reared sea stars seem to cope well and keep growing at higher temperatures. This bodes well for the possible future release of sunflower sea stars back into an ocean noticeably warmer than it was when the species was last widespread and abundant. There are no immediate plans for a sea star release programme. But if remnant populations don't recover by themselves, rearing more in aquariums maintains the possibility of one day returning the species to the wild.

Plans to set free captive-reared animals often provoke questions of ethics and concerns of messing with natural systems. It's true that plenty of ecological disasters have been triggered by people moving species around the planet, although most of these were species released a long way outside their natural range, such as the giant African land snails and Florida rosy wolfsnails brought to the South Pacific. On the contrary, many breeding programmes, with great care and consideration, have saved species from almost certain extinction. Were it not for captive-breeding efforts around the world, there wouldn't be scimitar-horned oryx in the deserts of central Africa or candy-striped endemic tree snails crawling through the forests of Polynesia or giant tortoises chewing on prickly pear cactus trees on Española Island in the Galápagos.

I see no good reason not to try to do the same for ocean-going species that are in most urgent need of help and can feasibly be reared in captivity.* Frankly, too much is already changing in the Anthropocene ocean to be precious about keeping some notional version of wild nature untouched by human hands. Millions of captive-reared salmon and trout are released into the ocean every year to boost fisheries. Why not do the same for endangered species? How glorious it would be to see giant sunflower sea stars hunting once again alongside sea otters, offering even more hope for the future of kelp forests.

A different seaweed forest exists far from shore. It doesn't grow upwards from the seabed but forms a detached canopy floating at the surface of the Sargasso Sea, a 1.5-million-square-mile region of the Atlantic Ocean to the east of Bermuda, the only sea on earth that has no coastlines, bounded instead by rotating currents. Inside this gyre lies a network of islands composed of golden *Sargassum* seaweeds,† their tangled mats of serrated leaves suspended by small, round bladders filled with gas. Like an upside-down rain forest, this unique habitat (the only one of its kind) creates shelter and food for a rich ecosystem of animal life. Sea spiders, sea slugs, and snails creep through the canopy, and sea anemones fix to the weeds like flowers. Sargassum crabs and sargassum shrimp live exclusively in this drifting forest, as does the sargassum anglerfish, which is brilliantly camouflaged to match its weedy habitat and uses its modified fins to clamber through the undergrowth and sneak up on prey.

In 2011, *Sargassum* suddenly started appearing where it hadn't been seen before. Colossal quantities began washing up on coastlines in Brazil and Mexico, along the US Gulf Coast, and on numerous Caribbean islands. Every summer since then, more *Sargassum* has

---

*I doubt it will ever be possible to rear such animals as great white sharks or blue whales in captivity, and I hope it never comes to that.

†The Sargasso Sea forest contains two (out of several hundred) *Sargassum* species, *Sargassum natans* and *S. fluitans*.

piled up on beaches, creating a dangerous public nuisance that's disastrous for tourism industries, ruining beachgoers' vacations. Decomposing piles of *Sargassum* release toxic hydrogen sulphide gas that stinks of rotten eggs, and there are worries too about pathogenic bacteria in the seaweed flotsam. Clean-up efforts are costing millions of dollars every year.

Coastal ecosystems are also being harmed because thick mats of *Sargassum* drifting into coastlines block the sunlight needed by seagrass meadows and coral reefs to flourish. Sea turtle hatchlings are emerging from their sandy nests on beaches only to encounter impenetrable mountains of stranded *Sargassum* in their path to the sea. Tragically, the palm-size turtles are getting trapped by the very same seaweeds that should offer them sanctuary when they swim out to the floating forest.

The source of this scourge has been spotted from space. Satellites have recorded a huge clump of *Sargassum*, up to five thousand miles long and three hundred miles wide, stretching all the way across the Atlantic, from the coast of West Africa to the Caribbean, in an area to the south of the Sargasso Sea that used to be open blue ocean. Scientists named it the Great Atlantic Sargassum Belt.

The most obvious culprit to blame for the explosion was *Sargassum* escaping from the Sargasso Sea, and yet studies showed that in fact this is a distinct southerly population that had previously never proliferated. Increasing sea temperatures are likely playing their part in this dramatic expansion for the simple reason that warmth speeds up seaweed growth. A critical connection between ocean and land is also largely responsible. At the centre of this disaster is the Amazon Basin, where accelerating deforestation and burgeoning soya plantations and cattle ranches are releasing excess nutrients into the Orinoco and Amazon Rivers and out to the Atlantic. Likewise, land-based runoff from farmland and sewage systems in North America's Mississippi Basin is also adding to the nutrient load offshore. Specifically, increasing amounts of nitrogen have been linked to the sudden boom in *Sargassum*. And with no circulating currents to contain the seaweed, as happens in the Sargasso Sea, the Atlantic bloom is being swept westwards towards land.

An ideal solution has yet to be found for getting rid of *Sargassum* after it has washed up on the shore. Composting and using it as fertiliser are not straightforward options, because *Sargassum* contains significant amounts of arsenic, which would contaminate soils and groundwater. Other ideas include pressing the weeds into building blocks or processing the seaweed mass, along with the plastic debris that gets caught up in it, to make biofuels. A company called Seaweed Generation is developing robotic collectors that would gather the floating *Sargassum* mats, bundle them up, and sink them into the deep ocean several miles down, in the process removing carbon from the atmosphere. The ecological impacts this would have are still to be fully explored, from the floating ecosystems at the surface that could also get scooped up, to the deep-sea animals that may, or may not, appreciate the extra food.

Even if effective ways are invented to clear beaches and help safeguard coastal ecosystems from *Sargassum*, this problematic seaweed will keep on arriving unless something can be done to stop the rampant destruction of terrestrial forests and the surge of farmland taking their place. The message from the Great Atlantic Sargassum Belt is that the future of earth's land and ocean are bound tightly together.

While efforts are ongoing to clear up the *Sargassum* deluge from the Caribbean to Florida, conservationists and scientists farther north have been working hard for the past two decades to bring back a long-lost green ecosystem. Like vast underwater prairies carpeting tens of thousands of acres of seabed, meadows of eelgrass used to thrive in coastal lagoons of the US state of Virginia. In the 1930s, a deadly pandemic broke out of seagrass wasting disease, caused by a slime mould called *Labyrinthula*. Combined with a devastating hurricane, this completely eradicated all of Virginia's underwater meadows.

For the next seventy years, no eelgrass grew in the inshore lagoons, although it was gradually returning to nearby Chesapeake Bay, which had also been stripped bare by the disease. Then, early in the twenty-first century, the situation turned around. Locals had noticed small patches of eelgrass in the lagoons, and scientists from Virginia Institute of Marine Science found the conditions were right for meadows to grow—if there were enough eelgrass plants and their seeds to kick-start the populations.

Thus began a programme to actively replant Virginia's missing eelgrass. Teams of scientists and volunteers worked together to gather up seedpods from existing meadows in the Chesapeake and scatter them in dense patches in empty areas of Hog Island Bay, Spider Crab Bay, Cobb Bay, and South Bay. Over the course of twenty years, more than seventy million seeds were sown, which quickly germinated, grew, and began producing their own seeds, and so the eelgrass meadows have spread. From around five hundred replanted acres, close to nine thousand acres are now covered in meadows.

The regreening of Virginia's lagoons has been the world's most successful seagrass restoration project. It's inspiring similar attempts elsewhere to bring back the ocean's underwater meadows, which are highly threatened by pollution and sediments pouring off land and destruction by boat anchors, trawlers, and dredgers. Seagrass meadows grow along the coasts of every continent except Antarctica, and already a third have disappeared globally, some at a horrifying rate: Casco Bay, an inlet in the Gulf of Maine, lost more than half its eelgrass meadows, from 5,012 to 2,286 acres, in just four years, between 2018 and 2022.

The seventy or so species of seagrasses, including eelgrass, play a similarly critical role in the ocean as kelp forests: they buffer waves, protect coastlines from erosion, and provide habitat for a rich mix of other species. As the recovering Virginia lagoons are showing, when meadows return, so do a host of animals. Here, crab and fish populations have rebounded, including large shoals of silver perch and pinfish. Tundra swans and redhead ducks are among the birds that are calling in at the aquatic grasslands in greater numbers than a few decades ago. Scientists have also reintroduced a now-thriving population of bay scallops, which rely on the eelgrass, resting on the blades at an early stage in their life cycle before settling down on the seabed.

Virginia's thriving eelgrass ecosystems are also improving water quality in the lagoons, trapping sediments in their roots and creating sparkling-clear waters. And the underwater grasses are storing more carbon and nitrogen in the seabed. Globally, seagrass meadows likely store close to twenty billion tons of carbon, equal to more than half of the global annual emissions in the mid-2020s. Keeping existing seagrass meadows intact will prevent the release of a great deal more carbon into the atmosphere. And that carbon capture could increase further if more seagrasses were helped to recover. A 2022 study projecting the future of seagrass meadows highlighted the importance of not only protecting seagrasses but helping to restore them too. Combining conservation efforts with restoration programmes, like the one in Virginia, could see underwater meadows increase by more than a third by 2070, effectively dialling back the damage done over past decades.

Likewise, mangrove forests will likely do much better in the years ahead with a blend of conservation and effective restoration. In 105 countries, mangroves grow between the tides on sheltered shorelines, where their looping, twisted roots and trunks flood daily, then get exposed to air and sun when the tide falls. In the later decades of the twentieth century, 1 per cent of these semiaquatic tropical forests were being lost every year, most of them cut down to make way for agriculture and fish farms, a rate of deforestation that has since been reduced; a further 2 per cent were lost between 2000 and 2016.

Historically dismissed as disease-ridden swamps, mangrove forests are another of the sea's green habitats that provide critical benefits for coastal communities, creating storm buffers, nurturing countless young fish and other animals, and supporting the livelihoods of millions of small-scale fishers.

Globally, mangrove forests lock up close to ten billion tons of carbon in their roots, trunks, and soils. Many restoration programmes have chased the dream of increasing carbon sequestration but not always with good results. Scandalous amounts of money and goodwill have been wasted as projects have carelessly jumped on a greenwashed bandwagon, poking millions of seedpods, the shape and size of cigars, into the seabed, only for all the seedlings to die.

The Philippines, for instance, which lost nearly three-quarters of its mangrove forests in the last hundred years, saw one of the most intensive and pointless efforts to restore mangrove forests. Over the course of twenty years, conservationists planted millions of mangrove seeds over an area of more than one hundred thousand acres. Some seeds germinated and began to grow, but most were doomed. A later survey found the new mangrove trees were almost entirely dead, dying, or dismally stunted. Restoration efforts failed because planters didn't take into account the mangroves' biology and the conditions they need to survive. Across the Philippines, and in many other restoration projects, seeds have been planted in places that would never have supported mangrove trees; they were stuck into shorelines of the wrong elevation and tidal regime; some were even planted on top of seagrass meadows, destroying one threatened ecosystem in failed attempts to grow another. Far more important than planting seeds is to ensure the hydrological conditions are just right for mangroves to grow—for instance, by digging away sediments or breaking down dams so there's just enough but not too much seawater flooding in and out every day. Mangrove seeds are buoyant and float for days or months on ocean currents, some drifting thousands of miles before

sprouting roots to anchor themselves in place. If the shoreline conditions are right, seeds will drift in, and damaged or lost forests will
naturally rejuvenate.

Compared to drifting mangrove seeds, kelp spores don't tend to travel
far. Depending on the species, the next generation of kelp can disperse
a few miles or almost no distance at all. Many kelp spores simply scatter
among the holdfasts of their parents. The shady, sheltered canopy of
adult kelp is commonly where sporelings grow best. Too much light
can cause tender young kelp to lose its pigments and bleach white,
while chunks of its tissue rot away and die. And the fronds of adult kelp
undulating in the swell can sweep away sea urchins and help protect
sporelings from being eaten. This means that efforts to restore kelp
forests are most likely to be successful when there are large surviving
forests nearby. The ocean's underwater forests need existing forests to
grow, which raises a problem when there are none for miles around.
Then it's not enough for kelp restorationists to manipulate grazing
and predatory species. They also need to try to regrow the forests.

Japan has the longest history of kelp restoration. *Isoyake** is the
term for declining kelp forests, and there are records going back
centuries of efforts to help them recover, commonly by constructing
artificial reefs for kelp spores to settle on. Fishers in the early part of
the eighteenth century threw stones onto barren areas of seabed to
encourage kelp regrowth, and essentially the same practice remains
popular today. Over the past few decades, off the Pacific coast of
Shizuoka Prefecture, not far from the foothills of Mount Fuji, concrete blocks have been installed inside healthy kelp forests, providing substrate for spores to fix on. Moving the sporeling-covered
blocks to areas of *isoyake* has restored more than three square miles
of *Ecklonia* forest.

---

*Meaning "rocky-shore denudation" or "sea desertification."

It takes decades, centuries even, for a terrestrial tropical rain forest or an oak woodland to regrow. Meanwhile, a mature kelp forest can establish within a few years. Kelp restorationists are still in the experimental stages of figuring out how to make that happen in the ever-shifting conditions of the Anthropocene ocean.

In the 1980s, beaches in the Australian city of Sydney were frequently closed to swimmers because masses of poorly treated sewage were allowed to pour straight into the sea. Below the waterline, the pollution killed off dense stands of a jagged seaweed known as crayweed,* although the disappearance went unnoticed until much later. In 2007, a team of diving scientists surveyed the coastline and found dense crayweed canopies were common on the rocky reefs of New South Wales. But along more than forty miles of Sydney's metropolitan coastline, they didn't find a single seaweed blade. By then, the city's sewage was being diverted along pipes offshore, and water quality inshore had substantially improved. Still, though, the shallow, rocky reefs remained empty of crayweed.

In 2011, a team of scientists at the Sydney Institute of Marine Science decided to test whether crayweed could grow again in the empty areas. They took mature adults from existing seaweed forests north and south of Sydney and transplanted them into the forty-mile gap, fixing them to bare rocks with plastic mesh and cable ties.† Six months later, some of the transplants had survived, and they were busy scattering the next generation of young sporelings across the seabed.

From that initial success, Operation Crayweed was born. Restoration efforts were scaled up, initially paid for by a crowdfunding campaign in December 2015 that prompted people to "plant an underwater tree for Christmas." Support from members of the public

---

* *Phyllospora comosa* forms habitat that's used by rock lobsters, known locally as crayfish, hence the common name crayweed.

† Restorationists are well aware that deliberately adding plastics to the ocean is not ideal, and they are seeking alternatives that will be robust enough to withstand the waves and strong currents.

was critical in kick-starting the project, paving the way for state investment. Operation Crayweed is also reaching beyond the science of reforestation and rolling out art installations and exhibitions along the coast to make new connections between local people and the lost forests. Schoolchildren dressed up as sea dragons and octopuses have been parading along the Sydney seafront, imagining what it's like to be these animals living in the underwater forest that's regrowing just offshore. Previously, many Sydneysiders didn't realise the city's water quality had greatly improved, and they had no idea crayweed forests used to grow on their doorstep. Now, at more than a dozen sites across the city, people can look out to sea at the marker buoys and know that's where the forests are coming back, gradually filling in the gap in these easterly reaches of Australia's Great Southern Reef.

In another part of this immense network of underwater forests, ancient human connections that have remained unbroken for millennia are now at risk of coming to an end. In *lutruwita* (Tasmania), the shark tooth–shaped island south of the Australian mainland, Aboriginal people traditionally hunt for food in the giant kelp forests of their sea country and use the kelp as an important material to make objects such as water-carrying containers. Aboriginal women visit kelp forests at low tide to collect seashells, including maireener, or rainbow kelp shells, which they rub with sand to reveal the shining mother-of-pearl underneath. These and other tiny shells are pierced, threaded into necklaces, and used as gifts and tokens of honour. Maireener shells are now much harder to find, and shell necklaces could become a lost art because *lutruwita*'s giant kelp forests are disappearing.

In recent years, propelled by climate change, the warm ocean current that flows polewards along the east coast of mainland Australia has been pushing farther south. This is the prime reason why the seas around *lutruwita* are heating four times faster than the global average, and why the *lutruwita* giant kelp forests are dying. There are bays where, just a few decades ago, fishermen cut channels through the giant kelp to get their boats in and out, and now there's no kelp at all. Only 5 per cent of *lutruwita*'s giant kelp forests still stand, and that 5 per cent could hold the secret for the future of the forests.

People from the weetapoona Aboriginal Corporation have been collaborating with marine biologists from the University of Tasmania to trial a new form of restoration they hope will see the return of kelp to their sea country. They selected Trumpeter Bay, on the southeast coast of *lutruwita*, as a site where kelp have been outplanted in the hope they will kick-start the return of lost forests.

These outplantings originate in the surviving naturally occurring stands of kelp dotted around *lutruwita*. Cayne Layton and his team at the university visited some of the remaining patches of kelp forests and collected spore-producing fronds, leaving the intact adults behind. In the lab, the fronds released spores, which developed into microscopic kelp females and males, known as gametophytes, which look like tiny twigs. These form an important stage in kelp's unusual, two-phase life cycle, a part that's normally hidden from view. Minute females and males produce eggs and sperm, which fuse and grow into the large kelp that form the structure of a forest.

Conveniently, this miniature, gametophyte stage can be cooled and stored under red light, which arrests its development; and more gametophytes can easily be made by snapping the tiny twigs in two. It's a practice perfected in Japan and Korea, where kelp is important food, much of it reared by the aquaculture industry. Cultures of kelp gametophytes have been kept alive in cool storage for decades.

In *lutruwita*, Layton and colleagues store their kelp gametophytes in a refrigerator the size of a hotel minibar. This is a compact, living repository, the kelp equivalent of a seed bank. It provides material for Layton's studies in rearing lab-grown sporelings in aquarium tanks at different temperatures, to identify those that can naturally cope with heat. Some young kelp even grow well at seventy-four degrees Fahrenheit, way above temperatures the kelp parents would have experienced in *lutruwita*'s warming sea.

Layton's team reared more of these super-kelp strains and transplanted them into the wild, including in Trumpeter Bay. As expected in the turbulent seas of *lutruwita*, not all the trial outplantings have taken hold. But enough are surviving to show the technique works. Crucially, some of the super-kelp have now reached maturity in the wild and are producing their own spores, like the crayweeds in Sydney. This is the main aim of the *lutruwita* initiative, to put enough kelp back in the ocean to kick-start the natural cycles, so that ultimately forests regenerate by themselves—and hopefully keep growing as the ocean continues to warm.

There is no silver bullet for creating future-proof, self-sustaining underwater forests or, for that matter, any other important green habitats in the ocean. In *lutruwita* and elsewhere, restorationists are busy testing out ways to replant and restore kelp forests, seagrass meadows, and mangrove forests. They're showing that restoration is doable, but it's complicated and nuanced. Each species and habitat in each region will likely need its own methods and solutions. And that's going to require much more funding, in many more countries, to support the kinds of detailed research and scientific trials that are exploring what works best. So far, successes in restoring lost kelp forests have mostly been modest in size, but they are showing what's possible. The obvious next big steps will be finding ways to effectively scale up, while avoiding the pitfalls that other restoration efforts have crashed into.

The future of kelp forests will depend on finding practical ways of keeping these ecosystems alive in the changing ocean, ideally without having to sell out to carbon markets. And perhaps more than anything, it will depend on weaving underwater forests more deeply into people's lives and minds. The greater the number of people who know and care, the less likely it is that the ocean's forests will be allowed to disappear.

Chapter 9
Future Reefs

Several things I remember vividly from my first visit to a coral reef. The water was a lot warmer than I expected—it was like jumping into a bathtub—and I could see much farther into the distance than I ever had before underwater. After two years diving in British seas, I knew what it felt like when my face got so cold I returned speechless from a dive, and that one can lose sight of a dive buddy from only an arm's length away. Most of all, the first coral reef I saw was even more colourful than I imagined it possibly could be. There were fish in yellows, purples, and electric turquoise blues, and mauve corals and emerald sponges. All the colours were an obvious sign that I'd arrived in the tropics, a reality that I found exhilarating and terrifying all at once. I was fresh out of high school and slowly getting over a crippling home sickness I had not anticipated. Of course, a few days later, I wanted to stay forever, exploring the reefs, learning the names of everything that lived there, and doing my part, so I hoped, in helping to protect this extraordinary place from harm.

I was in Belize, on Turneffe Atoll, midway along the Mesoamerican Reef, which runs south from Cabo Catoche, Mexico, along more than five hundred miles of coastline, taking a sharp eastern turn to the Bay Islands of Honduras. The coral-reef complex there is the biggest in the world after Australia's Great Barrier Reef. I had joined a team of divers tasked with mapping the underwater habitats and species of the atoll. Our daily routine was to head to the reef, morning and afternoon, and swim along straight lines, noting down in waterproof notebooks the life forms we encountered along the way. Four scuba divers would work together, each focusing on a particular component of the ecosystem. One diver catalogued the corals, noting down species and estimating what percentage of the reef was covered in live growth of corals—a key indicator of reef health. Another diver looked for invertebrates, all the crabs, shrimp, sea cucumbers, and sea urchins. The third diver was the fish spotter, my favourite underwater assignment. I might have seen more than five hundred species, and out of those I got to know well a hundred or so: hogfish and porkfish; blennies and ballyhoos; midnight, princess, and stoplight parrotfish; queen, grey, and French angelfish; golden, shy, and indigo hamlets; squirrelfish, trunkfish, soapfish, and jawfish.

The fourth diver in the group was responsible for navigating the rest of the team through the water and carrying a line to a floating buoy so the boat captain at the surface would know where we were. While I was doing that job, steering the rest of the team along their straight lines, I began to notice the reef around me was changing.

To navigate while diving, I used an underwater compass, setting a bearing and making sure to keep the needle in line as I swam along. A trick I soon learned was to find my bearing, fix my eyes on a large coral or sponge in the right heading, and swim towards that. A month or so into the expedition, I realised I was picking out and aiming at pale-coloured corals. They shone through the water and were the easiest to make out in the distance—but they hadn't been there during our earlier dives. The underwater seascape was leaching colour and turning white.

Started to notice a lot of coral bleaching, especially the mountainous star.

That line from my dive logbook from October 4, 1995, referred to a species of *Orbicella*, a common Caribbean coral. By then I had seen many of these huge mounds, which from afar looked like olive-green blankets draped over boulders and up close were covered in small, raised bumps, some of them outlined in a neon-green ring. Those bumps were coral polyps, which lived together in the hundreds and thousands and built colonies up to ten feet across. An individual coral polyp with its soft tentacles extended looks like a little flower nestled in a stony cup, which the polyp secretes around itself from the mineral calcium carbonate. *Orbicella* and hundreds of other coral species are generally known as stony corals, or hard corals, because of these limestone skeletons, which feel sharp to the touch. Lodged inside living tissue of a coral polyp are millions of microscopic spheres of single-celled algae known as zooxanthellae.* These algae are photosynthetic, soaking up sunlight and providing food for the whole coral colony in exchange for a secluded place to live in the shallows with a good supply of sunshine. It's a symbiosis that both corals and zooxanthellae benefit from, but the relationship can break down when conditions become stressful, such as when the sea around them heats up. The warmth shifts the algae into overdrive, and they photosynthesise much faster than normal and produce lots of damaging oxygen-free radicals. The polyps respond by ejecting the zooxanthellae from their bodies. Pigments in the zooxanthellae are what make corals colourful, and when they're gone, all that's left is a thin, transparent layer of coral tissue, which shows the bone-white limestone skeleton underneath. It looks like someone poured a bottle of toilet cleaner over the colony.

A scribbled note in my dive log from Belize mentions that recent warm, calm weather all over the Caribbean was causing outbreaks of coral bleaching. At the time, I knew about bleaching only in an

---

*Pronounced *zoo-zan-thellee.*

abstract sense, and evidently, I had no idea what was really at stake. A puzzling remark in my logbook reads:

This is the movement of biodiversity as we watch—exciting but maybe something to worry about?

It was the first mass coral bleaching in Belize in living memory. My dive buddies and I were among the first to knowingly witness the colour of these reefs fading away. Temperatures in Belizean waters that summer were almost one degree Celsius warmer than at the same time the previous year. For weeks, the temperature stayed high enough to stress many different types of corals and trigger bleaching along hundreds of miles of reef. A similar scenario was playing out across the region. That year saw the first known cases of mass bleaching on reefs in Cuba and Honduras; and coral reefs turned white in the Cayman Islands, Jamaica, Dominican Republic, Puerto Rico, Curaçao, and Bonaire.

When corals bleach, they don't necessarily die right away. Without their zooxanthellae, most corals struggle to get enough food, but if they can keep going long enough, their polyps will eventually absorb new algae from the seawater around them. Then the colonies regain their colour and carry on growing.

In Belize, the bleached corals began to show signs of the living tissue dying off. It could have been much worse, but in the nick of time, the atmospheric conditions shifted, and hurricanes stirred. I remember sitting on the beach at night, watching thunderstorms rage in the distance. And for a time, our base camp stayed on evacuation alert as several hurricanes passed through the region. I didn't know it at the time, but that hurricane season cooled the sea enough to ease the coral bleaching. Within six months, many coral colonies in Belize had recovered.

But this was only the beginning of the troubles for Belizean corals. Three years later, in 1998, another mass bleaching struck, much worse than the first, when a massive ocean heatwave, associated with one of the most powerful El Niño events on record, swept around the planet. In 2005, the reefs of Belize bleached again.

Early in my studies of coral reefs, I was caught up in the same desires that I bet many other marine biologists have felt. I wanted to see reefs for myself and try to wrap my head around these staggeringly diverse ecosystems. Coral reefs grow in shallow, tropical waters around the world, in more than one hundred countries, with major clusters in the Caribbean Sea, on islands dotted through the Pacific Ocean, in the western Indian Ocean, in the Red Sea, and along the east and west coasts of Australia; the most biodiverse reefs are in the Philippines, Indonesia, Papua New Guinea, and the Solomon Islands, a region known as the Coral Triangle. Collectively, the world's coral reefs cover less than 2 per cent of the ocean surface, an area roughly equal in size to Ecuador,* and yet they pack in one in every four known ocean species. Counting and cataloguing the number of species that exist in the ocean goes something like this: fish, octopus, shark, reef shark; sea cucumber, sea urchin, crab, reef crab; worm, worm, worm, reef worm.

A healthy coral reef flaunts its diversity and sheer abundance of life to anyone who sticks their head in the water and looks. Even more life is small and hidden away within the reef's recesses, requiring more careful looking. Nature photographer David Liittschwager created an intimate view of reef life when he nestled a square metal frame, each side one foot long, onto a reef in Moʻorea in French Polynesia. He then catalogued and photographed every living organism visible to the naked eye that swam, crawled, or floated through that cubic foot of water during the course of a day. His crowded, composite image shows just how much life exists, even in one small space on a reef.

---

*The global area of tropical corals is approximately 110,000 square miles.

The unique biodiversity alone makes coral reefs supremely important parts of the living planet, and there are many other reasons they matter. In purely economic terms, coral reefs are a global asset estimated to generate close to $3 trillion each year in goods and services, roughly equal to the global commercial banking sector. Reefs support tourism outfits and attract visitors from all around the world who want to experience these dazzling ecosystems. The value of reefs lies in plenty besides tourism revenues. Coral reefs hug coastlines and guard them against storms and erosion; they form nurseries for fish and other animals that are caught in surrounding seas, and they create untold, deep cultural connections to the communities that have always lived alongside them. Reefs are central to the lives of coastal people across the tropics. Worldwide, more than one hundred million people live within an hour's walk of a coral reef; close to a billion people live within sixty miles. Most of these people live in low- and middle-income countries, and the security of their food, livelihoods, and homes is directly underpinned by healthy reefs. These are the people whose lives are being transformed as the world's reefs change.

Much has changed on Belize's coral reefs in the years since I got to know them. I feel a mix of emotions knowing that the first coral reefs I ever studied are not there anymore, not in a form that I would recognise from my first tropical dives. I've come to appreciate how lucky I was, belonging to one of the last generations of young marine biologists who studied coral reefs without a looming sense of the ocean unravelling. That note from my dive logbook about bleaching shows how differently I was thinking about reefs then compared to now.

Guilt has since caught up with me for my contributions to the downfall of reefs. I have flown across the ocean many times, playing my part as a rich visitor, leaving trails of carbon in the skies. And for a long while, I carelessly assumed the biggest changes in the ocean still lay way off in some unspecified point in the future. It's obvious now that reef life was already shifting and altering around me; it just took me time to realise what was happening.

There are still coral reefs in Belize, but they're very different than they used to be. For more than a million years, reefs in the Caribbean were dominated by a small set of stony coral species that grew fast and created the ecosystem's complex limestone architecture. Staghorn and elkhorn corals, reaching their branches skywards in dense thickets, and massive boulders of *Orbicella* all played their key parts in building reefs. Over the past few decades, these foundational species have dramatically declined. In their place are smaller corals that grow much more slowly and don't lay down as much reef-building limestone. There are also sponges and soft corals, which don't make stiff limestone skeletons but grow in colourful fronds, fans, and feather dusters that sway and thrum in the current. Large seaweeds take up more space on reefs than they used to. These are novel ecosystems assembled by species that are coping with gradual environmental change as well as the sharp and increasingly common catastrophes that the ocean in the Anthropocene is delivering.

Across the region, many coral reefs are doing just as badly as those in Belize. In the past thirty years, corals on three-quarters of reefs across the Caribbean have declined. In 1998, mass bleaching killed off 8 per cent of the world's stony corals. The survivors set about rebuilding the damaged ecosystems, releasing larvae, which settled and grew. It took ten years for reefs to regain their coral cover, but it didn't last long. In the following decade (2009–18), at least 14 per cent of stony corals worldwide were killed—that's more than all the corals currently living on Australia's reefs. This century, coral cover on tropical reefs has been episodically ratcheting further and further down.

The lost corals were blasted, smothered, and poisoned, eaten by outbreaks of crown-of-thorns starfish, snapped off for aquarium displays, and killed by diseases. Most of all, though, coral reefs are getting sucker-punched by the climate crisis from all directions. Hurricanes are becoming more powerful and more likely to flatten reefs. Heat-stressed corals are more vulnerable to sickness and disease. Warming seas are losing oxygen, which in many places is stressing corals and will likely get a lot worse in the years ahead.

Mass coral bleaching kills corals across hundreds and thousands of square miles of reef within a matter of months. Most worrying are outbreaks that impact entire regions. In the summer of 2023, reefs yet again bleached throughout the Caribbean, from Cuba and Mexico to Costa Rica and Colombia. That year, an ocean heat-wave in Florida drove sea surface temperatures above one hundred degrees Fahrenheit for the first time on record, and coral bleaching was devastating.

The heatwaves that trigger mass bleaching are striking worldwide more frequently, giving corals less time in between to recover. The Great Barrier Reef was hit by mass coral bleaching in 1998, 2002, 2016, 2017, 2020, and 2022. The 2022 event was the first to occur in a year when the Pacific Ocean was not expected to be so hot. In past years, mass bleaching was only likely in association with a strong El Niño, the periodic climatic phenomenon that pushes up sea temperatures over large tracts of the ocean, which climate change is making more frequent and intense. The cooler phase, La Niña, used to offer corals respite. But now mass bleaching can happen in any hot summer, regardless of which part of the El Niño–La Niña cycle the world is in.

Reefs also have to contend with another climate impact caused by humanity's carbon dioxide emissions absorbing into the ocean, caus-ing the pH of seawater to fall. This ocean acidification is reducing the availability of dissolved carbonate ions in seawater, the molecules that corals need to build their limestone skeletons. Other import-ant organisms also need a good supply of carbonate ions to grow, including algae that incorporate limestone in their tissues and grow in pink and orange crusts over reefs, like layers of thick paint. Stony corals are the bricks that form a reef's foundation, and encrusting coralline algae is the cement that binds the framework together.

To better understand what could happen to reefs in a warmer, more acidic ocean, scientists in Australia have built multiple miniature patch reefs in eighty-gallon aquarium tanks in a laboratory. They carefully assembled diverse mixes of corals and seaweeds, fishes, sponges, sea cucumbers, and other animals. Then they wound the clock forwards and exposed these mini-reefs to conditions predicted for the end of the century. The experiment ran for a year and a half, in which time some corals fared better than others. The winners were coral species that live as solitary polyps and don't have chunky limestone skeletons. The losers were coral species responsible for building the limestone reef structures. They were impacted most when bathed in seawater that was not only warmer but also more acidic. Living in these conditions, they grew weaker skeletons—a coral equivalent of osteoporosis. This foretells of times ahead, possibly for thousands of years to come, when wild reefs may not be able to keep pace with rising seas and won't grow upwards fast enough to stay living in the sunniest shallow waters. Reef-building species of stony corals can't survive well in deeper waters because there's not enough sunlight for their zooxanthellae to grow and supply their food. Even though they are ocean-dwelling animals, coral reefs can drown.

The endgame for coral reefs as we know them could come when there's nowhere left in shallow seas with the right chemistry to allow stony corals and encrusting algae to grow. Instead of building and maintaining their limestone ramparts, reefs could start dissolving. Predictions of when this could happen remain highly uncertain. It could be as soon as 2030 or perhaps not until midway through the twenty-second century.

All these threats combine to depict the future of coral reefs in various shades of gloom. These are without doubt some of the world's most vulnerable ecosystems. Coral reefs are also some of the best-studied parts of the ocean. Thousands of scientists are staring gimlet-eyed at reefs and attempting to understand how and why these ecosystems are transforming. And yet, there are still reasons to be hopeful.

Surveys in 2022 recorded the highest overall cover of coral on parts of the Great Barrier Reef in thirty-six years of monitoring, despite repeated bouts of bleaching and outbreaks of crown-of-thorns starfish. A few reefs were almost entirely covered in sprawling colonies of corals.

Generally, heatwaves don't strike everywhere, all at once, with equal intensity, so while some reefs are getting stressed out and overheated, others remain cooler and healthier. Also, some reefs cope better than others with being baked at high temperatures, likely because of their past experiences. The thermal history of a reef matters. Those that have lived through previous temperature spikes seem less likely to bleach than others that haven't undergone such extremes, partly because the most vulnerable corals are already dead. Among the survivors are signs that corals are toughening up and beginning to adapt to their warming ocean. In Palau, a cluster of remote islands in the western Pacific, reefs are apparently becoming more heat tolerant. A heatwave in 2010 caused widespread bleaching but seven years later, when similar hot conditions returned, there was little to no coral bleaching. For now, scientists haven't determined why Palau's corals are surviving heat better: if individual corals are acclimatizing or if there are genetic shifts taking place. On reefs in Panama, *Pocillopora* corals, which look like little cauliflowers, have been coping better with heatwaves as time has gone by. The key to their survival has been an alteration in the varieties of zooxanthellae living inside their bodies. They switch their algae for a more heat-tolerant variety that naturally occurs in the sea, and it makes them less inclined to bleach when the temperature rises. There are also broader hints that corals are adapting. Globally, since the 1990s, the average temperature that triggers the onset of mass bleaching has increased by a half degree Celsius.

Amid the dark shadows on today's reefs, there are bright spots. Twenty years' worth of underwater surveys on three thousand tropical reefs reveal a few dozen that shine out and are in a healthier condition than expected, based on a variety of factors that influence coral cover, such as water depth, hurricane damage, and the temperature regime. Bright spots are dotted across the globe, from reefs in Cauca on the Pacific coast of Colombia to Maui in Hawai'i, from Okinawa in southern Japan to Kien Giang off southwestern Vietnam; others are located in New Caledonia, the Philippines, Indonesia, and Malaysia, on the Andaman Sea coast of Myanmar, and in Ari Atoll in the Maldives. These reefs are doing better than the local conditions would seem to allow—and creating more room for hope.

Tropical reefs in shallow seas are critically important and frighteningly threatened, but they're only a part of the story of the world's coral reefs. A new vision for the future of coral reefs is emerging in parts of the ocean that are challenging to get to and that I've never visited. Often I've hovered beside steep walls of coral, gazed into the yawning blue below, and felt a strong urge to carry on down. I've seen giant fans and tall spirals of coral twisting up from the reef below. Shoals of fish have swooped overhead, then raced into the depths and out of sight. I've watched sea snakes wind their way to the surface to catch a breath before plunging back down beneath me, drawing curves through the water, and always I've resisted the temptation to follow them. Cumulatively, I've logged many days' worth of scuba dives, but I've spent fewer than fifteen minutes of my life diving deeper than 130 feet. Much deeper, and I would get drunk on the nitrogen in the compressed air I'm breathing or fall unconscious from the toxic high pressure of oxygen. But coral reefs don't stop at 130 feet, and an increasing number of diving scientists don't either.

To unlock these depths, divers use equipment known as closed-circuit rebreathers, which instead of bubbling air into the water, as with a standard scuba kit, divers rebreathe their exhalations over and over. The technology was pioneered in the 1970s with a system called the Electrolung. A diver's breaths are circulated through a scrubber to remove exhaled carbon dioxide and past an electronic sensor that monitors the gases and automatically keeps the oxygen at a safe level, topping up as necessary from a small cylinder. It's critical to breathe not too much or too little oxygen; either can make a diver pass out, which quickly becomes lethal a long way underwater. Tragically, that does still sometimes happen. More scientists are undertaking the long training regime to use this technical equipment as safely as possible. Like pilots learning to fly an aeroplane, rebreather divers first learn how to do it, then log many hours of supervised diving time. Once fully qualified, divers can go on very long, very deep dives, lasting four or five hours, as far as five hundred feet down, allowing them to plunge into this indigo realm in bubble-free tranquillity and explore a region of coral reefs that used to be almost entirely out of bounds.

Between one hundred and five hundred feet down is the mesophotic zone. Here lie coral ecosystems that continue from shallower reefs and transition into a space that's shared by species from nearer the surface and others that are found only deeper down. It lies in between the sunny surface seas and the dark "deep sea" proper, where sunlight is too weak to power photosynthesis. In the mesophotic, meaning "middle light," there's still just enough illumination for living organisms to use. Seaweeds grow in the upper reaches of mesophotic reefs, their pigments adapted to absorb the faint remnants of light seeping down. Stony corals with zooxanthellae inside their bodies grow to at least 210 feet down. Deeper in the mesophotic grow other types of corals that don't have symbiotic algal partners to draw food from and instead entirely feed themselves. These include black corals with dark, shiny skeletons and octocorals that grab minute prey from the water with their eight-tentacled polyps. The mesophotic is the zone where coral ecosystems switch from being dependent on sunlight to surviving in semi-darkness.

Compared to the well-studied, scuba-accessible shallows, very little is known about the mesophotic zone. Nevertheless, the reefs here are clearly important, since they cover a far larger area of habitat than all shallow reefs combined. The Great Barrier Reef likely has an equivalent area of reef below one hundred feet as above. Globally, around 80 per cent of potential coral-reef habitat lies in the mesophotic. Of those reefs, only a small subset has been explored and studied so far, and enough is already known to show such reefs support unique biodiversity, of a composition unlike anywhere else in the ocean.

The mesophotic contains fish species that nobody has seen before. For every hour a rebreather diver spends searching the lower parts of this zone, they find an average of two species of fish that are new to science. Many of the deep-only species seem to occupy a small geographical range; they live only in one tiny part of the ocean, which for reef fish is unusual. Many mesophotic fish have stunning colours and patterns, like the rose-veiled fairy wrasse,* which lives on reefs more than two hundred feet underwater on the coral atolls of the Maldives, with its crimson-dipped head, golden body, and cobalt-fringed fins. The latigo fairy wrasse was found in the mesophotic zone beneath one of the busiest shipping lanes in the Philippines; this fish has pinstripes across its face and a metallic blue spot on its dorsal fin, and the male of the species has a scintillating, iridescent tail and long, whiplike pelvic fins, which he flicks in eye-catching displays put on for potential mates and rival males. On Kure Atoll in the Northwestern Hawai'ian Islands, 300 feet down, lives Obama's basslet, a

---

* *Cirrhilabrus finifenmaa. Finifenmaa* means "rose" in the Maldivian Dhivehi language. This was one of the first species found and described in the Maldives by a Maldivian researcher.

small fish with a yellowish-pink body and a thin, bright-yellow line running through its eyes. It was named in honour of President Barack Obama and his efforts to preserve the natural environment. A few weeks after the fish's discovery, Obama announced the expansion of the Papahānaumokuākea Marine National Monument, which now encompasses the Obama's basslets' deep-water home.

Scientists are also finding some incredibly healthy and vibrant coral reefs in the mesophotic. In Tahiti, in 2021, divers visited a previously unknown reef, two miles long and between one hundred and two hundred feet deep, where colonies of coral cover every available piece of the seabed. Seen from above, they look like great piles of spiral shavings from carefully sharpened pencils. And these corals showed no signs of the mass coral bleaching that swept through the region three years earlier.

Reefs like these have spawned the hopeful idea that the mesophotic zone could be safe from the worst impacts of the Anthropocene, a deep oasis hidden away from troubles concentrated nearer the surface. Generally, the deeper underwater, the colder and darker it gets, so it stands to reason that deeper reefs are less likely to suffer from heatwaves and coral bleaching (light intensity and heat are both triggers for bleaching). Mesophotic reefs also lie deep enough to avoid getting smashed apart by hurricanes, and they lie below the reach of some methods of fishing.

Deeper reefs are indeed showing they can be less vulnerable to the climate crisis than their stressed, overheated neighbours above. Near to where divers found the deep reef in Tahiti, scientists studied two other French Polynesian reefs during a mass coral bleaching in 2019. Off both Moʻorea and Makatea islands, the proportion of bleached coral colonies declined dramatically with depth.* Below two hundred feet, there was almost no bleaching at all.

---

*These are only the corals that normally have algae symbionts; azooxanthellate corals can't bleach.

In some cases, though, thermal relief in the deep may be only temporary. In the 2016 heatwave on the Great Barrier Reef, fewer corals bleached in the upper parts of the mesophotic, at around 130 feet, compared to the shallows, because a cool current from below happened to sweep in while the heatwave was at its peak. At other times of year, the difference in temperature between the surface and deeper water is not as notable. Future heatwaves may not be so well timed.

As deep-diving scientists have gotten to know the mesophotic better, they've been exploring another promising possibility for the future of coral reefs. Perhaps these deeper, healthier reefs could come to the rescue of damaged reefs at the surface. Just as mangrove seeds floating from intact forests can help regenerate damaged areas, mesophotic corals and fishes could perform a similar service, although only if certain conditions prevail. First, there need to be species that span the boundary between mesophotic and shallow reefs. Depending on where in the world they look, scientists are finding depth generalist species among the corals. For instance, surveys in American Samoa have found almost two hundred coral species that live on shallow reefs, a dozen that live only in the mesophotic below one hundred feet, and sixty-three that occupy both zones. But the deeper corals will be of use to the shallower reefs only if the populations are mixing. It's no use if mesophotic corals keep to themselves, and their eggs and larvae don't venture nearer to the surface. Indeed, genetic studies are showing that some coral species do not mix, essentially subdividing populations by depth. This could be because physical barriers get in their way, such as currents sweeping down and not up, or there may be limits in how far the eggs and larvae move before settling, so they never make it to shallower reefs.

Fish have the possibility of roaming up and down throughout their lives between the mesophotic and the surface, and so they could use the greater depths to escape fisheries in shallower seas. In the Pacific, around the Mariana Islands, giant humphead wrasse, up to six feet long, are caught by divers spearfishing near the surface. More of them now live in mesophotic reefs than on shallower reefs, suggesting that the greater depths act as a de facto marine reserve and could become a last stand for this highly endangered species.

Exactly how important mesophotic reefs could be in helping shallower reefs recover remains uncertain. Scientists who dive frequently in the mesophotic are convinced these are distinct ecosystems, wholly separate from their shallow neighbours. What's more, they're seeing that the mesophotic is not in fact beyond the reach of human impacts. Invasive lionfish released in the Caribbean Sea have already spread into mesophotic reefs, potentially shifting the balance of these ecosystems. Hurricanes may not directly smash deeper corals, but storm-stirred debris and landslides can slump down steep slopes and smother ecosystems below. Plastic debris builds up at higher concentrations deeper underwater on coral reefs, peaking in the mesophotic, likely because stronger wave energy in the shallows sweeps plastics away, but when they rain down into the calmer depths, they tend to stay there. Many fisheries already exploit the mesophotic. Black corals in the mesophotic have been stripped out for the jewellery trade.

Regardless of how well connected they are to shallower seas, mesophotic reefs very much matter in their own right, for the ecosystems they harbour and the threats they face. And for now, they are poorly protected. Conservation plans for coral reefs are just beginning to include those at greater depths. Belize has long been a pioneer in protecting its seas and coasts. A century ago, in the 1920s, long before conservation went mainstream, the government set up a sanctuary on Half Moon Caye to safeguard the large colonies of nesting red-footed boobies. In 1982, it became the first marine protected area in Belize and in the whole of Central America. The country now has one of the most extensive networks of marine protected areas in the Caribbean. In 2019, the government tripled the highly protected no-take zones so they cover almost 12 per cent of the nation's waters, including extensive areas of mesophotic reefs.

Marine reserves are important for the health of coral reefs for many reasons: they can prevent the smashing of corals by anchors, trawlers, and dredgers, and they can help reef fish populations recover from overfishing and boost catches in nearby fisheries. But they won't be enough to guarantee that coral reefs survive unscathed throughout the Anthropocene ocean. They're just not cut out to hold back the problems that threaten reefs the most.

A two-decade study in Belize surveyed fifteen sites across the reefs and found that stony corals declined by just the same amount inside and outside reserves. During the twenty-year time span, Belizean reefs were struck twice by mass coral bleaching, devastated by an outbreak of yellow-band disease, and hit by seven hurricanes. All these problems are linked to the climate crisis, and none of them paid any attention to the watery boundaries of marine reserves. Several other studies have similarly found no great difference in bleaching on protected versus unprotected reefs in other parts of the world.

It's possible that, given enough time and enforcement of fishing regulations, coral reefs inside marine reserves will become healthier, and some will be more resilient and better able to recover from the grimmest global threats. Early theories predicted that protecting reefs from fishing pressure would help corals thrive. Parrotfish have been thought to play a key part in reef health. Like their rainforest namesakes, these fish have dazzling colours, and their teeth are arranged in a sharp, beaklike form. They graze reefs, scraping surfaces clear of large seaweeds that could outcompete corals, overshadow and abrade young corals, and even poison them with toxic chemicals. It was generally thought that allowing parrotfish and other grazing fish to rebound inside reserves would help corals survive. But that theory hasn't been playing out neatly on reefs, and simplistic links between fishes, seaweeds, and corals may be weak, inconsistent, or nonexistent. That's not to say that fish are inconsequential for reef health, just that they can't be expected to bear the burden of saving reefs in the Anthropocene.

Even the most isolated and healthy reefs, such as those in the Chagos Archipelago in the central Indian Ocean, have been brutally hit by coral bleaching. In 1998, mass bleaching struck corals in the Chagos, and as happened elsewhere in the world, the reefs recovered, and corals regrew over the following decade. Then, in 2015 and 2016, while Pacific kelp forests were withering under the disastrous heatwave known as the Blob, sea temperatures were also rising across the tropics, and the reefs of Chagos suffered massive back-to-back bleaching events. For two years running, corals lost their colour, and the seascape faded to white. Close to 90 per cent of the dense thickets and wide tables of *Acropora* coral were killed.

Those scorching years were unprecedented. The destruction they caused was a huge wake-up call for scientists and conservationists, who watched as countless reefs bleached and corals died, including those in supposedly well-protected waters.

Still, there are glimmers of hope. In the Chagos Archipelago, when the reefs were struck by bleaching in 2016, a smaller portion of the corals died than in the previous year, suggesting the survivors had become more resistant to rising temperatures. And some reefs in Chagos are recovering faster than others, thanks in part to seabirds. On islands where tropicbirds, boobies, shearwaters, and frigate birds come to nest, nutrients from their droppings splatter on the ground and get washed out to sea. This runoff fertilises nearby reefs and encourages the growth of encrusting coralline algae, which cements reefs together and creates suitable surfaces for young corals to settle on. Long ago, visiting sailors released rats on some islands in the archipelago, and these rodent invaders have a keen appetite for seabird eggs. Rat-infested islands now have no seabird colonies and no nourishing guano. De-ratting islands is one approach to help restore seabird colonies and give recovering reefs an added boost.

Such efforts will likely contribute to reef health on a small scale, but ultimately the fate of coral reefs will be determined by how quickly heatwaves come along. As the interval between heatwaves shrinks, the less time reef ecosystems have to recover between the mass bleaching events they trigger. And the only way to limit the frequency and intensity of heatwaves is to limit greenhouse gases in the atmosphere.

Coral reef researchers and conservationists may differ in their opinions over what to do about the coral crisis—whether marine reserves are the key, for instance, and whether parrotfish really help—but on one matter, everybody agrees. The most hopeful version of reefs in the future will happen only if carbon emissions are drastically cut. Climate and ocean experts at the Intergovernmental Panel on Climate Change forecast that if humanity continues with business as usual, coral reefs as we know them today will mostly be gone by century's end. If global temperature rise can be kept below 1.5 degrees Celsius, then maybe as much as one-third of corals stand a chance of surviving. And as the chances diminish that emissions will be driven down fast and far enough, more scientists and conservationists are deciding that the time has come to make alternative plans to try to keep corals and their reefs intact.

A few years ago, behind the scenes at a public aquarium in Florida, I learned that corals have a strong, distinctive smell. The aquarist who was showing me around pulled out a fist-size branching colony from a gurgling tank of seawater and waved it under my nose. It smelt like turpentine, and I tried to imagine the stink that wafts from a reef full of corals, all of them exuding chemicals as predator deterrents.

In that aquarium were two dozen species of Floridian corals, among them emerald-green cactus corals, brain corals, staghorn and

HELEN SCALES

elkhorn corals. I peered at fuzzy brown dots of new baby corals that
were just a few weeks old, born when their parents had been placed
together in a bucket at new moon and had spawned. Seen up close,
with their peculiar coralline commingling of animal and stone, all
these corals seemed robust. And yet, a pile of dead, white skeletons
on the floor was proof of how sensitive they can be. Those corals had
all bleached and died because an aquarist had moved them around
their tank into spots where the illuminating lamps were a fraction
brighter. The coral colonies weren't accustomed to so much light,
and it killed them.

The aquarium staff were growing corals not only to put on display to the public but to send to scientists who are working out
how to keep them alive and encourage them to reproduce. Some of
the corals I saw may have ended up being planted out in the wild.
The number of coral restoration projects has been exponentially
increasing as more efforts are made to breathe life back into damaged
ecosystems. They aim to boost the cover of stony corals as the key
metric for reef health and something that can be manually improved.
A popular technique is to chip off small nubbins of branching corals from healthy colonies and transplant them onto degraded areas,
cementing or tying them in place on the seabed. Propagating corals
in aquariums is another way to do it.

As the ocean becomes hotter and more acidic, reef restorationists
increasingly want corals that have been engineered to survive the
Anthropocene. Designer, future-proof corals are not a pipe dream.
In laboratories, scientists have already begun to enhance the ability of
corals to withstand heat. One approach for toughening them up is a
process known as experimental or assisted evolution. At its heart is an
ancient practice that humans have been performing for millennia, in
the way that our ancestors bred crops and domesticated animals. This
involves selecting the animals or plants that have characteristics of
greatest interest—the strongest horses, the biggest ears of wheat, the
cutest puppies—then having those individuals breed and pass on their

qualities to the next generation, and repeat. In the Anthropocene, generations of wild corals have the potential to adapt naturally to their changing environment, but it's unlikely to happen fast enough for them to escape extinction. This is why scientists are working to speed up the process by breeding more heat-tolerant corals. Hybridisation is another old technique that's being brought into play for corals. Pairing up different wild species can result in hybrid offspring that are fitter than either of their parents.

Breeding and evolving corals in captivity through multiple generations takes time, partly because spawning naturally occurs only once a year for many corals. Researchers are largely focusing instead on the rich mix of microbes living on and inside corals, which grow and reproduce much faster than the corals themselves. Important targets are the symbiotic algae that live inside corals and influence how sensitive they are to bleaching. Conveniently, zooxanthellae survive well outside corals and can be cultured in laboratories, where they divide and produce a new generation within a matter of days. Experimental evolution of zooxanthellae has already led to some impressive results. Over the course of one year, researchers incrementally raised the temperature in a culture of zooxanthellae; at each stage, they picked out strains that were surviving and growing best, then turned up the heat some more and repeated the process, again and again. By the end, they had zooxanthellae that were growing well at temperatures over ninety-three degrees Fahrenheit.

The next step is to see whether these experimentally evolved algae can help corals survive the heat. Corals in the wild naturally shuffle and switch their algae, and they can be nudged to do the same in captivity. In one study, young corals were given heatproof zooxanthellae, and after ten months at 80.6 degrees Fahrenheit, they had grown to twice the size of other corals with the wild-type algae. Then the researchers simulated a heatwave, cranking up the temperature in the experimental aquariums to 87.8 degrees

Fahrenheit for forty-one days, and watched as the corals with regular zooxanthellae bleached. The corals with the heat-evolved variety stayed colourful and survived.

Manipulating other parts of the corals' microbiome can also help boost their health and resilience. Just as humans have communities of microbes living inside our bodies, without which we can't live healthy lives, so do corals. A coral's microbiome includes bacteria, viruses, and microscopic fungi, which protect them from stress and disease by providing vitamins, antioxidants, and antimicrobial compounds. This opens the possibility of performing the coral equivalent of faecal transplants in humans, a successful therapy that involves a healthy person donating samples of gut microbes, which are then used to inoculate people suffering from various gastrointestinal disorders. It is not yet a standard procedure for coral reefs, but there are signs that it could work, even with transplants conducted within the same reef.

Off the island of Phuket in Thailand, divers collected fragments of naturally heat-resistant corals that grow on reef flats where the shallow waters get periodically simmered by the sun at low tide. Scientists stripped off the living tissue from these coral samples and used the resulting slurry to inoculate other, more sensitive corals that had been growing in gentler conditions on the reef. These inoculations made the corals substantially more heat-resistant when researchers dialled up the temperature in their tanks. Genetic tests suggest that particular strains of bacteria were transferred and fortified the corals. A goal for this kind of research is to culture probiotic treatments that would give corals the right blend of bacteria in their microbiomes to help them survive at higher temperatures.

A new and no doubt tempting molecular tool already available to coral restorationists is gene editing. CRISPR* technology involves cutting and pasting specific sections of DNA code, making it

---

*CRISPR stands for Clustered Regularly Interspaced Short Palindromic Repeats.

possible to create designer organisms with desirable genes added in or unwanted genes cut out. Experts have not yet deployed this technology to engineer corals, but they are using it to better understand what makes some corals particularly tough.

A breakthrough came in 2020, when a team led by researchers at Stanford University used CRISPR to identify a gene that plays a critical part in corals' resistance to heat stress. They cut out this gene, known as heat shock transcription factor 1 (HSF1), from coral larvae. Without HSF1, the larvae became much more susceptible to rising heat, indicating this gene does something important in protecting corals from heat stress, although at this stage no one knows exactly what. Pasting more copies of the HSF1 gene into coral genomes could potentially boost their resistance, although there are likely other genes involved, all interacting in ways that scientists have yet to untangle.

CRISPR could also be used to find genes involved in other aspects of coral health, including their tolerance to acidification, pollutants, and pathogens. A promising place to look for these is among the corals' many highly usual genes, known as unigenes. These are so unlike all known gene sequences in other living organisms, it's impossible to predict what they do.* Unigenes could potentially boost coral health via mechanisms that don't exist in other organisms, and they could give researchers a whole new way of understanding what makes corals tick.

In the past few years, spurred on by the accelerating impacts of ocean warming, major research programmes have started exploring what technologies have to offer the future of reefs. An Australian initiative, with a budget of AUD$92 million, began in 2020 to investigate

---

*Many genes are similar enough among different organisms that, from the DNA sequence alone, geneticists can tell if it's a gene for, say, light receptors in a retina or a skin pigment cell. But this is not the case with unigenes.

various options to help the Great Barrier Reef resist, adapt, and recover from the climate crisis. These tactics range from biologically engineering heatproof corals to geoengineering methods that would dim sunlight above reefs by creating mists or fogs of seawater or releasing blankets of bubbles.

Scientists will identify the most promising methods to save as many as possible of the thousands of reefs and islands that make up the Great Barrier Reef and then, it is hoped, apply them to reefs in other parts of the world. But there's no guarantee any of these efforts will work, which is one reason a backup plan of sorts is running alongside these research programmes. For a site on the coast of northern Queensland, architects have designed an eye-catching circular building, inspired by *Fungia* corals, which look like upside-down mushrooms. The building will become a living coral biobank, filled with aquariums in which every one of the world's eight hundred or so species of stony corals will be kept in safe isolation from the Anthropocene ocean.

Elsewhere, coral species are gathered up, and their cells, sperm, and eggs are frozen. It's a similar scheme to seed banks, which aim to preserve all the world's plants, so people in the future can use them to breed the crops they need or replant species that are lost from the wild. Coral DNA is also being sequenced and archived to preserve the genetic codes that would be lost forever if those species went extinct. And for a growing collection of species, extinction is becoming a distinct possibility. The last full assessment, in 2008, showed that one-third of all stony corals are threatened with extinction. In the Caribbean, twenty-six coral species are now placed in the Red List's most high-risk category, Critically Endangered. This includes pillar coral, a species that used to grow in fingerlike colonies all along the Mesoamerican Reef, from Florida to Trinidad and Tobago, but it's being wiped out, like many other Caribbean corals, by the newly arrived and catchily named stony coral tissue loss disease, which can infect hundreds of feet of reef in a single day.

Biobanking and cryopreservation are pragmatic options for corals. The information contained in preserved tissues and genetic codes could prove useful for future restoration in ways nobody has thought of yet. However, none of these projects are cure-alls for sick reefs, and crucially, efforts must continue to slash carbon emissions and prevent damage to and demolition of more ecosystems. While the belief that technology can fix the troubles of the living planet is alluring, the animals won't come marching back, two by two, and the ocean isn't going to simply bounce back to normal. It will take gargantuan endeavours to avoid a dystopian future where all that's left of the wild ocean are genetic and digital memories locked away in archives on land of once diverse and complex ecosystems.

While scientists are busy engineering corals and testing other solutions to help ensure reef building continues into the Anthropocene, even greater technological challenges are still to come. To have any meaningful effect in the ocean, the scale of coral-reef restoration will need to massively expand. Reef restoration has so far typically been done on a microscale, with projects operating across hundreds of square yards of reef. The problem is that, just in the past decade, warming seas and bleaching have devastated thousands of square miles of reef.

Current methods of reef restoration are immensely labour-intensive. Most rely on scuba divers installing structures underwater and fixing onto them coral fragments and colonies. Entire armies of well-meaning scuba-diving tourists lending a hand wouldn't be enough to scale up restoration efforts.

To go global, reef restoration will need a techno-centric transformation on par with the industrialisation of agriculture. Steps in the process would need to be mechanised and automated. Machinery could prepare the seabed—much as tractors prepare fields for planting crops—clearing away loose coral rubble or spraying bio-glues to bind up loose material that would otherwise abrade and smother small coral recruits. Other machinery could sense and forecast when remaining healthy coral reefs are spawning, then swoop in to scoop up floating slicks of coral larvae, including millions that wouldn't survive anyway because they would drift into open seas, and deliver them to depleted reefs.

Coral factories on land, or perhaps floating out at sea, will need to churn out many varieties of heat-tolerant colonies. To maximise their chances of survival, the young corals will need to be carefully planted out, perhaps with the kinds of precision techniques that are now being introduced to agriculture. Rather than homogenising the landscape by planting endless acres of monoculture and spraying entire fields with fertilisers and pesticides, precision farming involves working at a much finer resolution—for example, autonomous robots deliver water and fertiliser to individual plants and, equipped with artificial intelligence, accurately determine whether a plant is diseased and needs dosing with pesticides.

It's not beyond the bounds of reality to imagine fleets of underwater robots scanning the topography of an area of seabed and making decisions about the best places to plant corals. The robots could select a coral species from its onboard manifest, locate a spot with exactly the right light and angle for it to grow well, fix it in place with a squeeze of quick-setting eco-cement, give it a dab of probiotic treatment, and then move on to the next one. The underwater robots could work in synchrony with drones at the surface that spray fine mists of seawater into the skies to reflect the sun's heat and cool the sea while the new corals are settling in below.

This would require bespoke technologies to be developed, because no existing devices are available to do the job. The remote-operated underwater vehicles in current use by ocean scientists were originally developed by the oil and gas industry to work on offshore drilling rigs in deep, calm waters. Scientists have also built autonomous vehicles that steer themselves through the deep ocean gathering data. These machines would likely struggle to navigate around the rugged topography and turbulent waters of shallow coral reefs just a few yards below the surface, let alone to be dexterous enough to manipulate individual coral colonies.

Given enough funding, teams of engineers and scientists could no doubt invent technologies to make large-scale coral restoration a reality, but financing will not be straightforward. Restoration projects for other habitats, such as mangroves and terrestrial forests, are commonly funded by carbon-trading and offsetting schemes. But coral reefs are not substantial enough carbon sinks to be traded on blue carbon markets.* An alternative for funding reef restoration is to tap into the value the reefs hold in protecting coastlines from storms and flooding. Globally, tropical storms are the most common and costliest natural disasters, and healthy coral reefs are one of the most effective natural barriers against storm impacts. Just in the United States and its territories, coral reefs fringe close to two thousand miles of at-risk, low-lying coasts, including in Florida, Hawai'i, American Samoa, Puerto Rico, and Guam. These reefs help protect tens of thousands of lives and save an estimated US$1.8 billion each year that would otherwise be needed to repair storm-damaged homes, commercial buildings, and infrastructure. A possibility that has yet to be fully explored would be to divert some of the billions spent on mitigating coastal hazards—building flood defences, for instance—towards coral restoration.

Money could be raised some other way, perhaps through a new mechanism to capture the economic value of the very existence of

---

*Following the example of terrestrial carbon offsetting schemes, blue carbon is a term applied to the carbon sequestered by marine ecosystems, such as mangrove forests and seagrass meadows. Blue carbon credits can be created when areas of habitat are protected or restored, and the credits traded by greenhouse gas offsetting programmes. Major forest carbon offsets on land have come under heavy criticism for being largely worthless for the environment and potentially making global heating worse.

species and biodiversity, or by using the fund that richer nations are pledging to assist lower-income nations to adapt to climate change. However it's done, a restoration economy for coral reefs would raise some deep ethical issues.

The damage to coral reefs lies front and centre among the global injustices of the changing ocean. Most people who depend on coral reefs for their food and livelihoods, and to protect their homes and coasts, live in countries that contribute the least to global carbon emissions. The climate crisis that's killing corals and devastating reefs is caused by carbon emitted by nations that, for the most part, don't have their own tropical reefs. There are a few exceptions, notably the United States with its Floridian and Hawai'ian reefs, and Australia with its Great Barrier Reef. Both nations are technological leaders in coral-reef restoration and are devoting considerable resources to research and development.* This means that if restoration is to be rolled out more widely, it will inevitably require a one-way flow of technological know-how, as well as financing and labour, from high-income nations where most research is happening, to low- and middle-income nations where most of the world's coral reefs exist.

Reef restorationists will need to avoid unintentionally repeating mistakes made over the centuries by colonialists who imposed their ideas of how the natural world should be managed and used, and how it should look. Colonial powers dramatically transformed landscapes and rearranged the world's biodiversity by introducing animals and plants to hunt, rear, and cultivate, or even simply to remind them of home. Reef restorationists aren't proposing anything as preposterous as bringing rabbits and camels to Australia or English house sparrows to the United States, but they will make decisions about the future of reefs. And the outcome could look very different depending on who gets to make those decisions.

---

*While at the same time not devoting nearly enough resources, many critics say, to reducing the nations' carbon emissions.

Governments in countries with lucrative tourism industries might decide to pay to install heatproof reefs of a type that overseas visitors consider to be beautiful and worth flying around the world to see. These sorts of decisions are already being made—for instance, in Raja Ampat, Indonesia, a programme is underway to reintroduce zebra sharks to reefs where many shark species have been overfished and depleted. The choice of the zebra shark is based on several practical matters, including the fact that they breed well in captivity, and that their living egg cases can be easily moved from the aquariums where they were born and flown internationally to coral reefs on the other side of the world. Zebra sharks also happen to be attractive, with their rounded snouts and speckled skin, and they are docile and easy to see lying on the seabed, making them a favourite species among scuba divers. There's nothing inherently wrong with bringing back species that visitors want to see, and the approach can work. But these sorts of decisions will influence how reefs will be. It's hard to imagine reintroduction programmes attempting to boost local populations of species that diving tourists are more fearful of, say, or that they deem too ugly or boring.

When coral reefs fade to white, they dramatically reveal how the ocean is changing. Climate impacts play out in front of people's eyes from one day to the next, week to week. Bleaching reefs are impossible to ignore, and they deliver to us a sense of helplessness and desperation to do something, anything, to stop the damage from happening and go back to the way things were. Restoration fills that need to take action. What used to be a marginal patching-up of damaged parts of individual reefs is morphing into a global endeavour.

Not everybody agrees this is the best way forwards, and a battle for the soul of coral reefs is gathering pace. Some reef experts contend that it's already too late for any form of restoration because conditions in the ocean can no longer support reef growth as it was known a decade or two ago. Focus instead, they urge, on helping reefs, with their novel mixes of species, find a place in the Anthropocene ocean. Instead of concentrating on coral cover, consider other measures of reef health, such as the number of fish and amount of food they support, and the ability of these ecosystems to keep on functioning.

Many still advocate for reef protection, campaigning for more marine reserves, to ease the threats their watery boundaries can hold back. Others argue for techno-centric approaches to restoration—from biobanking to engineering heatproof corals—which are often judged to be the extreme solutions necessary to grapple with the existential threats to reefs. And yet these steps are labelled as radical because they involve cutting-edge technologies and deliberately changing coral biology, which carry inherent risks and dangers that something unforeseen could go wrong. Restoration is not a radical method for saving coral reefs because it can go only as far as fixing some of the symptoms of the Anthropocene, while it does nothing to address the source of the problems. A perversely chilling vision of the future sees engineered, heatproof coral reefs growing in countries that can afford them, while the ocean continues to heat and carbon emissions continue unabated. Restoration of reefs could still be deemed a success even if nothing at all is done about the climate crisis.

Unhitching humanity from business as usual, shifting the underlying drivers that cause so many problems, and finding new ways of living with the changing ocean is where truly radical views of the future lie.

Chapter 10
Living in the Future Ocean

The future of the ocean is not yet determined. What lies ahead will depend on how exactly the most critical changes in the climate play out—how hot the seas become, how fast and high they rise, how quickly oxygen ebbs and carbon climbs, how storms are stirred and where they strike. And it will depend on how humanity responds to the changes that are well underway, and the choices people make from this point forwards. A range of possibilities could still unfold, but plans are being laid down by entrepreneurs and industrialists, who are assembling their vision for the future and steering the ways people will live with and use the Anthropocene ocean.

Cities set adrift at sea or built underwater are science-fiction staples. Today architects are putting these imaginings into practice (although for now chiefly above the waterline) in places that could otherwise become unlivable. The construction of the world's first truly floating city is slated for the Maldives archipelago in the northern reaches of the Indian Ocean, a cluster of low-lying islands mostly standing less than three feet above current sea level. Candy-coloured houses will have picture windows overlooking a sparkling turquoise lagoon. People will stroll and cycle along sandy paths and over bridges connecting the city's hexagonal segments, which will link together like the honeycomb patterns of brain corals. The modular units are to be fixed to a massive underwater concrete structure screwed to the seabed with telescopic steel stilts, allowing the buildings to gently rise and fall with the waves. The city will float inside a five-hundred-acre lagoon bordered by sand barrier islands. For added protection, foam-glass structures will be fixed beneath the city for new corals to settle and grow on, perhaps transplanted from other reefs around the islands. Solar power for twenty thousand people will be harnessed within the city; sewage will be treated locally and used as compost for the displays of tropical flowers; instead of air conditioning, cool water will be pumped up from the deep sea into the lagoon.*

The Maldives' floating city could lead the way for more of this new kind of urban ocean living. This venture is a private-public partnership between a Dutch architectural firm and the Maldivian government, championed by former president and committed climate campaigner Mohamed Nasheed. In 2009, President Nasheed held an underwater cabinet meeting; he and his ministers, wearing scuba gear, knelt on the seabed writing on waterproof slates. They called on the rest of the world to help fight against climate change and save their vulnerable nation from drowning. Nasheed had also raised the possibility of purchasing land elsewhere to relocate the entire population, which has grown to more than a half million people. Now the focus is on finding ways to keep the Maldivian homeland, and if the building schedule goes according to plan, this first floating city will be up and running by 2027. Designers don't intend this to be a luxury tourist resort but a practical solution for living above rising seas. With a reported starting price of $150,000 for a studio apartment, international investors will no doubt snap up their slice of tropical paradise and the residence permit that will

---

*It's not entirely clear how the lagoon water can be cooled enough to make a difference for residents without chilling and killing off the corals at the same time.

be thrown in with it. Whether an average Maldivian fishing family will be able to raise enough capital is another matter.*

On the opposite side of the globe, efforts are already underway to clean up the plastic debris floating in the ocean. The Ocean Cleanup, a nonprofit organisation, was founded in 2013 by a then-teenage entrepreneur, Boylan Slat, from the Netherlands. Outraged by disastrous plastic pollution, Slat raised millions of dollars and began sending out ships towing U-shaped barriers to skim floating plastic from the infamous Great Pacific Garbage Patch. In April 2023, the Ocean Cleanup announced the removal of its two hundredth metric ton of plastic from this slowly spinning gyre. It's estimated that at least fourteen million metric tons of plastics enter the ocean every year. For that reason alone, we need to focus on reducing the production of plastics.

When it comes to cleaning up existing plastic pollution, many scientists and conservationists are worried about the method used to skim off floating plastics. The surface of the sea is a wide, flat ecosystem, home to a mix of delicate organisms that float and drift with the winds and currents. Many of these animals evolved to match the colour of their surroundings and are various shades of indigo and cobalt blue. *Velella* is a jelly-like creature with a little sail sticking up to catch the breeze; *Porpita* looks like a round blue button edged with a fringe of stinging tentacles; *Janthina janthina* are deep purple snails that hang down from the surface on frothy rafts of bubbles. On an eighty-day survey undertaken while sailing across the Pacific from Hawai'i to San Francisco, scientists found that these three blue animals live in the garbage patch. The same currents that sweep up the floating plastics also gather these animals together, and they occupy the same regions of the sea surface. It follows that scooping up plastics will likely scoop up these and other animals,

---

*According to the World Bank, the average gross domestic product (GDP) per capita in the Maldives in 2021 was just over $10,000.

threatening the survival of species—a form of unintentional bycatch equivalent to oceanic sharks getting snagged on longlines. These blue-tinted surface dwellers are important food for predators such as sea turtles and seabirds and form critical links to other ecosystems, which could be broken by plastic clean-up efforts. Experts caution that the impacts of plastic collectors on these living communities haven't been taken seriously enough or properly assessed. Meanwhile, investors are pouring money into this method that picks out only the big bits of floating trash and creates little incentive to stop making so much plastic in the first place.

While some initiatives currently in development, including those exploring ways to clean up plastics, aim to reduce humanity's impact on the ocean, others are aggressively ramping up exploitation. In shipyards in China, new vessels are being built that will hasten the practice of super-intensive industrial fishing. Their target will be the shoals of krill swimming in the icy seas surrounding the Antarctic Peninsula. Most of these ships are so huge they wouldn't fit diagonally across a football field. Among them, a 460-foot-long krill trawler will be the biggest, most advanced of its kind, capable of sucking more krill out of the ocean than any vessel before it. Russia also plans to re-enter the Antarctic krill-fishing business, having exited in 2010, and India may soon join the fray in the Southern Ocean.

The way things are going, more people around the world will soon be eating farmed seafood that was reared on Antarctic krill. Aquaculture is the fastest-growing sector in the food industry. In the past few decades, the global annual catch of wild fish has stagnated and levelled off; since the late 1980s, it has fluctuated between roughly eighty and ninety million metric tons. At the same time, aquaculture has been relentlessly rising year on year. Today, approximately half of all the aquatic animals people eat come from the wild, and the other half from aquaculture, including a lot of species that are fed meal made from wild-caught ocean species. Krill are in high demand for meal because other species have already been overexploited and can no longer be caught in large enough quantities. Apparently, krill also make ideal food for farmed salmon and shrimp, the two most popular species in ocean farming: krill enhances these species' growth, resulting in high-quality products. A push for more krill fishing in the remote waters of Antarctica would strengthen the view that the ocean exists chiefly as a resource for humans to use by whatever methods generate the most profit.

Similarly, within the next few years, an entirely new industry could begin exploiting more ocean resources. Mining magnates are intent on establishing the world's first deep-sea mines and becoming the first people to extract profits from the immense depths of the ocean. They dream of a future ocean with gigantic machinery working over the deep seabed to excavate rocks containing metal ores. These are not the first plans for mining the deep. For a time in the mid-twentieth century, this was just one of many futuristic fantasies of how people might operate in the ocean, alongside building human colonies in the abyss and learning to talk to whales. Earlier deep-sea mining schemes fizzled out when fluctuating ore prices, political uncertainties, and a lack of technological know-how put investors and technocrats off. Now it's been forced back onto the global agenda by governments and corporations determined to make it happen this time.

A glimpse of this future ocean appeared recently, when a prominent mining corporation, the Metals Company, sent a ship to the central Pacific to test mining equipment designed to excavate seabed rocks, known as polymetallic nodules, which look like misshapen lumps of coal. These nodules take millions of years to accrete and grow from chemicals in seawater, in one of the slowest known geological processes on earth. If they're stripped away by miners, these nodules won't return for millennia, and the unique, biodiverse ecosystems they support will be lost—the ghostly-white octopuses and tiny "water bear" tardigrades, the lemon-yellow sea cucumbers, the delicate corals and sponges, plus thousands of other, as yet undiscovered life forms that inhabit the nodule fields.

Late in 2022, the Metals Company dragged up more than three thousand metric tons of nodules from the abyss to its surface production vessel, the *Hidden Gem*, during its test operation in the Pacific. Scientists hired to work with the company leaked video footage showing dirty plumes of sediment being discharged over the side of the *Hidden Gem* into the ocean after the rocks were processed on board.

The Maldives' floating city, the Ocean Cleanup's capture of floating plastic, plans to expand industrial Antarctic krill fishing, and deep-sea mining are just four possible solutions to four of the most important problems humanity faces in terms of the future ocean: how to live by the changing ocean, how to clean it up, how to feed people, and how (and whether) to extract other ocean resources. All four solutions are part of what's becoming a prevailing way of thinking. They adopt largely techno-centric perspectives, based on the belief that humans can invent their way out of trouble. And they adopt the implicit assumption of continuing business as usual. These visions of the future do nothing about the underlying problems that are causing the ocean to change; they lean instead towards adaptation and making the best of a bad situation, and some of them forge ahead with new versions of the problems that created this mess in the first place. And to a greater or lesser extent, they tend to be highly unequal in the winners and losers they create. Under these and similar scenarios, some people and some parts of the living ocean will do very well, while many more will do a whole lot worse.

Decisions such as these are not inevitable, no matter what industrialists and devotees of unrelenting economic growth might claim. There are other options, other ways of doing things and other decisions that can still be made for the future of the ocean. The accelerating pace of climate change and the biodiversity crisis is making the need to act ever more urgent. Meanwhile, powerful vested interests in damaging industries will fight tooth and nail to resist changes to the status quo that threaten to undermine their profits. Pushing against them will not be easy, but it's by no means impossible. Action is happening, and alternative views for how to use and protect the ocean are taking hold. Many exist in small ways and can be amplified and grown; others are already forging a bold path ahead. The final pages of this book outline some of these options. They are not intended to be a complete blueprint but rather an invitation to think differently and be part of a push for a better future for the ocean.

How to Live by the Changing Ocean

In 2015, a final shipload of soil arrived at the English county of Essex after it was dug from beneath the streets of London to build tunnels for a new underground railway line. In all, more than three million metric tons of material was excavated and transported forty miles to the estuary, where it was used to raise up the level of the land by five feet and make a network of winding creeks, mudflats, and shallow lagoons. Centuries ago, Wallasea Island was part of wildlife-rich marshlands that wove along the Essex coast until they were dug up, enclosed in seawalls, and converted into farmland. The aim of the current project is to begin bringing back those marshlands and help future-proof the low-lying coast. It's one of Europe's most ambitious plans to re-create coastal wetlands that act as natural sea defences. Close to two thousand acres of farmland have been transformed into grasslands and salt marsh. Samphire, sea lavender, and other salt-tolerant plants are the botanical engineers creating the foundation for the ecosystem, which slows down water flow and makes coasts less prone to erosion and flooding.

The edges of the ocean have always played a deep-rooted part in human lives, now more than ever. In recent decades, many coastlines have become heavily industrialised and far more densely populated than the hinterland. Urban areas on low-lying coasts are expanding fastest, especially in Southeast Asia and China. Most megacities are coastal, from Los Angeles to Tokyo, Shanghai to Mumbai, Lagos to New York.

Across the world's populated coastlines, one billion people live on land that lies at most thirty feet above the current high-tide lines, and 230 million people live below three feet of elevation. These places are all prone to flooding and storm damage, and those risks are only going to get worse as the climate crisis worsens. Sea levels are rising and speeding up as they go. The twentieth century saw the seas rise by approximately a hand's span with fingers splayed out. So far this century, levels have already risen by a pinky finger's length; by century's end they are expected to rise by around an arm's length, and ten feet or more can't be ruled out, depending on what happens with the breakup of Antarctica's ice sheet. For people living along coasts, what matters isn't simply the incremental rise in seas but the way it raises the chances of extreme flooding, especially when high tides and storm surges combine. What used to be once-in-a-century extreme high water will become annual events in low-lying areas by mid-century and along most coasts by 2100—even if global warming is kept under 1.5 degrees Celsius. In the tropics, as the seas warm, they feed hurricanes, creating more intense and devastating storms with more rainfall, causing even more flooding.

Deciding what to do about all this is one of the greatest challenges that humanity faces in the coming years. Up until now, the standard strategy has been to build higher and stronger walls between people and the ocean. Seawalls, surge barriers, levees, and other engineered installations can work predictably and very well, right up until the moment when they don't anymore. In New Orleans in August 2005, when Hurricane Katrina ripped through, more than fifty failures in the levee system flooded most of the city for weeks. African-American neighbourhoods were most severely damaged, and people living in them, alongside elderly people and poorer members of the city's communities, were the ones most likely to die from the disaster.

These types of hard infrastructure often don't solve a problem but pass it on, interrupting natural flows of sediment and causing coastlines to erode elsewhere. They're also unaffordable outside of densely populated cities in wealthy countries. In poorer regions, hard engineering is generally not a realistic option, and neither are floating cities or any other big-ticket substitutes for coastal life as it used to be.

An alternative mind-set is beginning to gain traction around the world. Instead of pitting humans against the changing ocean, more ecological and equitable solutions are coming into play, and people are tuning in to the possibilities of protecting coastlines with tidal wetlands that grow between the high and low tide marks on the shore. Along temperate shores, salt marshes such as those at Wallasea Island are important wetlands. On tropical shores, mangrove trees grow at the edges of the sea with their roots dipped in salt water. Both these wetland habitats act as storm buffers. They dampen the power and height of waves, and the plants trap sediments among their roots and stems, which reduces the chances of coastlines eroding and getting washed away. And unlike hard engineering, these living systems have the potential, given the right conditions, to grow upwards and inland and keep pace as the seas continue to rise.

Roughly a third of the human population currently living on low-lying coasts already gains protection from wetlands, with the majority of those coastal dwellers living in China, Vietnam, India, Germany, and the Netherlands. The most obvious way to help protect those people is to keep existing wetlands as intact and healthy as possible. A huge opportunity exists to safeguard such coastal habitats growing in and around cities. From Port Harcourt in the Niger delta of Nigeria to Surabaya in Indonesia, Chattogram in Bangladesh to Haikou in China, urban wetlands will continue to benefit city dwellers if they are well looked after and, ideally, given space inland to move into and expand landwards as sea levels rise.

A trickier matter is deciding how to re-establish wetlands that are already degraded or were lost long ago, or even to create entirely new areas of habitat. There's no simple formula for how to restore and nurture wetlands to protect people and coastlines. Much depends on the local conditions, the species of plants, and the kinds of storms that strike. The best way forwards is to embrace that uncertainty. Rather than marching in with a fixed idea of what to do, restoration projects can be more experimental, with monitoring and testing along the way to see what's working and what's not.

How to Clean the Ocean

Walk into a supermarket in France, and there will be displays of fresh vegetables and fruits arranged loosely in colourful piles. Shoppers help themselves, filling bags brought from home or paper sacks from the store. Since January 1, 2022, there has been a national ban on plastic packaging for fresh produce, with some exceptions, including tender varieties like blueberries and cherry tomatoes. Manufacturers have a few more years to find suitable alternatives for those, and by 2026, all whole fruits and vegetables will be plastic-free across the country.

The fight against single-use plastics is the most successful and high-profile ocean campaign globally in recent times. Plastic pollution is capturing attention and stimulating action because it's impossible to ignore the ugly mess it makes of the world around us, and it's obvious where all the plastic is coming from. The award-winning image of a seahorse with its tail wrapped around a plastic Q-tip, taken by nature photographer Justin Hofman, portrays the absurdity in a nutshell.

Plastic manufacture kicked into gear after the end of the Second World War, and since then, more than eighty-three hundred megatons of this synthetic, durable wonder stuff have been produced; more than half of it has been made since 2002. Currently, four hundred million metric tons of new plastics are made each year; less than 10 per cent of the total is recycled, and much of the rest is used just once and then thrown away, often ending up in the ocean. Fortunately, more people than ever are disgusted by this and want plastic pollution to end. A 2022 survey of more than twenty thousand people in twenty-eight countries showed that, on average, eight out of ten support a ban on single-use plastics. Immense pressure from the public has already forced many countries to impose bans and restrictions on throwaway items like grocery bags. Countries such as France are showing it is possible to stand up to the petrochemical giants that are behind the surge in plastic production. Coal, oil, and natural gas are the raw materials used to make more than 98 per cent of all synthetic plastics. Corporations extracting those resources have made a calculated pivot away from producing fossil fuels, largely owing to falling demand as the green-energy sector expands, and instead are making more plastics and deliberately stimulating demand for copious amounts of cheap, single-use products. Oil and gas giants are addicted to the outrageous profits they're making—in the hundreds of billions of dollars each year—and they will do whatever they can to keep those profits coming. Pushing against that is a huge challenge, especially given the massive lobbying powers of the petrochemical industry, but it is happening. Local and national campaigns against plastic pollution have been a gateway to expanding the issue, and a global rebellion against plastics is stepping up a gear.

In 2022, negotiations began at the United Nations for an international treaty on plastics. An early round of discussions in Paris showed that most nations want to limit the production of plastics and are in favour of banning the most harmful types as well as the toxic additives that are used to make products colourful, inflammable, flexible, or tough, including polyfluoroalkyl and perfluoroalkyl substances (PFASs), or "forever chemicals." The majority of nations also insist the treaty should be not voluntary but global and legally binding. Even some major users of plastics are in favour of tough regulations, including Coca-Cola and Unilever, both of which have come under increasing public scrutiny for the plastic pollution their products create.

A plastics treaty wouldn't be the first time a blanket ban has been imposed on pollution that threatens the health of people and the planet. In the 1980s, the growing hole in the ozone layer led to rapid global action and the universal adoption of the Montreal Protocol, which phased out chlorofluorocarbons (CFCs) used in aerosol sprays and refrigerators. Alternatives to CFCs were found, and the ozone layer over Antarctica is slowly healing.

Of course, there is resistance to a binding plastics treaty from a powerful minority of plastic-producing nations, including India, China, and the United States. And rather than limiting production and banning the worst of the offending materials, manufacturers want the focus to be on recycling. Overall, however, governments around the world are taking the issue of plastic pollution seriously, and if the negotiations stay on course, by the end of 2024 a new, binding treaty will be in place to start to bring the plastic juggernaut under control.

The means to do this already exist. Boosting the reuse and recycling of products offers the chance to bring down plastic production worldwide by around 50 per cent. Bottle-return schemes drastically increase recycling rates, especially when the price is right. Across the United States, for instance, the average recycling rate for plastic bottles is 17 per cent. In the states of Massachusetts and Connecticut, where manufacturers, distributors, and retailers jointly pay five cents for every bottle returned, the recycling rate is around 40 per cent. In Oregon and Michigan, where the per-bottle deposit is ten cents, the return rate is closer to 90 per cent.

Another important mechanism for curbing plastic pollution will be for governments to stop paying out subsidies that prop up the fossil fuel industry. Analysis by the International Monetary Fund showed that in 2020, global subsidies were close to $6 trillion—or $11 million a minute—in the form of tax breaks or direct payments to reduce the costs of producing coal, oil, and gas; fixing artificially low fossil fuel prices; and subsidising exploration and development of new oil and gas fields. There is tremendous pushback from oil and gas giants that risk seeing their profits take a knock, but progress has been made, and dozens of countries are reforming their subsidy policies. In 2023, US president Joe Biden unveiled a budget proposal to scrap oil and gas subsidies—which, whether or not it makes it through Congress, sends a strong signal from the White House.

Low-impact alternatives to fossil-fuel-based plastics are already in development around the world. For instance, a German start-up, Traceless, is making rigid plastics, films, and coatings that, in two to nine weeks, break down completely in a home compost heap or municipal facility, leaving only carbon dioxide and water. The materials used, though plant-based, don't require additional land to grow crops but come from existing agricultural wastes and residues left over from the brewing industry, all of which would otherwise be thrown away. And if these bioplastics do escape into the environment, they will cause no harm to animals that eat them.

Cutting worldwide plastic production by 80 per cent by 2040 is practical and affordable—it would cost a lot, around $65 billion a year, but that's roughly half the sum currently invested in the plastics industry worldwide. What's more, it would bring benefits worth trillions of dollars by reducing the harm done to people and the environment. It would save countless human lives, reduce suffering, and undo enormous inequalities. Diseases and debilitating conditions are rife among those who work in plastics manufacturing and disposal industries and those who live in neighbourhoods near those facilities; they face increased risks of lung and breast cancer, leukaemia, lymphoma, cardiovascular disease, premature births, reduced fertility, and much more. The world's poorest nations will benefit the most from reductions in plastic pollution, as will people living in disempowered and marginalised communities, especially indigenous groups, women, and children. These people are the least responsible for creating the problem of plastics; they gain the least from them, and they suffer the most. Many rely on seafood for nutrition, which exposes them to plastics and toxic chemicals in their contaminated food. And many live in communities that are threatened by more severe and frequent flooding, because plastic trash blocks drainage systems, and on small island nations with beaches strewn in plastics that float in from far away.

A vision of the cleaner ocean is well within sight, now that the public and governments have woken up to the problem and are taking action. Once the tide has turned on new plastics pouring into the environment, the ocean itself will help reduce and remove existing pollution. Sunlight breaks plastics into smaller pieces, and naturally occurring bacteria get to work. Scientists have found plastic-eating bacteria living in the ocean, and their studies suggest these may fully break down at least 1 per cent of the available plastics per year. While these and other bacteria and enzymes could one day be used to help remove difficult-to-recycle plastics from landfills nobody is seriously considering releasing engineered bacteria into the ocean to speed up plastic degradation. The risks of something going wrong are simply too high. However, even without enhancing the natural breakdown, by the end of the century, the ocean could be much less polluted than today.

How to Fish in the Anthropocene Ocean

Along the coast of the US state of Maine, shellfish and seaweed farms are popping up, many of them owned and run by women, and together they're changing the way seafood is locally produced and consumed. Festoons of golden kelp and other seaweeds are strung from lines at the sea surface; suspended wire cages contain oysters and scallops, and mussels cling to hanging ropes.

Lady Shuckers is a company that sells and markets oysters from sixteen of the twenty-three Maine oyster farms that are owned by women, including Amanda Moeser of Lanes Island Oysters in Yarmouth, Emily Selinger of Emily's Oysters in Freeport, and Kim Grindle of the Islesboro Oyster Company. Among the ocean farmers encouraging people to include more nutritious seaweed in their diet is Briana Warner, chief executive officer of Atlantic Sea Farms, which produces kimchi, salads, and veggie burgers made of kelp.

Maine's female ocean farmers give various reasons why they participate much more in aquaculture than in the lobster industry, which has dominated the state for decades; women own fewer than 5 per cent of the lobster-fishing licences but close to a quarter of the permits for oyster and seaweed farms. Many see their farms as a chance to operate in a supportive and diverse workplace, with fewer barriers to participation. Women make up to half of the members of local aquaculture associations and advisory councils— while there's good reason the other organisations are generally called lobster*men's* associations. Some women ocean farmers speak of feeling drawn to growing rather than hunting. As one farmer said, "I see seaweed as a way for women to enter this realm because the history of fisheries is all exploitation, and that's not a female quality." Also present in the minds of many women involved in aquaculture are the growing threats to the lobster industry from overfishing and climate change and the need to find alternative approaches to producing seafood. "It is time to transfer to more of a female approach to the ocean," one of the women said. "It needs a mentality of cultivation and investment."

Elsewhere, many more women are pioneering this new generation of ocean farms. The United Kingdom's largest offshore seaweed farm, SeaGrown, based in the North Sea coastal town of Scarborough, was cofounded by marine scientist professor Laura Robinson. Tomi Marsh had been fishing the seas of Alaska from her own vessels for decades before setting up OceansAlaska in Ketchikan, where a seaweed farm and hatchery for oysters and geoducks supplies other ocean farms. In San Diego, Leslie Booher cofounded Sunken

Seaweed, where she works closely with academics to study how her farm is cleaning up local waterways.

These women are not only helping to shift the ingrained gender bias in the seafood industry; they're leading the way in a global movement to make aquaculture more ecologically sustainable. Instead of rearing animals like salmon and shrimp that are fed on meal made from wild-caught fish, they focus on growing seafood that feeds itself and in the process cleans the ocean. Bivalve molluscs, such as oysters and mussels, are filter feeders, drawing plankton from the seawater around them. Seaweeds produce their own food from sunlight and nutrients naturally dissolved in seawater. This type of aquaculture has many benefits. It improves water quality by removing excess nitrates and phosphates pouring off farmland and from sewage outfalls, it sequesters carbon, and it buffers against local ocean acidification.

Regenerative ocean farms like these are among the kinds of operations that need to be the focus for the future of seafood—together with well-run, sustainable fisheries—rather than the destructive, industrial-scale operations that are causing so much damage to the planet. Thousands of industrial vessels ply the ocean, ranging from eighty-foot longliners to four-hundred-foot supertrawlers. They have the greatest fishing power and use the most environmentally brutal types of fishing gear; they drag huge, heavy trawl nets across the seabed, wiping out thousand-year-old deep-water corals and all other life forms in their path; they set out miles of longlines and draw in purse seines that trap, hook, and kill millions of endangered sharks, dolphins, and sea turtles every year. And they burn colossal quantities of fossil fuel, giving the food they produce a super-high carbon footprint.

For the future ocean to sustainably feed as many people as possible—crucially, people who rely most on the seas for nutrition—industrial fishing needs to radically change and ideally be dramatically scaled back, most urgently for certain types of fishing operations in certain places.

Corporations from a handful of wealthy countries dominate industrial fishing and have aggressive lobbying powers and vested interests. Despite that, fishery reforms are gradually happening and showing that change is possible.

After decades of campaigns and negotiations, in 2022 an agreement was reached at the World Trade Organization (WTO) to rein in the subsidies governments pay to prop up industrial fisheries. These subsidies, worth billions of dollars a year, have been a massive driving force behind overfishing. Much of the money subsidises fuel costs and boosts destructive fishing capacity by encouraging the building of bigger boats with bigger engines, privileging larger companies over smaller-scale producers, and facilitating the behemoths such as those that hoover up Antarctic krill and deplete more of the ocean's vital, living biomass, ton by ton.

The 2022 WTO agreement didn't include everything conservationists and scientists were hoping for. At the last minute, several key points were dropped in order to get all 164 member states to agree, including any specific mention of subsidies that encourage overfishing. These may be addressed at a later date. Nevertheless, this was a major milestone, the first binding, multilateral agreement to help reduce fishing impacts globally, and experts expect it will stimulate further action as it begins to push fisheries in the right direction.

For now, the WTO will focus on prohibiting subsidies for vessels that target depleted populations of animals and those that operate in the high seas, the remote waters beyond national boundaries that cover two-thirds of the global ocean. Subsidies are keeping afloat many high-seas fisheries that would otherwise not turn a profit.

Under the new agreement, nations will also be required to crack down on subsidies supporting illegal, unreported, and unregulated fishing. These kinds of fisheries are notorious for flouting rules aimed at protecting endangered species, such as the vessels that trespass into the Galápagos Marine Reserve and leave with their holds full of sharks.

Curbing illegal and high-seas fishing will also reduce human suffering. Working and living conditions are often appalling on vessels that stay out at sea for months, even years, at a time. Investigations of industrial fisheries have found cases of human trafficking, debt bondage, forced confinement, physical abuse, and even murder. Out in distant waters, atrocities of modern slavery go unseen and unpunished. Removing subsidies will force more of these unethical operations out of business.

In March 2023, another milestone for the ocean was reached, which likewise took decades to negotiate. Member states of the United Nations gathered in New York and agreed to a new treaty to protect the high seas. At the heart of this is a legal framework that will help to bring the rampant exploitation of the high seas under control, to conserve wildlife and establish vast new marine reserves. There will be a new conference of parties, like those overseeing the global climate, in which UN member states can be held to account for how they operate in the high seas. It means the distant parts of the ocean will no longer be overlooked and ignored.

The industrial fishing trade urgently needs to change the deals rich fishing nations strike with poorer countries in order to gain access to their waters. Broadly speaking, the history of global fishing has seen highly industrialised nations overexploiting their nearby seas, then moving into more distant regions so they can keep catching more fish. Governments, many of them in Africa, sell access agreements to foreign industrial fishing fleets, including those from China, Russia, and the European Union, in particular Spain. The prices for these licences are a paltry sum compared to the amount of money the catches sell for. European countries pay on average 8 per cent of the value of the fish they catch off West Africa; China pays on average 4 per cent. These foreign fisheries are paying very little to snatch away fish from nations that rely most on healthy seas for jobs and food.

Progress is desperately needed to halt the damage foreign vessels are inflicting on habitats and species, and to protect people's lives. In recent years, surging numbers of people from Senegal have braved the ocean in tiny canoes to try to reach Europe. Many are former fishers who have watched as foreign fleets have wrecked their way of life, ransacked local fish and habitats, and made the seas treacherous for them to work in. They see no other option. A popular gateway to Europe is the Spanish-owned Canary Islands, nine hundred miles north of Senegal. Thus, the country that sends huge industrial ships to West Africa is seeing ever more small, precarious boats filled with desperate people heading back in its direction. Every year, hundreds of migrants starve and drown en route.

Governments that sell licences to foreign fleets need instead to phase them out and put their citizens first, prioritising their health and livelihoods. And governments in richer nations, especially those in the European Union that profess to be environmental and human rights leaders, should be disgraced for aggressively negotiating and buying licences that effectively steal fish from hungry mouths and stoke the migrant crisis. Some headway was made when China cancelled foreign permits with three of its national companies for breaking fishing regulations and operating illegally off West Africa. Much more needs to be done to end these unethical and ecologically ruinous agreements.

In a future ocean that's fished more ethically and sustainably—with strict limits on industrial fishing and greater protection for habitats and species—the seafood on supermarket shelves, fishmonger counters, and restaurant menus will no doubt be different from what we see today. Costs will go up for some products, reflecting more accurately the true costs of production; some will be harder to come by, and some will be gone altogether; other alternative, affordable, and sustainable varieties will appear. And none of that is entirely new or unheard of. Seafood markets have always shifted, and consumers have adapted to different foods and prices. I remember that, during my childhood, salmon was an occasional treat and not the cheap dish it's become with the industrialisation of fish farming. Conversely, in the nineteenth century in Europe and North America, some of the cheapest, most abundant seafoods eaten by the masses were oysters and lobsters.

Completely new options are also being invented for seafood that's never been anywhere near the ocean. As part of the growing alternative-protein industry attempting to wean people off planet-damaging meat and fish, start-up companies are producing laboratory-grown seafood. Companies in California are investing millions in growing sushi-grade bluefin tuna and coho salmon sashimi. In 2023, an Israeli food-tech company partnered with a Singapore-based enterprise to give diners their first taste of 3D-printed fillets of grouper. There are also regional specialities in the works, from Russian sturgeon to fish swim bladders for traditional fish-maw soup in Hong Kong. Lobster, mahi-mahi, yellowtail, and shrimp are also on the alt-protein menu, although for now mostly behind closed doors.

The manufacturing process involves taking small samples of cells from living fish or crustaceans and growing them in vats, called bioreactors, and feeding them liquid nutrients. The resulting cell culture is then either shaped, on an edible fillet-shaped scaffold, or turned into bio-ink and squirted into desired shapes using a 3D printer.

Assuming these ventures get regulatory approval, there will be early adopters among ethically minded and adventurous diners, but the big question is whether a critical mass of consumers will join the ocean-free seafood party. It's a stretch to expect high enough volumes will be produced to ease pressure on wild fisheries, and the ventures could backfire and stimulate greater overall demand for seafood. And if this is going to become the next big thing, prices will have to come down; the nutrient feeds are expensive, and the production processes use a lot of energy. In 2019, one company produced a plate of eight shrimp dumplings at a cost of more than twenty thousand dollars per pound, compared to less than five per pound for shrimp reared in aquaculture ponds; another start-up produced a two-hundred-dollar salmon sushi roll.

New technologies will also help consumers of wild and farmed seafood to know exactly what they're eating, where it came from, and who caught it. Blockchain is now being tested to eradicate widespread fisheries fraud. Originally created for managing Bitcoin and other cryptocurrencies, blockchain creates an incorruptible digital ledger that keeps records of transactions from fishers to retailers and consumers, which will eventually prevent the smuggling of illegal and unsustainable seafood into the market. Current estimates indicate that around a third of wild-caught fish imported into the United States is caught illegally, but consumers have no way of knowing the provenance of most of the seafood they buy.

With all that's available now and in the future, it should be possible for seafood diners to choose from a broad array of species caught and carefully farmed; there will be good-value food available from low-impact, regenerative ocean farms and from fisheries that are properly managed, with well-enforced regulations governing the types of fishing gear used and the times and places where fishing happens, to ensure habitats aren't damaged and wild populations are not depleted.

How to Use Ocean Resources

In the Pacific Ocean, more than a hundred miles off the coast of British Columbia, Canada, a shipful of research scientists recently found a giant underwater volcano with shimmering warm water seeping out of it. Almost a mile beneath the surface, the seamount's summit was covered in colourful forests of deep-sea corals and sponges, and among them were nestled giant golden egg cases, each more than a foot long. Flying up from the deeper abyss was a spiny skate, a ghostly-white, diamond-shaped relative of the flapper skates of the Atlantic and likewise more than six feet long. The scientists soon saw this was a female, because she had an egg case emerging from her body—the first time anyone had seen a skate in the process of laying her egg in the deep sea. Thousands more skates joined her on the seamount. Although the total number was impossible to count, the team estimated that one million, perhaps even five million, skate eggs were laid on that seamount. The female skates likely migrate to this spot from great distances across the Pacific basin, knowing this is the place to come for warm waters that are just the right temperature to incubate their eggs and speed their growth; otherwise, it takes three years or longer for them to hatch in cold waters of the deep ocean.

At around the same time, southwards in the Pacific off the coast of Costa Rica, another team of scientists were studying a previously unexplored seamount when they came across a deep-sea octopus nursery, only the fourth ever found. Hundreds of mauve-coloured octopus mothers lay across the flanks of the mountain, more than nine thousand feet underwater, their suckered arms wrapped over their bodies, protecting their egg clutches from predators. The scientists watched as coin-size baby octopuses emerged from their eggs and swam away with pulses of their eight tiny arms.

Meanwhile, across the Pacific on its northwestern rim, a research team has been studying the first seamount to be successfully mined. Rocky crusts on underwater volcanoes are a target for deep-sea mining companies eager to begin exploiting them for the metals they contain, in particular cobalt. In 2020, in the waters of Japan, more than a mile deep, a small part of the Takuyo-Daigo Seamount was drilled and extracted by a fifteen-ton, remotely operated mining machine that looked like a digger on caterpillar tracks, with a twenty-inch-wide cutter head. During less than two hours, the machine mined four hundred feet of the seamount's surface and removed fourteen hundred pounds of crust.

The test mine was trifling in size compared to the full-scale commercial operations that are planned. And yet, scientists surveying the site before and after the test saw that the ecosystem had been drastically altered. As expected, squashed, dead wildlife, including corals, sponges, and sea cucumbers, lay in the path of the crawling machine. Far more shocking, a year later, the area surrounding the mined site was still substantially depleted of life. Fish and shrimp were around half as abundant as before the test. They'd been scared off and not come back, long after the machine was taken away and the scene had quietened, presumably because the area was still too disturbed and their prey too contaminated. Studies of the small test set off loud alarm bells that mining seamounts would be even more devastating to deep-sea life than had been thought previously.

Amid a constant stream of discoveries of life in the ocean, it's plain to see that deep-sea mining would be catastrophic for the health and vibrancy of the planet. As researchers explore and study more of the deep, the stakes become ever higher, as they uncover vital habitats on which species depend and see how everything matters—each seamount, each hydrothermal vent, each square foot of abyssal plain.

The year 2023 marked a turning point in plans to begin mining the deep sea. At a series of key meetings at the headquarters of the International Seabed Authority (ISA) in Jamaica, deep-sea mining companies anticipated receiving a green light to commence their commercial operations. Out in the high seas, the seabed is officially the common heritage of humanity—it is a natural asset shared among everyone alive today and with future generations to come—and the ISA is the organisation charged with deciding on behalf of all humanity whether to permit deep-sea mining, and how, when, and by whom.* Companies hungry to start turning a profit from deep-sea mining were met at the ISA's meetings in 2023 with a growing wall of opposition. More than twenty nations are calling for a pause or moratorium on the industry. Canada, Brazil, Chile, Germany, Switzerland, Sweden, Finland, Spain, Aotearoa (New Zealand), and Costa Rica are among the countries urging the ISA stop the rush to begin mining;† Palau, Fiji, Samoa, and the Federated States of Micronesia have formed a moratorium alliance; the European Parliament has called for a moratorium; and the French Parliament voted in favour of a full ban on the industry.‡

Joining the chorus of concern are the voices of indigenous peoples whose lives are closely entwined with the areas nearest the potential first wave of mining sites in the Pacific. Campaigners presented a declaration to the ISA signed by more than one thousand representatives from thirty-four Pacific countries and fifty-six indigenous groups who collectively deny their consent to deep-sea mining. In the words of the declaration:

> Cultures across the Pacific consider the ocean to be sacred space for creation, a provider, an ancestor, and a link to places and people across the horizon. We would no more harm the ocean than we would a member of our family. And as with our family, we depend on each other for survival. . . . We refuse to allow any further harm to our sacred ocean.

---

*The ISA comprises 167 member states and the European Union.

†The UK government dragged its heals on the matter, amid considerable pushback including from those in power. For instance, in a letter to *The Times* in July 2023, former Conservative Party leader William Hague wrote: "The right question to ask at the International Seabed Authority is not 'Shall we find a way to do this?' but rather 'Are you completely mad?'" Finally, in October that year, the UK government capitulated and announced its support for the proposed moratorium on mining licenses.

‡The United States is not a member of the ISA and so does not attend these meetings.

Corporate backers and partners, seeing which way the wind is blowing, have been exiting the deep-sea mining industry, including Lockheed Martin and the shipping giant Maersk, which sold all its shares in the Metals Company. International corporations pledging not to use metals from the deep in their supply chains include Google, battery manufacturer Samsung SDI, and car makers Volvo, Volkswagen, and BMW, stating environmental concerns as a major reason for steering clear of the industry.

At the July 2023 meeting in Jamaica, following ardent calls from member states to debate the issue of a moratorium, ISA officials finally agreed that when talks resumed in 2024 they would, for the first time, allow formal discussions about environmental safeguarding and the possibility of a precautionary pause in deep-sea mining. The ISA also resisted pressure from a few vocal countries and companies to permit mining to start right away and kicked the issue two years down the line. A provisional deadline of July 2025 was set for completing the regulations that would oversee deep-sea mining. Known as the mining code, this contentious document has already been a work in progress for many years. Technically, mining can commence only once those regulations are in place. There is still a possibility a company will apply for a full mining licence from the ISA before the code is finalised, exploiting a legal loophole created in 2020 by the Micronesian island nation of Nauru in partnership with the Metals Company, intended to accelerate their mining plans. But any premature applications would not necessarily be approved, and so there is no smooth path open for mining to begin imminently.

Crucially, the mining code would dictate how mining can be managed to avoid harming the ocean environment, which is a key responsibility of the ISA. Hundreds of scientists around the world agree that it will take an absolute minimum of ten years of dedicated, independent, well-funded global research to gather enough data to even begin considering whether it's possible to responsibly mine the deep sea.

A long list of important topics and questions needs investigating. Even the simplest matter of cataloguing the species that exist in the deep will require immense, coordinated research programmes. There are more difficult questions to investigate to reveal how deep-sea ecosystems work. How do deep-sea corals reproduce? (Nobody has ever seen one spawning.) Why do so many species visit seamounts, and how important are they for the functioning of the entire ocean?

We also need to understand much better the impacts of mining huge areas of seabed—individual mines would excavate hundreds of square miles of the abyss each year and operate nonstop for decades, and dozens of these mines would be operating simultaneously. This is not a simple matter of questioning whether mining will impact the ocean—it's obvious that it would cause widespread, irreversible damage by removing habitat and killing species. The key challenge is to fully grasp just how bad those impacts would be. How much would deep-sea mining worsen the climate crisis by interfering with stores of carbon in the seabed and altering the ocean's ability to sequester more carbon from the atmosphere? What will whales and other megafauna do when their migration routes become noisy and polluted? How much pollution will mining stir up, including toxic heavy metals and radioactive particles from polymetallic nodules? Already studies suggest human food webs will be contaminated, as fish such as tuna swim through the areas earmarked for mining, and it would become more of a problem as the ocean warms and more populations are expected to shift into mined zones.

As deep-sea research continues, arguments in favour of deep-sea mining will continue to weaken. The main focus of pro-mining campaigns has been the demand for certain metallic elements to manufacture batteries for electric vehicles. Electrifying global fleets of cars and trucks would no doubt require immense amounts of resources, including a lot of metal. However, it's highly premature to presume which metals will be in greatest demand in the years ahead.

Building batteries for electric vehicles is one of the world's fastest-paced industries. New designs are frequently being released as manufacturers compete to make the most affordable, fast-charging, long-lasting batteries. And the metals they use are quickly changing. Until a couple of years ago, industry talk focused on cobalt, a key element in early-generation hybrid and electric cars. This deeply problematic metal is produced in mines in the Democratic Republic of the Congo, in an industry with a disastrous human rights record. Prospective deep-sea miners declared their virtuous intentions of sidestepping that horrendous industry and instead extracting cobalt from the deep. Now, however, electric car batteries are being built that contain little or no cobalt. The metals that could be extracted from the deep sea, including cobalt and lithium, can be swapped out. Chinese manufacturers are releasing the first car batteries made from sodium, a metal that is not in limited supply and won't be dug up from the deep sea.

In ten years, the world will be a very different place. Vehicle technologies will have progressed beyond anything that exists today. Scientists will have continued making mind-blowing discoveries in the ocean, uncovering species nobody imagined, and learnt so much more about the inner workings of these vast, interconnected living spaces that help make life possible everywhere else on the planet. With the tide turning on the deep-sea mining industry, and ever more people realising just what's at stake, hope is growing that swaths of the living ocean that could have ended up being sacrificed for the profit of a few will instead be saved for the benefit of everyone.

Living together on this blue planet, we are all ocean people. We all depend on healthy seas for the air we breathe, for the falling rain, for the liveable world we inhabit. For millions of people, a healthy ocean means food and jobs. It is within reach of every one of us to be a force for good in the ocean and join the growing movement to keep ocean life as vibrant and abundant as possible, even while the Anthropocene swiftly changes around us.

A starting place is at home, wherever that is. The choices we all make as consumers are important. Express your buying power at the checkout counter; support ethical, responsible businesses; ask questions about where products have come from, how they were made, and who made them. Get informed and help others in your life do the same.

If you choose to eat seafood, you have a direct line between your body and the ocean, and you can decide to use that link in a positive way. You can seek out the options that tread most lightly on sea life and give your business to the people working hardest to make a sustainable, ethical living from the ocean.

Support businesses that are part of the emerging circular economy and are offering alternative ways of producing and consuming goods, including rental rather than ownership, repair instead of throwing away. See how you can cut back on plastic packaging; there are ever more companies out there trying to help you do that.

Much of this takes effort, money, and time, which you won't always have—none of us do. So make sure you feel good when you can make better choices, and try not to feel guilty when you can't.

Recognise that the actions you take do matter, though they can go only so far. None of us can save the ocean by ourselves. But you can reach out wider. Look to your networks and find ways to influence them. Now that environmental activism has gone mainstream, every office, every school, every industry has people who want to make a difference and do better for the planet. Find them, join them, be one of the leaders.

When it comes to the food you eat and the products you buy, you can exert your influence higher up the supply chain. Supermarkets have immense power. They decide where so much of our food comes from, and they do shift their ways when consumers pile on the pressure. Use social media to name and shame companies that are filling the ocean with pointless plastics. Join campaigns that are calling out the worst offenders and demanding change. In Britain and Germany, supermarkets responding to environmental campaigns are putting pressure on the European Union to improve its tuna fisheries in the Indian Ocean. France wouldn't have banned plastic-wrapped fresh produce if supermarket customers hadn't been up in arms. These kinds of campaigns can and do work.

It is critical for the ocean, and the whole living planet, that carbon emissions are cut as soon and as deeply as possible. Already, there's a global campaign underway to starve fossil fuel corporations of capital. Influential organisations and institutions, from churches and pension funds to universities and banks, are phasing out their investments in the industry. Leaders include the French bank Crédit Mutuel, which in 2020 divested all its fossil fuel financing; other banks making major divestments include the German Deutsche Bank and the State Bank of India. After a five-year campaign by students, academics, and politicians, the University of Cambridge pledged in 2020 to divest its £3.5 billion endowment from fossil fuel corporations by the end of the decade, and many other British universities are making similar commitments. Among American universities, Harvard University announced in 2021 it will move to divest its $42 billion endowment from fossil fuels; other divestors include New York, Cornell, Boston, and Brown Universities. You can be part of this by supporting the businesses and groups that are boldly pushing back against fossil fuel dominance. And if you work in a business or organisation with capital to invest, be part of this push and join the movement.

The future of the ocean will be determined at the coasts and far inland, in assembly halls, boardrooms, and voting booths. Next time you step up to vote, do so as if the environment matters. Call on your elected representatives. Their job is to stand up for constituents like you and take your views seriously.

We all live in a world with an ocean full of remarkable, beautiful, and strange living things, creatures we can dream about and maybe see one day. We can all feel the same sorrow when those wonders are allowed to fade away, and we can all take action to push towards a better future. My greatest source of hope comes from knowing that ever more people are embracing this idea and strengthening the connections between us all and the edges of the land and out into the wide, wild ocean.

Epilogue

Not long ago, I went swimming at one of my favourite spots in Brittany, where I scramble over rocks, pull on a dive mask, and slip into the cold sea to explore the seaweed-covered rocks, search for the tiniest cowrie shells, and watch for the tails of pipefish twisting through the greenery. It was the eighth of August, a perfect date because for the first time after several years of exploring this part of the French Atlantic coast, I saw an octopus.

It caught my attention with a wave of one of its eight arms, and before my conscious mind had time to register what it was, the inner voice that always narrates my underwater explorations silently called out, *Suckers!* If I hadn't seen that supple, tapering arm with circular suction cups lined up along it, largest at the body end and leading to impossibly tiny ones at the tip, I'm sure I would have missed the octopus entirely. It shrank into the seaweed garden and became almost invisible, matching its skin colour and texture to its surroundings. All I could make out was one eye watching me, white with a horizontal black iris striped across it.

That octopus encounter, and another I had a little while later, sum up for me the strange hybrid mix of glories and troubles of the Anthropocene ocean.

It was a common octopus. Historically, it was considered a single, cosmopolitan species living in disjointed populations in temperate seas across the globe. However, recent studies of its genes revealed the common octopus to be what's known as a cryptic species complex, a group whose members all look alike but are dissimilar enough at a molecular level to count as separate species, in this case at least six octopuses that live along different coastlines around the world. Octopuses that live in the Mediterranean and in the Atlantic between North Africa and the English Channel have kept the original name, *Octopus vulgaris*. Others have been assigned new names, including *Octopus americanus* in the Americas; *Octopus djinda* and *Octopus tetricus* in southwest and southeast Australia, respectively; and *Octopus sinensis* in the East China Sea. These species are all sensitive to climate change in slightly different ways, which means that in future warmer seas, some will do better than others. Some octopuses are predicted to lose only small parts of their habitats where the waters will become too hot for them. Some species are expected to shift towards the poles. And some could disappear from large parts of their current range. By the end of the century, unless carbon emissions are brought down, species from this cryptic complex could be lost entirely from the Caribbean and the Indian Ocean island of Madagascar, where octopus fisheries are a significant source of food and income.

Over the past forty years, the global catch of octopuses has doubled. As other ocean species have become overexploited, octopuses are increasingly taking their place in seafood markets. There are also plans to begin farming *Octopus vulgaris* for food, despite huge worries about the ethics and ecological impacts of mass-rearing these highly intelligent and notoriously solitary predators. A company in the Spanish Canary Islands intends to produce a million octopuses a year in a thousand communal tanks inside a two-storey building at the port of Las Palmas. The animals will be killed by plunging them into freezing water, a method that is untested in octopuses but has been shown to cause a slow, cruel death in fish.

I choose not to eat octopuses, for various reasons including that thoughtful look in their eyes. That's not to say that I think nobody should eat them. It is possible to catch wild octopuses sustainably and ethically. But that's not what's happening in Brittany. When huge numbers suddenly appeared along the coast in 2021, an octopus-fishing bonanza began. Before then, octopuses were not a common sight along the northwestern coast of France. Within a couple of years, fishers were catching hundreds of tons and earning a fortune selling them to fish markets in Spain (for now, there's no appetite for *poulpes* in Breton cuisine). Nobody yet knows exactly what caused this population boom, or how long it might last, but it has happened before. At the very end of the nineteenth century, there was an octopus frenzy in southern England and northern France. The London *Fishing Gazette* reported in October 1900 that octopuses had been so abundant along the Brittany coast the previous year that it was almost impossible to turn over a stone on a beach without finding one or more hiding underneath. After a storm, hundreds of dead octopuses washed up on the shore and were carted away to sell as manure.

Another British newspaper explained in 1900 that the presence of so many octopuses was due to the "excessive heat of recent summers." Warming seas today, especially during the winter months, could have a part to play in the rise of octopuses around the coasts of France and England, potentially allowing more of their larvae to survive and grow to adulthood. Another factor could be a general lack of large predators in the region, such as seals and dolphins, which might otherwise have kept octopus numbers in check. While a direct link can't be drawn, it's a poignant fact that while octopuses are plentiful in France, dolphins have been washing up dead and mutilated along the same stretch of coastline, likely after they were caught and drowned in industrial trawl nets and then dumped over the sides of fishing vessels.

In the late 1890s, British and French fishers complained bitterly about the surfeit of octopuses stealing their catches of crabs, lobsters, and oysters, describing them as pests and loathsome beasts. More than a century later, fishers in Brittany are again infuriated that these eight-armed cephalopods still have a fondness for feasting on catches inside fishing nets and traps.

I witnessed this brazen habit a few days after seeing that first octopus. I took my nephew and his partner for a snorkel at the octopus spot, hoping we might get lucky and see it again. We searched through the seaweeds, and I pointed out sea stars and blue-rayed limpets, but we didn't spy any seaweed mimics watching us back. My nephew did, though, come across a cluster of abalone on the sand, and he dived down and picked up a half dozen big, gleaming shells. Until then, I had only ever seen live abalone a few times and had never found such large, intact shells; they're flattened and ear-shaped, and these ones fit all the way over my ear with room to spare.

The abalones we found were treasure enough, so we headed back towards the beach. On the way, my nephew's partner was the first to spot the fish trap resting on the kelp a few feet from the surface. Sitting inside was a large red octopus. Several of its arms were wrapped around chunks of bait, including a fish's head and tail. The octopus could easily have climbed out of the trap, but it seemed content where it was, surrounded by its free feast. For long, peaceful minutes, we watched the octopus in stunned silence, while it huffed and breathed through its siphon tube, and we held tight to our abalone shells. I now keep one of them on top of the piano, where the light catches its oily, iridescent interior and casts bright dots through the row of eight holes through which the living abalone reproduced, pooped, and breathed—right up until the moment it was prised off a rock by, I bet, a strong, suckered arm. The pile of shells we found on the seabed must have been a midden of the leftovers from abalone feasts, piled up outside an octopus's den. I like my shell all the more knowing that the creature inside was probably eaten by an octopus. I'll go back next summer to see if I can find some more.

Acknowledgments

This book arose from more than two decades of exploring the ocean, combined with two years thinking of little else but what the future may hold for it. Countless people along the way have taught me, talked with me, taken me places, dived with me, shown me things, explained to me their discoveries and ideas, and most of all fostered my fascination in what lies underwater. My great thanks to you all. From the explorations that appear in this book, special thanks to my dive buddies all those years ago in Belize, in particular Alice el Kilany, and later to John Bruno for introducing me to my first misplaced lionfish.

The book was written at a time when, for various reasons, I was disinclined to fly off to distant places, but I went on a few trips by land and sea to explore parts of the ocean I had not yet seen. Thanks to Jon Dunn for encouraging me to come to Shetland and for hosting, together with Sarah Cuttle, quite the best dinner party beneath the bright, northern midnight skies. My thanks to Billy Arthur for guiding me through the enchanting underwater forests of Shetland. Thanks to Bryce Stewart and Áine Purcell-Milton for chats about ocean protection in Arran and advice on good snorkelling spots.

My thanks for various conversations about the ocean and its future to Matthew Witt, Jake Davies, Jason Hodin, Cayne Layton, Luiz Rocha, Erika Gress, Kylie Lev, and Yi-Kai Tea. Thanks to Ali Hood, Ian Campbell, Al Edwards, John Bruno, Rachel Millar, and Sarah

Hamylton for reading and commenting on early drafts of chapters and for sharing your honest thoughts.

It's an absolute pleasure to be working with the teams at Grove on both sides of the Atlantic. Thanks to George Gibson for guidance and enthusiasm and for patiently waiting for my return from the waves to chat. Thanks to Clare Drysdale and Peter Blackstock for heartily embracing my oceanic explorations, and to Karen Duffy and John Mark Boling for so brilliantly handling publicity. Thank you to Amy Hughes for helping shape the manuscript with yet another impeccable copyedit, and to Emily Burns for all the critical finishing touches. My deep thanks to my agent, Margaret Sutherland Brown, for indispensable support, advice, and untiring cheering on, and to Melissa Sarver White for superbly handling the international translations. And my continuing gratitude to my retired agent, Emma Sweeney, and to Simon Winchester for crucial early encouragement. Without them both I doubt any of this would be happening at all.

My love and appreciation, as always, to all my family and friends who continue to celebrate and sustain me through my writing and watery life, and especially to David Thorp and Lydia Sefton-Minns for finding that amazing octopus. And my love to Ivan, and thanks for being by my side above and below the waterline. I wonder what we're going to find together next.

Photo Credits

Additional Resources

Many organisations around the world are working hard to safeguard the ocean and ocean life. Support them in any way you can, be that with your time and expertise, or with your passion and enthusiasm to learn. Some offer memberships and accept donations.

The following list gives a small selection, including organisations focused on certain habitats and species mentioned in this book, and it's by no means complete. Be sure to search in your local area too. If your town or city has an aquarium or a science or natural history museum, those institutions are often a good place to start.

ORGANISATIONS CAMPAIGNING TO PROTECT THE OCEAN
 Blue Marine Foundation www.bluemarinefoundation.com
 Mission Blue www.mission-blue.org
 Surfers Against Sewage www.sas.org.uk
 Sustainable Ocean Alliance www.soalliance.org

REGION-SPECIFIC GROUPS
 Australian Marine Conservation Society www.marineconservation.org.au
 COAST (Community of Arran Seabed Trust) www.arrancoast.com
 Marine Conservation Society (UK) www.mcsuk.org
 Oceana (international and regional branches) www.oceana.org
 Our Seas Our Future (Aotearoa/New Zealand) www.osof.org

SPECIES AND HABITATS
 Angel Shark Project www.angelsharkproject.com
 Deep-Sea Conservation Coalition www.savethehighseas.org
 Great Southern Reef www.greatsouthernreef.com
 Kelp Forest Alliance www.kelpforestalliance.com

North Coast Cetacean Society (BC Whales) www.bcwhales.org
Orca Conservancy www.orcaconservancy.org
Project Seagrass www.projectseagrass.org
The Shark Trust www.sharktrust.org
Wetlands International www.wetlands.org

FOR DIVERS
Seasearch (UK) www.seasearch.org.uk
PADI Project Aware www.padi.com/aware
Reef Check www.reefcheck.org

GUIDANCE ON MAKING BETTER SEAFOOD CHOICES
Good Fish Guide, Marine Conservation Society (UK) www.mcsuk.org
    /goodfishguide
Monterey Bay Aquarium, Seafood Watch (US) www.seafoodwatch.org
GoodFish (Australia) www.goodfish.org.au

Notes

Prelude

xii **Scientists have named this condition.** Hayley S. Charlton-Howard et al., "'Plasticosis': Characterising Macro- and Microplastic-Associated Fibrosis in Seabird Tissues," *Journal of Hazardous Materials* 450 (2023): 131090, https://doi.org/10.1016/j.jhazmat.2023.131090.

xiii **scientists recently discovered how northern elephant seals.** Jessica M. Kendall-Bar et al., "Brain Activity of Diving Seals Reveals Short Sleep Cycles at Depth," *Science* 380, no. 6642 (2023): 260–65, https://doi.org/10.1126/science.adf0566.

xiii **scientists tracked scalloped hammerhead sharks.** Mark Meekan and Adrian Gleiss, "Free-Diving Sharks," *Science* 380, no. 6645 (2023): 583–84, https://doi.org/10.1126/science.adg8452.

xiv **a population of at least a thousand.** Elitza S. Germanov et al., "Residency, Movement Patterns, Behavior and Demographics of Reef Manta Rays in Komodo National Park," *PeerJ* 10 (2022): e13302, https://doi.org/10.7717/peerj.13302.

xiv **off the coast of Ecuador.** Kanina Harty et al., "Demographics and Dynamics of the World's Largest Known Population of Oceanic Manta Rays *Mobula birostris* in Coastal Ecuador," *Marine Ecology Progress Series* 700 (2022): 145–59, https://doi.org/10.3354/meps14189.

xix **road map.** IPCC, *Climate Change 2023: Synthesis Report; Contribution of Working Groups I, II and III to the Sixth Assessment Report of the Intergovernmental Panel on Climate Change*, ed. H. Lee et al. (Geneva, Switzerland: IPCC), doi:10.59327/IPCC/AR6-9789291691647.

Chapter 1

6 **study of trilobite fossils.** John R. Paterson et al., "Trilobite Evolutionary Rates Constrain the Duration of the Cambrian Explosion," *Proceedings of the National Academy of Sciences* 116, no. 10 (2019): 4394–99, https://www.pnas.org/cgi/doi/10.1073/pnas.1819366116.

7 **ways many trilobites lived.** Richard Fortey, *Trilobite! Eyewitness to Evolution* (London: HarperCollins, 2001).

10 **The cause was likely a spell.** Justin L. Penn et al., "Temperature-Dependent Hypoxia Explains Biogeography and Severity of End-Permian Marine Mass Extinction," *Science* 362, no. 6419 (2018), http://dx.doi.org/10.1126/science.aat1327.

13 **fossilised *Diandongosaurus*.** Qiling Liu et al., "An Injured Pachypleurosaur (Diapsida: Sauropterygia) from the Middle Triassic Luoping Biota Indicating Predation Pressure in the Mesozoic," *Scientific Reports* 11 (2021): 21818, https://doi.org/10.1038/s41598-021-01309-z.

14 **sixteen-foot ichthyosaur.** Da-Yong Jiang et al., "Evidence Supporting Predation of 4-m Marine Reptile by Triassic Megapredator," *iScience* 23, no. 9 (2020): 101347, https://doi.org/10.1016/j.isci.2020.101347.

16 **interactive digital map.** Alexis Rojas et al., "A Multiscale View of the Phanerozoic Fossil Record Reveals the Three Major Biotic Transitions," *Communications Biology* 4 (2021): 309, https://doi.org/10.1038/s42003-021-01805-y.

17 **dusty old theory.** Neil Brocklehurst et al., "Mammaliaform Extinctions as a Driver of the Morphological Radiation of Cenozoic Mammals," *Current Biology* 31, no. 13 (2021): 2955–63, https://doi.org/10.1016/j.cub.2021.04.044.

17 **Their method detected.** Jennifer Cuthill et al., "Impacts of Speciation and Extinction Measured by an Evolutionary Decay Clock," *Nature* 588 (2020): 636–41, https://doi.org/10.1038/s41586-020-3003-4.

25 **This near-extinction.** Elizabeth Sibert and Leah Rubin, "An Early Miocene Extinction in Pelagic Sharks," *Science* 372, no. 6546 (2021): 1105–7, doi:10.1126/science.aaz3549. Several other groups of scientists have questioned some of the methods Sibert and Rubin used to identify the near extinction of sharks nineteen million years ago; see ibid., links to "Comment" and "Response" at foot of article.

26 **walking-shark populations.** Christine L. Dudgeon et al., "Walking, Swimming or Hitching a Ride? Phylogenetics and Biogeography of the Walking Shark Genus *Hemiscyllium*," *Marine and Freshwater Research* 71, no. 9 (2020): 1107–17, https://doi.org/10.1071/MF19163.

CHAPTER 2

32 **commercial crab fishery.** The red king crab fishery in the Russian region of the Barents Sea was certified by the Marine Stewardship Council in 2018. This is not an eradication fishery but an introduced species being fished just as native species are, with the aim of maintaining catches over the long term. Marine Stewardship Council, "Russian Red King Crab Fishery Is MSC Certified in World First," February 23, 2018, https://www.msc.org/media-centre/press-releases/press-release/russian-red-king-crab-fishery-is-msc-certified-in-world-first.

35 **tiger sharks are venturing.** Neil Hammerschlag et al., "Ocean Warming Alters the Distributional Range, Migratory Timing, and Spatial Protections of an Apex Predator, the Tiger Shark (*Galeocerdo cuvier*)," *Global Change Biology* 28, no. 6 (2021): 1990–2005, https://doi.org/10.1111/gcb.16045.

35   **great white sharks have started.** Kisei R. Tanaka et al., "North Pacific Warming Shifts the Juvenile Range of a Marine Apex Predator," *Science Reports* 11 (2021): 3373, https://doi.org/10.1038/s41598-021-82424-9.

37   **increasing their maximum depth.** Shahar Chaikin et al., "Cold-Water Species Deepen to Escape Warm Water Temperatures," *Global Ecology and Biogeography* 31 (2022): 75–88, http://dx.doi.org/10.1111/geb.13414.

38   **ocean will have deoxygenated.** Dan Laffoley and John M. Baxter (eds.), *Ocean Deoxygenation: Everyone's Problem; Causes, Impacts, Consequences and Solutions* (Gland, Switzerland: IUCN, 2019), https://portals.iucn.org/library /sites/library/files/documents/2019-048-En.pdf.

41   **lionfish will occupy.** C. Turan, "Species Distribution Modelling of Invasive Alien Species; *Pterois miles* for Current Distribution and Future Suitable Habitats," *Global Journal of Environmental Science and Management* 6, no. 4 (2020): 429–40, https://doi.org/10.22034/gjesm.2020.04.01.

42   **lionfish will gradually make a year-round move.** Brian D. Grieve et al., "Range Expansion of the Invasive Lionfish in the Northwest Atlantic with Climate Change," *Marine Ecology Progress Series* 546 (2016): 225–37, doi:10.3354/meps11638.

42   **eating fairy basslets.** Kurt E. Ingeman, "Lionfish Cause Increased Mortality Rates and Drive Local Extirpation of Native Prey," *Marine Ecology Progress Series* 558 (2016): 235–45, https://www.jstor.org/stable/24897431.

42   **concerns for the social wrasse.** Luiz Rocha et al., "Invasive Lionfish Preying on Critically Endangered Reef Fish," *Coral Reefs* 34, no. 3 (2015): 803–6, doi:10.1007/s00338-015-1293-z.

45   **When asked in 2020.** Periklis Kleitou et al., "Conflicting Interests and Growing Importance of Non-Indigenous Species in Commercial and Recreational Fisheries of the Mediterranean Sea," *Fisheries Management and Ecology* 29 (2022): 169–82, doi:10.1111/fme.12531.

46   **US East Coast, trawl fisheries.** Eva A. Papaioannou et al., "Not All Those Who Wander Are Lost—Responses of Fishers' Communities to Shifts in the Distribution and Abundance of Fish," *Frontiers in Marine Science* 8 (2021), https://doi.org/10.3389/fmars.2021.669094.

46   **By 2050, catches around the Arctic.** Vicky W. Y. Lam et al., "Projected Change in Global Fisheries Revenues under Climate Change," *Scientific Reports* 6 (2016): 32607, https://doi.org/10.1038/srep32607.

46   **In a widening band.** Chhaya Chaudhary et al., "Global Warming Is Causing a More Pronounced Dip in Marine Species Richness around the Equator," *Proceedings of the National Academy of Sciences* 118, no. 15 (2021), https://doi.org/10.1073/pnas.2015094118.

47   **Predictions extending to 2050.** Lam, "Projected Change."

47   **harder for fishers to make a living.** William W. L. Cheung et al., "Shrinking of Fishes Exacerbates Impacts of Global Ocean Changes on Marine Ecosystems," *Nature Climate Change* 3 (2013): 254–58, https://doi.org /10.1038/nclimate1691.

48 **One study predicts that these kinds.** E. W. Tekwa et al., "Body Size and Food-Web Interactions Mediate Species Range Shifts under Warming," *Proceedings of the Royal Society B* 289 (2022): 20212755, https://doi.org/10.1098/rspb.2021.2755.

49 **shifting whale populations will alter.** Angela R. Szesciorka and Kathleen M. Stafford, "Sea Ice Directs Changes in Bowhead Whale Phenology through the Bering Strait," *Movement Ecology* 11 (2023): 8, https://doi.org/10.1186/s40462-023-00374-5.

49 **Orcas are now hunting.** Kyle J. Lefort et al., "Killer Whale Abundance and Predicted Narwhal Consumption in the Canadian Arctic," *Global Change Biology* 26, no. 8 (2020): 4276–83, https://doi.org/10.1111/gcb.15152.

49 **Even those narwhals.** Greg A. Breed et al., "Sustained Disruption of Narwhal Habitat Use and Behavior in the Presence of Arctic Killer Whales," *Proceedings of the National Academy of Sciences* 114, no. 10 (2017): 2628–33, http://www.pnas.org/cgi/doi/10.1073/pnas.1611707114.

49 **Bowhead whales in the region.** Cory Matthews et al., "Killer Whale Presence Drives Bowhead Whale Selection for Sea Ice in Arctic Seascapes of Fear," *Proceedings of the National Academy of Sciences* 117, no. 12 (2020): 6590–98, https://www.pnas.org/cgi/doi/10.1073/pnas.1911761117.

50 **One such regime shift.** Mads Peter Heide-Jørgensen et al., "A Regime Shift in the Southeast Greenland Marine Ecosystem," *Global Change Biology* 29, no. 3 (2022): 668–85, doi:10.1111/gcb.16494.

52 **Experts now think we've passed the point.** Yeon-Hee Kim et al., "Observationally-Constrained Projections of an Ice-Free Arctic Even under a Low Emission Scenario," *Nature Communications* 14 (2023): 3139, https://doi.org/10.1038/s41467-023-38511-8.

CHAPTER 3

60 **"It is extraordinary."** Apsley Cherry-Garrard, *The Worst Journey in the World: Antarctic, 1910–1913* (London, Bombay, and Sydney: Constable and Company, 1922).

63 **Halley Bay colony was abandoned.** Peter T. Fretwell and Philip N. Trathan, "Emperors on Thin Ice: Three Years of Breeding Failure at Halley Bay," *Antarctic Science* 31, no. 3 (2019): 133–38, https://doi.org/10.1017/S0954102019000099.

64 **The following year, even more.** Graham Readfearn, "'Everyone Should Be Concerned': Antarctic Sea Ice Reaches Lowest Levels Ever Recorded," *Guardian* (UK), March 4, 2023, https://www.theguardian.com/world/2023/mar/04/everyone-should-be-concerned-antarctic-sea-ice-reaches-lowest-levels-ever-recorded.

65 **collapse of colonies in the Bellingshausen Sea.** Peter T. Fretwell et al., "Record Low 2022 Antarctic Sea Ice Led to Catastrophic Breeding Failure of Emperor Penguins," *Communications Earth and Environment* 4 (2023): 273, https://doi.org/10.1038/s43247-023-00927-x.

65 **most detailed study to date.** Stéphanie Jenouvrier et al., "The Paris Agreement Objectives Will Likely Halt Future Declines of Emperor Penguins," *Global Change Biology* 26, no. 3 (2019): 1170–84, doi:10.1111/gcb.14864.

67 **2023 study of their genetics.** Sally C. Y. Lau et al., "Genomic Evidence for West Antarctic Ice Sheet Collapse during the Last Interglacial Period" (preprint, January 31, 2023, https://doi.org/10.1101/2023.01.29.525778).

74 **number coming to nest.** Megan A. Cimino et al., "Projected Asymmetric Response of Adélie Penguins to Antarctic Climate Change," *Scientific Reports* 6 (2016): 28785, doi:10.1038/srep28785.

74 **chinstrap colonies.** Noah Strycker et al., "A Global Population Assessment of the Chinstrap Penguin (*Pygoscelis antarctica*)," *Scientific Reports* 10 (2020): 19474, https://doi.org/10.1038/s41598-020-76479-3.

75 **Since 2000, the krill catch.** Carolyn J. Hogg et al., "Protect the Antarctic Peninsula—Before It's Too Late," *Nature* 586 (2020): 496–99, https://doi.org/10.1038/d41586-020-02939-5.

75 **ships may be competing with local wildlife.** George M. Watters et al., "Long-Term Observations from Antarctica Demonstrate That Mismatched Scales of Fisheries Management and Predator-Prey Interaction Lead to Erroneous Conclusions about Precaution," *Scientific Reports* 10 (2020): 2314, https://doi.org/10.1038/s41598-020-59223-9.

CHAPTER 4

80 **A 1969 book about sharks.** Thomas H. Lineaweaver and Richard H. Backus, *The Natural History of Sharks* (Philadelphia: J. B. Lippincott, 1969), 58.

80 **A 1984 report named them.** Leonard J. V. Compagno, *FAO Species Catalogue*, vol. 4, *Sharks of the World*, pt. 2, *Carcharhiniformes* (Rome: United Nations Development Programme, Food and Agriculture Organisation of the United Nations, 1984).

81 **These large sharks that were once so plentiful.** Chelsey N. Young and John K. Carlson, "The Biology and Conservation Status of the Oceanic Whitetip Shark (*Carcharhinus longimanus*) and Future Directions for Recovery," *Reviews in Fish Biology and Fisheries* 30 (2020): 293–312, https://doi.org/10.1007/s11160-020-09601-3.

81 **one-third of all known shark species.** Nicholas K. Dulvy et al., "Overfishing Drives Over One-Third of All Sharks and Rays toward a Global Extinction Crisis," *Current Biology* 31, no. 21 (2021): 4773–87. https://doi.org/10.1016/j.cub.2021.08.062.

82 **declined by 71 per cent.** Nathan Pacoureau et al., "Half a Century of Global Decline in Oceanic Sharks and Rays," *Nature* 589 (2021): 567–71, https://doi.org/10.1038/s41586-020-03173-9.

84 **number of sharks killed.** Ian Campbell, personal communication, April 2023.

84 **In 2018, observers.** Gonzalo Mucientes et al., "Unreported Discards of Internationally Protected Pelagic Sharks in a Global Fishing Hotspot Are Potentially Large," *Biological Conservation* 269 (2022): 109534, https://doi.org/10.1016/j.biocon.2022.109534.

84 **Now researchers are using the publicly.** Global Fishing Watch, https://globalfishingwatch.org/.

85 **One year's worth of satellite positioning data.** David A. Kroodsma et al., "Tracking the Global Footprint of Fisheries," *Science* 359, no. 6378 (2018): 904–8, https://doi.org/10.1126/science.aao5646. Another study of global fishing used reconstructed fish catches to work out the percentage of the ocean fished and found it to have reached 90 per cent in the latter part of the twentieth century; see David Tickler et al., "Far from Home: Distance Patterns of Global Fishing Fleets," *Science Advances* 4, no. 8 (2018): eaar3279, doi.10.1126/sciadv.aar327.

85 **Combining satellite data.** The study divided the ocean into one-degree grids, with sides of sixty-eight miles, which is the average length of an industrial longline. Nuno Queiroz et al., "Global Spatial Risk Assessment of Sharks under the Footprint of Fisheries," *Nature* 572 (2019): 461–66, https://doi.org/10.1038/s41586-019-1444-4.

86 **estimate for the annual global death toll.** Boris Worm et al., "Global Catches, Exploitation Rates, and Rebuilding Options for Sharks," *Marine Policy* 40 (2013): 194–204, http://dx.doi.org/10.1016/j.marpol.2012.12.034.

86 **number of daggernose sharks.** Rosangela Lessa et al., "Close to Extinction? The Collapse of the Endemic Daggernose Shark (*Isogomphodon oxyrhynchus*) off Brazil," *Global Ecology and Conservation* 7 (2016): 70–81, https://doi.org/10.1016/j.gecco.2016.04.003.

88 **after 534 days, the eleven-inch male.** Steven Benjamins et al., "First Confirmed Complete Incubation of a Flapper Skate (*Dipturus intermedius*) Egg in Captivity," *Fish Biology* 99, no. 3 (2021): 1150–54, doi:10.1111/jfb.14816.

89 **Keystone predators.** Robert T. Paine, "Food Web Complexity and Species Diversity," *American Naturalist* 100, no. 910 (1966): 65–75, http://www.jstor.org/stable/2459379.

90 **The most controversial investigation.** Ransom A. Myers et al., "Cascading Effects of the Loss of Apex Predatory Sharks from a Coastal Ocean," *Science* 315, no. 5820 (2007): 315, 1846–50, https://doi.org/10.1126/science.1138657.

91 **laid bare in a 2016 study.** R. Dean Grubbs et al., "Critical Assessment and Ramifications of a Purported Marine Trophic Cascade," *Scientific Reports* 6 (2016): 20970, https://doi.org/10.1038/srep20970.

92 **Since 2000, marine biologists.** Neil Hammerschlag et al., "Disappearance of White Sharks Leads to the Novel Emergence of an Allopatric Apex Predator, the Sevengill Shark," *Scientific Reports* 9 (2019): 1908, https://doi.org/10.1038/s41598-018-37576-6.

92 **Their anxiety levels dropped.** Neil Hammerschlag et al., "Loss of an Apex Predator in the Wild Induces Physiological and Behavioural Changes

in Prey," *Biology Letters* 18, no. 1 (2022): 20210476, https://doi.org/10.1098/rsbl.2021.0476.

92 **Great white sharks had been scared.** Alison V. Towner et al., "Fear at the Top: Killer Whale Predation Drives White Shark Absence at South Africa's Largest Aggregation Site," *African Journal of Marine Science* 44, no. 2 (2022): 139–52, https://doi.org/10.2989/1814232X.2022.2066723.

92 **The arrival of orcas.** Tamlyn M. Engelbrecht et al., "Running Scared: When Predators Become Prey," *Ecosphere Naturalist* 10, no. 1 (2019): e02531, https://doi.org/10.1002/ecs2.2531.

93 **a team of diving scientists.** Robert J. Nowicki et al., "Loss of Predation Risk from Apex Predators Can Exacerbate Marine Tropicalization Caused by Extreme Climatic Events," *Journal of Animal Ecology* 90, no. 9 (2021): 2041–52, doi:10.1111/1365-2656.13424.

94 **Meanwhile, the Java stingaree.** Julia Constance et al., "*Urolophus javanicus. The IUCN Red List of Threatened Species* 2023," e.T60095A229337053. https://www.iucnredlist.org/species/60095/229337053. Accessed on 23 January 2024.

95 **A 2020 study gathered.** Julia M. Lawson et al., "Extinction Risk and Conservation of Critically Endangered Angel Sharks in the Eastern Atlantic and Mediterranean Sea," *ICES Journal of Marine Science* 77, no. 1 (2020): 12–29, doi:10.1093/icesjms/fsz222.

96 **other important strongholds.** Joanna Barker et al., "The Distribution, Ecology and Predicted Habitat Use of the Critically Endangered Angelshark (*Squatina squatina*) in Coastal Waters of Wales and the Central Irish Sea," *Fish Biology* 101, no. 3 (2020): 640–58, doi:10.1111/jfb.15133.

96 **conservationists, now armed.** Joanna Barker et al., *Wales Angelshark Action Plan* (London: Zoological Society of London, 2020); Cat Gordon et al., *Mediterranean Angel Sharks: Regional Action Plan* (United Kingdom: The Shark Trust, 2019); Joanna Barker et al., *Angelshark Action Plan for the Canary Islands* (London: Zoological Society of London, 2016).

99 **3 per cent of the global ocean.** Christine A. Ward-Paige and Boris Worm, "Global Evaluation of Shark Sanctuaries," *Global Environmental Change* 47 (2017): 174–89, https://doi.org/10.1016/j.gloenvcha.2017.09.005.

99 **survey of scuba divers' opinions.** Ibid.

100 **Close to three hundred thousand large pelagic sharks were likely caught.** Brendan D. Shea et al., "Quantifying Longline Bycatch Mortality for Pelagic Sharks in Western Pacific Shark Sanctuaries," *Science Advances* 9, no. 33 (2023): eadg3527, https://doi.org/10.1126/sciadv.adg3527.

100 **size of an individual reserve.** Median size of marine protected areas globally is 3.3 square kilometres; Central Park in New York is 3.4 square kilometres. Lisa Boonzaier and Daniel Pauly, "Marine Protection Targets: An Updated Assessment of Global Progress," *Oryx* 50, no. 1 (2015): 1–9, http://dx.doi.org/10.1017/S0030605315000848.

100 **catches of endangered elasmobranchs.** Manfredi Di Lorenzo et al.. "Small-Scale Fisheries Catch More Threatened Elasmobranchs inside

Partially Protected Areas than in Unprotected Areas," *Nature Communications* 13 (2022): 4381, https://doi.org/10.1038/s41467-022-32035-3.

103 **2021 study conducted in waters off Florida.** Nicholas M. Whitney et al., "Connecting Post-Release Mortality to the Physiological Stress Response of Large Coastal Sharks in a Commercial Longline Fishery," *PLoS One* 16, no. 9 (2021): e0255673, https://doi.org/10.1371/journal.pone .0255673.

103 **Sea trials in a small-scale.** Philip D. Doherty et al., "Efficacy of a Novel Shark Bycatch Mitigation Device in a Tuna Longline Fishery," *Current Biology* 32, no. 22 (2022): R1260–61, https://doi.org/10.1016/j.cub .2022.09.003.

103 **Illuminating gill nets.** Jesse F. Senko et al., "Net Illumination Reduces Fisheries Bycatch, Maintains Catch Value, and Increases Operational Efficiency," *Current Biology* 32, no. 4 (2022): 911–18, https://doi.org/10.1016/j.cub .2021.12.050.

105 **Scientists in Hong Kong.** Diego Cardeñosa et al., "CITES-Listed Sharks Remain among the Top Species in the Contemporary Fin Trade," *Conservation Letters* 11, no. 4 (2018): e12457, https://doi.org/10.1111/conl.12457.

105 **A turning point came in 2022.** Diego Cardeñosa et al., "Two Thirds of Species in a Global Shark Fin Trade Hub Are Threatened with Extinction: Conservation Potential of International Trade Regulations for Coastal Sharks," *Conservation Letters* 15, no. 5 (2022): e12910, https://doi.org/10.1111/conl.12910.

106 **Less than 10 per cent.** Colin A. Simpfendorfer and Nicholas K. Dulvy, "Bright Spots of Sustainable Shark Fishing," *Current Biology* 27, no. 3 (2017): R83–102, http://dx.doi.org/10.1016/j.cub.2016.12.017.

107 **A 2023 study of shark fisheries.** Nathan Pacoureau et al., "Conservation Successes and Challenges for Wide-Ranging Sharks and Rays," *Proceedings of the National Academy of Sciences* 120, no. 5 (2023): e2216891120, https://doi.org /10.1073/pnas.2216891120.

CHAPTER 5

109 **A necropsy revealed.** The concentration of PCBs in Lulu's body was 950 milligrams per kilogram of lipid; the threshold for severe impairment of marine mammals is around 40 milligrams per kilogram of lipid. Jean-Pierre Desforges et al., "Predicting Global Killer Whale Population Collapse from PCB Pollution," *Science* 361, no. 6409 (2018): 1373–76, https://doi.org /10.1126/science.aat1953.

110 **A recent study found that grandmothers.** Charli Grimes et al., "Post-reproductive Female Killer Whales Reduce Socially Inflicted Injuries in Their Male Offspring," *Current Biology* 33, no. 15 (2023): 3250–56, https: //doi.org/10.1016/j.cub.2023.06.039.

112 **In 1968, in the journal *Nature*.** R. W. Risebrough et al., "Polychlorinated Biphenyls in the Global Ecosystem," *Nature* 220 (1968): 1098–1102, https: //doi.org/10.1038/2201098a0.

113 **In the extreme depths of the Mariana Trench.** Alan J. Jamieson et al., "Bioaccumulation of Persistent Organic Pollutants in the Deepest Ocean Fauna," *Nature Ecology and Evolution* 1 (2017): 0051, https://doi.org/10.1038/s41559-016-0051.

113 **For decades, California sea lions.** Frances M. D. Gulland et al., "Persistent Contaminants and Herpesvirus OtHV1 Are Positively Associated with Cancer in Wild California Sea Lions (*Zalophus californianus*)," *Frontiers in Marine Science* 7 (2020), https://doi.org/10.3389/fmars.2020.602565.

114 **Around Iceland, orcas.** Anaïs Remili et al., "Individual Prey Specialization Drives PCBs in Icelandic Killer Whales," *Environmental Science and Technology* 55, no. 8 (2021): 4923–31, https://doi.org/10.1021/acs.est.0c08563.

114 **a group of scientists simulated.** Jean-Pierre Desforges et al., "Predicting Global Killer Whale Population Collapse from PCB Pollution," *Science* 361, no. 6409 (2018): 1373–76, https://doi.org/10.1126/science.aat1953.

114 **The model predicted.** There have been several rebuttals to the 2018 study; see ibid., eLetters. Some other orca experts think the model is too simplistic and the conclusions too sweeping. Some argued that if the models' assumptions were indeed realistic, orca populations would have already disappeared at the height of PCB production in the 1970s, which thankfully didn't happen.

115 **A study in the United States revealed.** David Q. Andrews and Olga V. Naidenko, "Population-Wide Exposure to Per- and Polyfluoroalkyl Substances from Drinking Water in the United States," *Environmental Science and Technology Letters* 7, no. 12 (2020): 931–36, https://doi.org/10.1021/acs.estlett.0c00713.

116 **legal battle by US lawyer Robert Bilott.** Nathaniel Rich, "The Lawyer Who Became DuPont's Worst Nightmare," *New York Times Magazine*, January 6, 2016.

116 **hid the findings of their studies.** Tom Perkins, "Chemical Giants Hid Dangers of 'Forever Chemicals' in Food Packaging," *Guardian* (UK), May 12, 2021, https://www.theguardian.com/environment/2021/may/12/chemical-giants-hid-dangers-pfas-forever-chemicals-food-packaging-dupont.

117 **excluding thousands of substances that won't be regulated.** Tom Perkins, "EPA's New Definition of PFAS Could Omit Thousands of 'Forever Chemicals,'" *Guardian* (UK), August 28, 2023, https://www.theguardian.com/environment/2023/aug/18/epa-new-definition-pfas-forever-chemicals.

117 **In 2001, General Electric was forced to pay to dredge New York's Hudson River.** Jane Martinson, "GE Hit with $450m Toxic Clean-Up Charge," *Guardian* (UK), August 1, 2001, https://www.theguardian.com/business/2001/aug/02/3.

118 **Pollutants in the bodies of striped dolphins.** Paul D. Jepson et al., "PCB Pollution Continues to Impact Populations of Orcas and Other Dolphins in European Waters," *Scientific Reports* 6 (2016): 18573, doi:10.1038/srep18573.

118 **The Franciscana dolphin.** Rosalinda C. Montone et al., "Temporal Trends of Persistent Organic Pollutant Contamination in Franciscana Dolphins from

the Southwestern Atlantic," *Environmental Research* 216, pt. 1 (2023): 114473, https://doi.org/10.1016/j.envres.2022.114473.

119 **Levels of PCBs in ringed and grey seals.** Karl Mauritsson et al., "Maternal Transfer and Long-Term Population Effects of PCBs in Baltic Grey Seals Using a New Toxicokinetic-Toxicodynamic Population Model," *Archives of Environmental Contamination and Toxicology* 83 (2022): 376394, https://doi.org/10.1007/s00244-022-00962-3; Thorsten B. H. Reusch et al., "The Baltic Sea as a Time Machine for the Future Coastal Ocean," *Science Advances* 4, no. 5 (2018): eaar8195.

119 **Recent estimates indicate.** Markus Eriksen et al., "A Growing Plastic Smog, Now Estimated to Be Over 170 Trillion Plastic Particles Afloat in the World's Oceans—Urgent Solutions Required," *PLoS One* 18, no. 3 (2023): e0281596, https://doi.org/10.1371/journal.pone.0281596.

121 **A 2022 study calculated.** Shirel R. Kahane-Rapport et al., "Field Measurements Reveal Exposure Risk to Microplastic Ingestion by Filter-Feeding Megafauna," *Nature Communications* 13 (2022): 6327, https://doi.org/10.1038/s41467-022-33334-5.

122 **The orcas' bodies are contaminated.** Kiah Lee et al., "Emerging Contaminants and New POPs (PFAS and HBCDD) in Endangered Southern Resident and Bigg's (Transient) Killer Whales (*Orcinus orca*): In Utero Maternal Transfer and Pollution Management Implications," *Environmental Science and Technology* 57, no. 1 (2023): 360–74, https://doi.org/10.1021/acs.est.2c04126.

123 **Trials of voluntary reduced speeds.** Rianna E. Burnham et al., "The Efficacy of Management Measures to Reduce Vessel Noise in Critical Habitat of Southern Resident Killer Whales in the Salish Sea," *Frontiers in Marine Science* 8 (2021), https://doi.org/10.3389/fmars.2021.664691.

123 **When ships passing through are slower.** Rob Williams et al., "Reducing Vessel Noise Increases Foraging in Endangered Killer Whales," *Marine Pollution Bulletin* 173, pt. A (2021): 112976, https://doi.org/10.1016/j.marpolbul.2021.112976.

124 **The film triggered public outcry.** Laure Boissat et al., "Nature Documentaries as Catalysts for Change: Mapping Out the 'Blackfish Effect,'" *People and Nature* 3, no. 6 (2021): 1179–92, https://doi.org/10.1002/pan3.10221.

124 **Among the most passionate advocates.** Squil-le-he-le Raynell Morris and Tah-Mahs Ellie Kinley, "One Stolen Whale, the Web of Life, and Our Collective Healing," *Fix/Grist*, October 28, 2021, https://grist.org/fix/opinion/lummi-nation-southern-resident-killer-whale-salish-sea-return/.

125 **scientists have tested their bodies.** Joseph G. Schnitzler et al., "Supporting Evidence for PCB Pollution Threatening Global Killer Whale Population," *Aquatic Toxicology* 206 (2019): 102–4, https://doi.org/10.1016/j.aquatox.2018.11.008.

126 **Dozens of sailors have reported.** Ruth Esteban et al., "Killer Whales of the Strait of Gibraltar, an Endangered Subpopulation Showing a Disruptive Behavior," *Marine Mammal Science* 38, no. 4 (2022): 1699–1709, doi:10.1111/mms.12947.

CHAPTER 6

133 **Over the course of fifteen years.** Lynn Waterhouse et al., "Recovery of Critically Endangered Nassau Grouper (*Epinephelus striatus*) in the Cayman Islands Following Targeted Conservation Actions," *Proceedings of the National Academy of Sciences* 117, no. 3 (2020): 1587–95, https://www.pnas.org/cgi/doi/10.1073/pnas.1917132117.

135 **prevent at least one black deed.** Laurence M. Huey, "Past and Present Status of the Northern Elephant Seal with a Note on the Guadalupe Fur Seal," *Journal of Mammalogy* 11 (1930): 188–194, https://doi.org/10.2307/1374066.

136 **fished as long ago as the Stone Age.** Adam J. Andrews et al., "Exploitation History of Atlantic Bluefin Tuna in the Eastern Atlantic and Mediterranean—Insights from Ancient Bones," *ICES Journal of Marine Science* 79, no. 2 (2022): 247–62, https://doi.org/10.1093/icesjms/fsab261.

140 **ICCAT soon earned.** Anjali Nayar, "Bad News for Tuna Is Bad News for CITES," *Nature*, March 23, 2010, https://doi.org/10.1038/news.2010.139.

141 **Off the west coast of Ireland.** Thomas W. Horton et al., "Evidence of Increased Occurrence of Atlantic Bluefin Tuna in Territorial Waters of the United Kingdom and Ireland," *ICES Journal of Marine Science* 78, no. 5 (2021): 1672–83, doi:10.1093/icesjms/fsab039.

141 **Bluefin tuna are also coming back.** Leif Nøttestad et al., "The Comeback of Atlantic Bluefin Tuna (*Thunnus thynnus*) to Norwegian Waters," *Fisheries Research* 231 (2020): 105689, https://doi.org/10.1016/j.fishres.2020.105689.

142 **the species was moved off the Red List.** The IUCN's 2021 text on the global population of Atlantic bluefin tuna concludes that "no change or an overall increase in the global population is probably most representative of the global status of the species." Bruce B. Collette et al., "Atlantic Bluefin Tuna, *Thunnus thynnus*," IUCN Red List of Threatened Species (2021): e.T21860A46913402, https://www.iucnredlist.org/species/21860/46913402.

142 **They've also recently been seen for the first time.** Brian R. MacKenzie et al., "A Cascade of Warming Impacts Brings Bluefin Tuna to Greenland Waters," *Global Change Biology* 20, no. 8 (2014): 2484–91, https://doi.org/10.1111/gcb.12597.

143 **A short while after the vote.** Karen McVeigh, "Revealed: Most of EU Delegation to Crucial Fishing Talks Made Up of Fishery Lobbyists," *Guardian* (UK), April 26, 2023.

146 **in 2020 scientists celebrated.** Susannah V. Calderan et al., "South Georgia Blue Whales Five Decades after the End of Whaling," *Endangered Species Research* 43 (2020): 359–73, https://doi.org/10.3354/esr01077.

CHAPTER 7

148 **Scientists from the University of York.** Ruth H. Thurstan and Callum M. Roberts, "Ecological Meltdown in the Firth of Clyde, Scotland: Two

Centuries of Change in a Coastal Marine Ecosystem," *PLoS One* 5, no. 7 (2010): e11767, https://doi.org/10.1371/journal.pone.0011767.

150 **In 1995, the pair set up.** Bryce D. Stewart et al., "Marine Conservation Begins at Home: How a Local Community and Protection of a Small Bay Sent Waves of Change around the UK and Beyond," *Frontiers in Marine Science* 7 (2020), https://doi.org/10.3389/fmars.2020.00076.

154 **In 2019, scientists sent an autonomous.** Veerle A. I. Huvenne and B. Thornton, *RRS* Discovery *Cruise DY108–109, 6 Sept–2 Oct 2019: CLASS—Climate-Linked Atlantic System Science Darwin Mounds Marine Protected Area Habitat Monitoring, BioCAM—First Equipment Trials, BLT—Recipes: Pilot Study*, National Oceanography Centre Cruise Report 66 (Southampton, UK: National Oceanography Centre, 2020), https://nora.nerc.ac.uk/id /eprint/526682/.

156 **Setting up the protected area in 2017.** Cassandra M. Brooks et al., "Reaching Consensus for Conserving the Global Commons: The Case of the Ross Sea, Antarctica," *Conservation Letters* 13, no. 1 (2020): e12676, https://doi.org /10.1111/conl.12676.

157 **more spiny lobsters.** Hunter S. Lenihan et al., "Increasing Spillover Enhances Southern California Spiny Lobster Catch along Marine Reserve Borders," *Ecosphere* 13, no. 6 (2022): e4110, https://doi.org/10.1002 /ecs2.4110.

157 **In Aotearoa, the effect.** Zoe Qu et al., "Economic Valuation of the Snapper Recruitment Effect from a Well-Established Temperate No-Take Marine Reserve on Adjacent Fisheries," *Marine Policy* 134 (2021): 104792, https://doi.org/10.1016/j.marpol.2021.104792.

158 **scientists analysed catch data.** Sarah Medoff et al., "Spillover Benefits from the World's Largest Fully Protected MPA," *Science* 378, no. 6617 (2022): 313–16, https://www.science.org/doi/10.1126/science.abn0098.

160 **system to track the right whales.** Derek P. Tittensor et al., "Integrating Climate Adaptation and Biodiversity Conservation in the Global Ocean," *Science Advances* 5, no. 11 (2019): eaay9969, https://doi.org/10.1126/sciadv .aay9969.

161 **by 2016, the pink corals.** Emma V. Sheehan et al., "Rewilding of Protected Areas Enhances Resilience of Marine Ecosystems to Extreme Climatic Events," *Frontiers in Marine Science* 8 (2021): 671427, https://doi.org /10.3389/fmars.2021.671427.

161 **A 2022 review of more than twenty thousand studies.** Juliette Jacquemot et al., "Ocean Conservation Boosts Climate Change Mitigation and Adaptation," *One Earth* 5, no. 10 (2022): 1126–38, https://doi.org/10.1016 /j.oneear.2022.09.002.

162 **Since 2001, more than a dozen.** "Minerals: Polymetallic Nodules," International Seabed Authority, https://www.isa.org.jm/exploration -contracts/polymetallic-nodules/.

162 **Biological surveys of the CCZ.** Muriel Rabone et al., "How Many Metazoan Species Live in the World's Largest Mineral Exploration

Region?" *Current Biology* 33, no. 12 (2023): 2383–96, https://doi.org/10.1016/j.cub.2023.04.052.

163 **study modelling the impacts of noise.** Rob Williams et al., "Noise from Deep-Sea Mining May Span Vast Ocean Areas," *Science* 377, no. 6602 (2022): 157–58, https://doi.org/10.1126/science.abo2804.

164 **vent mines could be interspersed.** Daniel C. Dunn et al., "A Strategy for the Conservation of Biodiversity on Mid-Ocean Ridges from Deep-Sea Mining," *Science Advances* 4, no. 7 (2018): eaar4313, https://doi.org/10.1126/sciadv.aar4313.

165 **A full survey of all the snails.** Elin A. Thomas et al., "A Global Red List for Hydrothermal Vent Molluscs," *Frontiers in Marine Science* 8 (2021): 713022, https://doi.org/10.3389/fmars.2021.713022.

166 **In the Mediterranean, 0.06 per cent.** Joachim Claudet et al., "Underprotected Marine Protected Areas in a Global Biodiversity Hotspot," *One Earth* 2, no. 4 (2020): 380–84, https://doi.org/10.1016/j.oneear.2020.03.008.

166 **Across the northeast Atlantic.** Julia Roessger et al., "Turning the Tide on Protection Illusions: The Underprotected MPAs of the 'OSPAR Regional Sea Convention,'" *Marine Policy* 142 (2022): 105109, https://doi.org/10.1016/j.marpol.2022.105109.

166 **European protected areas are home.** Manuel Dureuil et al., "Elevated Trawling inside Protected Areas Undermines Conservation Outcomes in a Global Fishing Hot Spot," *Science* 362, no. 6421 (2018): 1403–7, https://doi.org/10.1126/science.aau0561.

166 **almost all the protected areas are being legally dredged and bottom-trawled.** Karen McVeigh, "Fishing Industry Still 'Bulldozing' Seabed in 90% of UK Marine Protected Areas," *Guardian* (UK), May 31, 2022, https://www.theguardian.com/environment/2022/may/31/fishing-industry-still-bulldozing-seabed-in-90-of-uk-marine-protected-areas.

167 **Bill Ballantine wrote.** Mark J. Costello and Bill Ballantine, "Biodiversity Conservation Should Focus on No-Take Marine Reserves," *Science and Society* 30, no. 9 (2015): 507–9, https://doi.org/10.1016/j.tree.2015.06.011.

CHAPTER 8

171 **The latest estimates suggest kelp forests.** Aaron M. Eger et al., "The Value of Ecosystem Services in Global Marine Kelp Forests," *Nature Communications* 14 (2023): 1894, https://doi.org/10.1038/s41467-023-37385-0.

172 **In that one heatwave.** Thomas Wernberg et al., "Climate-Driven Regime Shift of a Temperate Marine Ecosystem," *Science* 353, no. 6295 (2016): 169–72, https://doi.org/10.1126/science.aad8745.

173 **successful campaign led to a ban.** Sussex Kelp Recovery Project, https://sussexkelp.org.uk/.

178 **Spiky armadas marched.** Karen Filbee-Dexter and Robert E. Scheibling, "Sea Urchin Barrens as Alternative Stable States of Collapsed Kelp Ecosystems," *Marine Ecology Progress Series* 495 (2014): 1–25, https://doi.org/10.3354/meps10573.

179 **otters' influence on eelgrass.** Brent B. Hughes et al., "Recovery of a
Top Predator Mediates Negative Eutrophic Effects on Seagrass," *Proceedings
of the National Academy of Sciences* 110, no. 38 (2013): 15313–18, https://www
.pnas.org/cgi/doi/10.1073/pnas.1302805110.

180 **To the north, off British Columbia.** Erin Foster et al., "Physical Dis-
turbance by Recovering Sea Otter Populations Increases Eelgrass Genetic
Diversity," *Science* 374, no. 6565 (2021): 333–36, https://doi.org/10.1126
/science.abf2343.

182 **study off the coast of Hokkaido.** Akira Watanuki et al., "Restoration
of Kelp Beds on an Urchin Barren: Removal of Sea Urchins by Citizen
Divers in Southwestern Hokkaido," *Bulletin of Fisheries Research Agency* 32
(2010): 83–87, http://www.fra.affrc.go.jp/bulletin/bull/bull32/83-87.pdf.

183 **study of two of Aotearoa's no-take zones.** Nick T. Shears and Russell
C. Babcock, "Marine Reserves Demonstrate Top-Down Control of Community Structure on Temperate Reefs," *Oecologia* 132 (2002): 131–42, https:
//doi.org/10.1007/s00442-002-0920-x.

186 **one group of scientists is suggesting.** Peter D. Roopnarine et al., "Impact
of the Extinct Megaherbivore Steller's Sea Cow (*Hydrodamalis gigas*) on Kelp
Forest Resilience," *Frontiers in Ecology and Evolution* 10 (2022): 983558, https:
//doi.org/10.3389/fevo.2022.983558.

187 **Subsequent analysis confirmed.** Armineh Barkhordarian et al.,
"Recent Marine Heatwaves in the North Pacific Warming Pool Can Be
Attributed to Rising Atmospheric Levels of Greenhouse Gases," *Communications Earth and Environment* 3 (2022): 131, https://doi.org/10.1038/s43247
-022-00461-2.

191 **At the centre of this disaster is the Amazon Basin.** Brian E. Lapointe
et al., "Nutrient Content and Stoichiometry of Pelagic *Sargassum* Reflects
Increasing Nitrogen Availability in the Atlantic Basin," *Nature Communications* 12 (2021): 3060, https://doi.org/10.1038/s41467-021-23135-7.

193 **programme to actively replant.** Robert J. Orth et al., "Restoration of
Seagrass Habitat Leads to Rapid Recovery of Coastal Ecosystem Services,"
Science Advances 6, no. 41 (2020): eabc6434, https://doi.org/10.1126/sciadv
.abc6434.

194 **seagrass meadows likely store.** James W. Fourqurean et al., "Seagrass
Ecosystems as a Globally Significant Carbon Stock," *Nature Geoscience* 5
(2012): 505–9, https://doi.org/10.1038/ngeo1477.

194 **2022 study projecting the future of seagrass.** Christina A. Buelow et al.,
"Ambitious Global Targets for Mangrove and Seagrass Recovery," *Current
Biology* 32, no. 7 (2022): 1641–49, https://doi.org/10.1016/j.cub.2022.02.013.

194 **1 per cent of these semiaquatic tropical forests.** Liza Goldberg et al.,
"Global Declines in Human-Driven Mangrove Loss," *Global Change Biology*
26 (2020): 5844–55, https://doi.org/10.1111/gcb.15275.

195 **mangrove forests lock up.** Daniel R. Richards et al., "Quantifying Net
Loss of Global Mangrove Carbon Stocks from 20 Years of Land Cover

Change," *Nature Communications* 11 (2020): 4260, https://doi.org/10.1038/s41467-020-18118-z.

197 **Operation Crayweed was born.** Operation Crayweed: Restoring Sydney's Underwater Forests, http://www.operationcrayweed.com/.

CHAPTER 9

204 **Within six months, many coral colonies.** Melanie D. Mcfield, "Coral Response during and after Mass Bleaching in Belize," *Bulletin of Marine Science* 64, no. 1 (1999): 155–72.

206 **Reefs are central to the lives.** Amy Sing Wong et al., "An Assessment of People Living by Coral Reefs over Space and Time," *Global Change Biology* 28, no. 23 (2022): 7139–53, https://doi.org/10.1111/gcb.16391.

207 **There are still coral reefs in Belize.** Catherine Alves et al., "Twenty Years of Change in Benthic Communities across the Belizean Barrier Reef," *PLoS One* 17, no. 1 (2022): e0249155, https://doi.org/10.1371/journal.pone.0249155.

207 **Across the region, many coral reefs.** Jeremy Jackson et al. (eds.), *Status and Trends of Caribbean Coral Reefs: 1970–2012* (Gland, Switzerland: Global Coral Reef Monitoring Network, IUCN, 2014).

207 **In 1998, mass bleaching.** The 8 per cent figure comes from a forty-year data set of underwater surveys on reefs, consisting of more than two million observations from over twelve thousand sites in seventy-three reef-bearing countries around the world. See David Souter et al. (eds.), *Status of Coral Reefs of the World: 2020 Report* (n.p.: Global Coral Reef Monitoring Network and International Coral Reef Initiative, 2020), https://doi.org/10.59387/WOTJ9184.

207 **14 per cent of stony corals worldwide were killed.** This is likely an underestimate because the most damaged reefs, with the lowest coral cover, are not always the ones people choose to survey. Another study estimates that fully half of the world's corals have died since 1950, although those figures are contentious among some experts, because they rely on a few early data points of coral cover that may not be as accurate or comparable to later surveys. See Tyler D. Eddy et al., "Global Decline in Capacity of Coral Reefs to Provide Ecosystem Services," *One Earth* 4, no. 9 (2021): 1278–85, https://doi.org/10.1016/j.oneear.2021.08.016.

207 **This century, coral cover.** Sterling B. Tebbett et al., "Benthic Composition Changes on Coral Reefs at Global Scales," *Nature Ecology and Evolution* 7 (2023): 71–81, https://doi.org/10.1038/s41559-022-01937-2.

208 **Heat-stressed corals are more vulnerable.** So far, scientists know of forty coral diseases that affect two hundred species across the world's tropical reefs, but they still understand little about what causes them, how they're transmitted, and what, if anything, can be done to protect reefs and help sick corals recover. See Juliano Morais et al., "A Global Synthesis of the Current Knowledge on the Taxonomic and Geographic Distribution of Major Coral

Diseases," *Environmental Advances* 8 (2022): 100231, https://doi.org/10.1016/j.envadv.2022.1002312.

208 **Warming seas are losing oxygen.** Ariel K. Pezner et al., "Increasing Hypoxia on Global Coral Reefs under Ocean Warming," *Nature Climate Change* 13 (2023): 403–9, https://doi.org/10.1038/s41558-023-01619-2.

208 **Mass coral bleaching kills corals.** Terry P. Hughes et al., "Spatial and Temporal Patterns of Mass Bleaching of Corals in the Anthropocene," *Science* 359, no. 6371 (2018): 80–83, https://doi.org/10.1126/science.aan8048.

209 **scientists in Australia have built.** Sophie G. Dove et al., "Ocean Warming and Acidification Uncouple Calcification from Calcifier Biomass Which Accelerates Coral Reef Decline," *Communications Earth and Environment* 1 (2020): 55, https://doi.org/10.1038/s43247-020-00054-x.

209 **It could be as soon as 2030.** Kay L. Davis et al., "Global Coral Reef Ecosystems Exhibit Declining Calcification and Increasing Primary Productivity," *Communications Earth and Environment* 2 (2021): 105, https://doi.org/10.1038/s43247-021-00168-w.

210 **Surveys in 2022 recorded.** AIMS Long-Term Monitoring Program, *Annual Summary Report of Coral Reef Condition 2020/2021* (n.p.: Australian Institute of Marine Science, 2021), https://www.aims.gov.au/reef-monitoring/gbr-condition-summary-2020-2021.

210 **seven years later . . . there was little to no coral bleaching.** Liam Lachs et al., "Emergent Increase in Coral Thermal Tolerance Reduces Mass Bleaching under Climate Change," *Nature Communications* 14 (2023): 4939, https://doi.org/10.1038/s41467-023-40601-6.

210 **On reefs in Panama, *Pocillopora*.** Ana M. Palacio-Castro et al., "Increased Dominance of Heat-Tolerant Symbionts Creates Resilient Coral Reefs in Near-Term Ocean Warming," *Proceedings of the National Academy of Sciences* 120, no. 8 (2023): e2202388120, https://doi.org/10.1073/pnas.2202388120.

210 **Globally, since the 1990s.** Shannon Sully et al., "A Global Analysis of Coral Bleaching over the Past Two Decades," *Nature Communications* 10 (2019): 1264, https://doi.org/10.1038/s41467-019-09238-2.

211 **Twenty years' worth of underwater surveys.** Shannon Sully et al., "Present and Future Bright and Dark Spots for Coral Reefs through Climate Change," *Global Change Biology* 28, no. 15 (2022): 4509–22, https://doi.org/10.1111/gcb.16083.

211 **Bright spots are dotted.** Ibid.

213 **Globally, around 80 per cent.** Richard L. Pyle and Joshua M. Copus, "Mesophotic Coral Ecosystems: Introduction and Overview," in *Mesophotic Coral Ecosystems*, ed. Yossi Loya et al., Coral Reefs of the World 12 (Cham, Switzerland: Springer, 2019), 3–27, https://doi.org/10.1007/978-3-319-92735-0_1.

213 **every hour a rebreather diver.** Hudson T. Pinheiro et al., "Deep Reef Fishes in the World's Epicenter of Marine Biodiversity," *Coral Reefs* 38 (2019): 985–95, https://doi.org/10.1007/s00338-019-01825-5.

213 **rose-veiled fairy wrasse.** Yi-Kai Tea et al., "*Cirrhilabrus finifenmaa* (Teleostei, Labridae), a New Species of Fairy Wrasse from the Maldives, with Comments on the Taxonomic Identity of *C. rubrisquamis* and *C. wakanda*," *ZooKeys* 1088 (2022): 65–80, https://doi.org/10.3897/zookeys.1088.78139.

213 **latigo fairy wrasse.** Yi-Kai Tea et al., "A New Species of Fairy Wrasse (Teleostei: Labridae: *Cirrhilabrus*) from Mesophotic Coral Ecosystems of the Verde Island Passage, Philippines," *Copeia* 108, no. 1 (2020): 91–102, https://doi.org/10.1643/CI-19-297.

214 **Obama's basslet.** Richard L. Pyle et al., "*Tosanoides obama*, a New Basslet (Perciformes, Percoidei, Serranidae) from Deep Coral Reefs in the Northwestern Hawaiian Islands," *ZooKeys* 641 (2016): 165–81, https://doi.org/10.3897/zookeys.641.11500.

215 **surveys in American Samoa.** Anthony D. Montgomery et al., "Community Similarity and Species Overlap between Habitats Provide Insight into the Deep Reef Refuge Hypothesis," *Scientific Reports* 11 (2021): 23787, https://doi.org/10.1038/s41598-021-03128-8.

216 **More of them now live in mesophotic reefs.** Steven J. Lindfield et al., "Mesophotic Depths as Refuge Areas for Fishery-Targeted Species on Coral Reefs," *Coral Reefs* 35 (2016): 125–37, https://doi.org/10.1007/s00338-015-1386-8.

216 **Scientists who dive frequently in the mesophotic.** Nicolas Loiseau et al., "Mesophotic Reefs Are Not Refugia for Neither Taxonomic nor Functional Diversity of Reef Fishes," *Coral Reefs* 42 (2023): 63–75, https://doi.org/10.1007/s00338-022-02311-1; Luiz A. Rocha et al., "Mesophotic Coral Ecosystems Are Threatened and Ecologically Distinct from Shallow Water Reefs," *Science* 361, no. 6399 (2018): 281–84, https://doi.org/10.1126/science.aaq1614; Paris Stefanoudis et al., "Low Connectivity between Shallow, Mesophotic and Rariphotic Zone Benthos," *Royal Society Open Science* 6, no. 9 (2019): 190958, http://dx.doi.org/10.1098/rsos.190958.

216 **Plastic debris builds up.** Hudson T. Pinheiro et al., "Plastic Pollution on the World's Coral Reefs," *Nature* 619 (2023): 311–16, https://doi.org/10.1038/s41586-023-06113-5.

217 **A two-decade study in Belize.** Catherine Alves et al., "Twenty Years of Change in Benthic Communities across the Belizean Barrier Reef," *PLoS One* 17, no. 1 (2022): e0249155, https://doi.org/10.1371/journal.pone.0249155.

217 **Several other studies have similarly found.** John F. Bruno et al., "Climate Change, Coral Loss, and the Curious Case of the Parrotfish Paradigm: Why Don't Marine Protected Areas Improve Reef Resilience?," *Annual Review of Marine Science* 11 (2019): 307–34, https://doi.org/10.1146/annurev-marine-010318-095300; Jack V. Johnson et al., "Marine Protected Areas Do Not Buffer Corals from Bleaching under Global Warming," *BMC Ecology and Evolution* 22 (2022): 58, https://doi.org/10.1186/s12862-022-02011-y.

218 **Close to 90 per cent.** Catherine E. I. Head et al., "Coral Bleaching Impacts from Back-to-Back 2015–2016 Thermal Anomalies in the Remote Central

Indian Ocean," *Coral Reefs* 38 (2019): 605–18, https://doi.org/10.1007/s00338 -019-01821-9.

218 **some reefs in Chagos are recovering.** Cassandra E. Benkwitt et al., "Seabird Nutrient Subsidies Alter Patterns of Algal Abundance and Fish Biomass on Coral Reefs following a Bleaching Event," *Global Change Biology* 25, no. 8 (2019): 2619–32, https://doi.org/10.1111/gcb.14643.

218 **De-ratting islands.** Nicholas A. J. Graham et al., "Seabirds Enhance Coral Reef Productivity and Functioning in the Absence of Invasive Rats," *Nature* 559 (2018): 250–53, https://doi.org/10.1038/s41586-018-0202-3.

219 **If global temperature rise can be kept.** Katja Frieler et al., "Limiting Global Warming to 2°C Is Unlikely to Save Most Coral Reefs," *Nature Climate Change* 3 (2013): 165–70, https://doi.org/10.1038/nclimate1674.

221 **researchers incrementally raised.** Leela J. Chakravarti and Madeleine J. H. van Oppen, "Experimental Evolution in Coral Photosymbionts as a Tool to Increase Thermal Tolerance," *Frontiers in Marine Science* 5 (2018), https://doi.org/10.3389/fmars.2018.00227.

221 **young corals were given heatproof zooxanthellae.** Kate Quigley et al., "Heat-Evolved Microalgal Symbionts Increase Thermal Bleaching Tolerance of Coral Juveniles without a Trade-Off against Growth" (preprint, *Current Biology*, 2021, https://doi.org/10.2139/ssrn.3981099).

222 **Off the island of Phuket.** Talisa Doering et al., "Towards Enhancing Coral Heat Tolerance: A 'Microbiome Transplantation' Treatment Using Inoculations of Homogenized Coral Tissues," *Microbiome* 9 (2021): 102, https://doi.org/10.1186/s40168-021-01053-6.

223 **A breakthrough came in 2020.** Madeleine J. H. van Oppen and John G. Oakeshott, "A Breakthrough in Understanding the Molecular Basis of Coral Heat Tolerance," *Proceedings of the National Academy of Sciences* 117, no. 46 (2020): 28546–48, https://doi.org/10.1073/pnas.2020201117.

223 **An Australian initiative.** Reef Restoration and Adaptation Program, https://gbrrestoration.org/.

224 **living coral biobank.** The Forever Reef Project, https://coralbiobank.org/.

227 **These reefs help protect.** Borja G. Reguero et al., "The Value of US Coral Reefs for Flood Risk Reduction," *Nature Sustainability* 4 (2021): 688–98, https://doi.org/10.1038/s41893-021-00706-6.

CHAPTER 10

233 **On an eighty-day survey.** Fiona Chong et al., "High Concentrations of Floating Neustonic Life in the Plastic-Rich North Pacific Garbage Patch," *PLoS Biology* 21, no. 5 (2023): e3001646, https://doi.org/10.1371/journal. pbio.3001646.

233 **It follows that scooping.** Matthew Spencer et al., "Estimating the Impact of New High Seas Activities on the Environment: The Effects of Ocean-Surface Macroplastic Removal on Sea Surface Ecosystems," *PeerJ* 11 (2023): e15021, https://doi.org/10.7717/peerj.15021.

238 **as the seas warm, they feed hurricanes.** See the IPCC's 2019 special report: *The Ocean and Cryosphere in a Changing Climate: Special Report of the Intergovernmental Panel on Climate Change*, ed. Hans-Otto Pörtner et al. (Cambridge: Cambridge University Press and IPCC, 2022), https://www.ipcc.ch/srocc/.

239 **A huge opportunity exists.** Tessa Mazor et al., "Large Conservation Opportunities Exist in >90% of Tropic-Subtropic Coastal Habitats Adjacent to Cities," *One Earth* 4, no. 7 (2023): 1004–15, https://doi.org/10.1016/j.oneear.2021.06.010.

241 **A 2022 survey.** "Three Quarters of People in Global Survey Want Single-Use Plastics Banned," Ipsos, February 22, 2022, https://www.ipsos.com/en/attitudes-towards-single-use-plastics.

243 **Diseases and debilitating conditions.** Philip J. Landrigan et al., "The Minderoo-Monaco Commission on Plastics and Human Health," *Annals of Global Health* 89, no. 1 (2023): 23, https://doi.org/10.5334/aogh.4056.

244 **Scientists have found plastic-eating bacteria.** Maaike Goudriaan et al., "A Stable Isotope Assay with ^{13}C-Labeled Polyethylene to Investigate Plastic Mineralization Mediated by *Rhodococcus ruber*," *Marine Pollution Bulletin* 186 (2023): 114369, https://doi.org/10.1016/j.marpolbul.2022.114369.

245 **Maine's female ocean farmers.** Loren McClenachan and Allie Moulton, "Transitions from Wild-Caught Fisheries to Shellfish and Seaweed Aquaculture Increase Gender Equity in Maine," *Marine Policy* 146 (2022): 105312, https://doi.org/10.1016/j.marpol.2022.105312.

247 **Corporations from a handful.** Douglas J. McCauley et al., "Wealthy Countries Dominate Industrial Fishing," *Science Advances* 4, no. 8 (2018): eaau2161, https://doi.org/10.1126/sciadv.aau2161.

247 **Subsidies are keeping afloat.** Enric Sala et al., "The Economics of Fishing the High Seas," *Science Advances* 4, no. 6 (2018): eaat2504, https://doi.org/10.1126/sciadv.aat2504.

248 **Out in distant waters, atrocities.** David Tickler et al., "Modern Slavery and the Race to Fish," *Nature Communications* 9 (2018): 4643, https://doi.org/10.1038/s41467-018-07118-9.

248 **European countries pay.** Dyhia Belhabib et al., "Euros vs. Yuan: Comparing European and Chinese Fishing Access in West Africa," *PLoS One* 10, no. 3 (2015): e0118351, https://doi.org/10.1371/journal.pone.0118351.

249 **In recent years, surging numbers.** Allwell Uwazuruike, "Migration and the Right to Survival: An Empirical Study of Three Fishing Communities in Senegal," *Journal of Rural Studies* 99 (2023): 71–78, https://doi.org/10.1016/j.jrurstud.2023.02.007.

251 **Current estimates indicate.** Ganapathiraju Pramod et al., "Estimates of Illegal and Unreported Fish in Seafood Imports to the USA," *Marine Policy* 48 (2014): 102–13, https://doi.org/10.1016/j.marpol.2014.03.019.

252 **first seamount to be successfully mined.** Travis W. Washburn et al., "Seamount Mining Test Provides Evidence of Ecological Impacts beyond

Deposition," *Current Biology* 33, no. 14 (2023): 3065–3071.E3, https://doi.org/10.1016/j.cub.2023.06.032.

254 **Campaigners presented a declaration.** Blue Climate Initiative, "Indigenous Voices for a Ban on Deep Sea Mining," https://www.blueclimateinitiative.org/say-no-to-deep-sea-mining.

255 **the possibility of a precautionary pause in deep-sea mining.** Karen McVeigh, "International Talks End Without Go-Ahead for Deep-Sea Mining," *Guardian* (UK), July 29, 2023, https://www.theguardian.com/environment/2023/jul/29/deep-sea-mining-international-talks-isa-jamaica.

256 **Already studies suggest human food webs.** Diva J. Amon et al., "Climate Change to Drive Increasing Overlap between Pacific Tuna Fisheries and Emerging Deep-Sea Mining Industry," *NPJ Ocean Sustainability* 2 (2023): 9, https://doi.org/10.1038/s44183-023-00016-8.

EPILOGUE

261 **recent studies of its genes.** Francisco Oliveira Borges et al., "Projecting Future Climate Change Impacts on the Distribution of the '*Octopus vulgaris* Species Complex,'" *Frontiers in Marine Science* 9 (2022), https://doi.org/10.3389/fmars.2022.1018766.

Index

Greenland

North
America

MACROCYSTIS

Deep-sea
Skate
Nursery

Southern
Residents
Orcas

Sunflower
Sea-star

Southern
Sea Otter

Clarion-Clipperton
Fracture Zone

Mesoamerican
Reef

Deep-sea
Octopus Nursery

Chesapeake
Bay

Cayman
Islands

Sargasso
Sea

Invasive
Lionfish

Great
Atlantic
Sargassum
Belt

South
America

Shetland

Darwin
Mounds

Isle of
Arran

Angelsharks

Gibraltar
Orcas

Africa

Atlantic Bluefin
Tuna

LESSONIA

Antarctic
Peninsula

Weddell
Sea

Halley Bay
Emperor Penguin
Colony

Antarctica

Geographic
South Pole

Ross
Sea

Magnetic
South Pole
(in 2023)

Ross Sea
Orcas

AARON JOHN GREGORY

= Invasive Lionfish

= Emperor Penguin Colony

= Angelsharks